The American
Woodland Garden

The American Woodland Garden

Capturing the Spirit
of the Deciduous Forest

Text and photography by
Rick Darke

TIMBER PRESS
Portland · Cambridge

HALF TITLE PAGE: Pen-and-ink drawing of sweetshrub, *Calycanthus floridus*, by Rick Darke.
FRONTISPIECE: A private woodland garden in northern Delaware captures the luminous quality of the deciduous forest when the sun's rays and direction are evident. It also demonstrates how central design elements (the weirs in the stream) can introduce order into an otherwise naturalistic, asymmetric landscape.

Published in 2002 by

Timber Press, Inc.
The Haseltine Building
133 S.W. Second Avenue, Suite 450
Portland, Oregon 97204, U.S.A.

Timber Press
2 Station Road
Swavesey
Cambridge CB4 5QJ, U.K.

Reprinted 2003

Printed through Colorcraft Ltd., Hong Kong
Designed by Susan Applegate

Library of Congress Cataloging-in-Publication Data

Darke, Rick.
    The American woodland garden: capturing the spirit of the deciduous forest/text and
  photography by Rick Darke.
      p. cm.
    Includes bibliographical references and index.
    ISBN 0-88192-545-4
    1. Woodland gardening—United States. 2. Woodland garden plants—United States. I. Title.

SB439.6 .D27 2002
635.9'77—dc21   2002020474

to MZ

Contents

Chapter Five: The Forest Palette 194

Preface

THIS BOOK IS NOT intended to be an encyclopedia but, rather, a synopsis: a portrait drawn from the ethos, the aesthetic, and the ecology of the eastern deciduous forest. It is aimed mainly at individual private gardeners who, like me, tend a modest piece of ground that is a part of the larger forest. It is also designed as a guide and visual reference for professionals, especially those keepers and interpreters of parks, streetscapes, and other public landscapes who must identify and promote the relevance of woodland environs to a burgeoning human population. I hope it will serve as a practical and compelling account that will be useful in the creation of designed gardens and in the conservation of nearby nature.

For many of us living in twenty-first-century North America, the deciduous forest is somewhere in our daily view, even if only at the periphery. The

A contemplative winter view from our
Pennsylvania garden to the woods.

usual phrase "eastern deciduous forest" hardly conveys the huge range of this area. Draw a vertical line dividing the United States in the middle, and the right half is the approximate domain of the deciduous forest. Though it today consists of a patchwork of remnants splintered from a once vast whole, more than half the U.S. population lives within its midst.

The deciduous forest is not and never was a homogeneous type of vegetation. Though always characterized by a predominance of deciduous hardwood tree species, it includes coniferous trees in much of it and evergreen hardwood species especially in the South. In sheer biomass and diversity, it reaches its zenith in the southern Appalachian Mountains, where rainfall is abundant, and it gradually changes in composition as precipitation diminishes to the west, and as winter temperatures drop to the north.

Although gardeners and foresters are often focused on trees, the forest community is an intricate complex including higher plants, animals, fungi, oxygen, carbon dioxide, water, minerals, and dead and decaying organic matter. It is a place of intense recycling and reuse, and because of this, the organic soils of the deciduous forest are often deep and rich. Much diversity of the deciduous forest owes to its vertical layering and to the many different organisms sharing space in any given square foot, extending from deep within soil layers to the skyscraping tops of trees. The forest's deciduous nature is the basis of its supreme seasonality, and the translucent quality of its predominant foliage makes it one of the most luminous landscapes on earth. By any standards, the magnificence of its autumn color display is unmatched in the world of plants.

This book is about the observation and appreciation of such characteristics and qualities, about seeing the forest for what it is and what it can be in both broad surrounds and intimate landscapes. It begins with an exploration of the forest aesthetic, relying on images of native woodland landscapes to depict and define the forest's unique dynamics and architecture in ways that may be directly inspirational to woodland gardeners. The second chapter tells the story of a nineteen-year study I've made (to date) of a woodland stream landscape, presenting it as a potential model for observation and distillation, and promoting the notion that concepts such as change over time, solstice, and equinox can be incorporated in the designed landscape. The third chapter is about woodland garden design as a synthesis of art, architecture, and forest ecology, with a strong emphasis on sustainability and stewardship. Chapter four is about the practical side of planting and maintenance, and the final chapter is a fairly in-depth look at the forest palette: a descriptive and visual portrait of many trees, shrubs, wildflowers, and ferns that might make up a garden in and of the deciduous woodlands. Readers who are also photographers may be interested to know that nearly every image in this book was taken with Kodachrome 64 ASA slide film using a Nikon FM2 camera. All were taken in natural light, and no flash or filters were used.

Today, though the notion of wilderness lingers as an ideal, in fact our hand is evident everywhere and "all the world's a garden." If that garden is to be eminently fit for human habitation while respecting the resources and requirements of other living communities, its making will depend partly on an understanding of ecological principles and partly on the creative skills and techniques that are in the gardener's domain. It has been my intention to produce a book that might represent such a synthesis, and it is my hope that it will be useful to others gardening with the American woodlands, wishing to capture the spirit of the deciduous forest.

Acknowledgments

I WANT TO THANK all those friends, family, and professional acquaintances who have shared the woods or their insights with me over the years, in particular Ted Browning, Hal Bruce, Bill Brumback, Jerry Darke, Marjorie Darke, Ken Druse, Nancy and William H. Frederick, Peter and Jasmin Gentling, Don Hamill, Dale Hendricks, Tim Hohn, Steve Holt, Donald "Dutch" Huttleston, Dick Lighty, George Longenecker, Jeff Lynch, FM Mooberry, Darrel Morrison, Jim Plyler, Melissa Powel, Claire Sawyers, W. Gary Smith, Fred Somers, Paul van Meter, Melinda Zoehrer, and Blade.

I'd also like to thank the following people who opened their gardens to me for photography: Sue and Doug Barton, Jean Bruns (Anderson Cottage), Mr. and Mrs. John H. Bryan Jr. (Crab Tree Farm), Pamela Copeland (Mount Cuba Center), Governor and Mrs. Pete du Pont (Patterns), Peter and Jasmin Gentling, Neil Grossman and Nancy Wolff, Nancy and William H. Frederick Jr. (Ashland Hollow), Dale Hendricks and Carol Curtis, Philip Johnson, Marge and Dick Lennihan, Dick and Sally Lighty (Springwood), Barbara and

Jerry Riegel, Mr. and Mrs. Jack W. Schuler (Crab Tree Farm), Louise Smith, Rod and Susan Ward, and Louise Wrinkle.

I'm grateful for the opportunities I've had to photograph in the following public landscapes: Arnold Arboretum, Birmingham Botanical Gardens, Blue Ridge Parkway, Connecticut College Arboretum, Grey Towers (Gifford Pinchot home), Grover Cleveland Park, Henry Foundation, James Rose House, Joyce Kilmer National Forest, Leonard J. Buck Garden, Longwood Gardens, Montgomery Pinetum, Morris Arboretum, Morton Arboretum, Rutgers Gardens, Scott Arboretum, Smoky Mountains National Park, Stonecrop, Suningive, White Clay Creek Preserve, and many additional semi-wild places.

I'm happily indebted to the people who contributed photographs to this book—Dan Benarcik (for *Gymnocladus* in autumn), Claire Sawyers (for the Scott Amphitheater in winter), and Melinda Zoehrer (for the Olana fence and *Iris cristata* 'Alba')—and to my brother, Jerry Darke, whose technical support on all manner of digital devices has been absolutely invaluable.

Finally, I want to express my special appreciation of all those at Timber Press for the passion and professionalism they bring to enriching the literature of the American landscape and garden.

CHAPTER ONE

A Forest Aesthetic

I'VE BEEN ENCHANTED by the woods since childhood. Though I've lived in various places, all have been within the borders of the North American deciduous forest. Asked what it is about the woodlands that I find so spellbinding, I'd probably say it is the strength and individuality of the seasons, but the images that come to mind are not simple changes in the weather. I'd perhaps picture myriad translucent leaves filling in the canopy, building a new roof over the spring woods while bathing it in a lime glow. I might recall sunlight streaming laserlike in the moist air that fills the forest in mid summer, or maybe the voluptuous curves of an ancient oak, silhouetted by the winter moon. Sound and scent memories are equally compelling; the wind's singing through high branches, the rustle of fall leaves underfoot, the sweetness of spring breezes, or autumn's intoxicating pungency. Such delights are among the dramas that play each year within the framework of the forest, and they are worthy of celebration in the garden.

Woodland gardening can be so much more than cultivating plants that bloom in the shade. Flowers are certainly part of the appeal; however, they are only one aspect of a garden designed to tickle all the senses, to stimulate the mind as well as the eye. A landscape aesthetic inspired by the complex dynamics and architecture of the forest is not only more humanly satisfying, it is more sympathetic to the natural processes that are essential to a healthy woodland environment.

Four seasonal glimpses of the deciduous forest in northern Delaware, here and overleaf.

OPPOSITE Beautiful in its simplicity, the forest is deep in dormancy on a rainy, fog-filled day in late February. Nearly absent of color, the landscape is reduced to black trees against white snow. Low light and the diffusing effects of the moist air have banished all shadows from the scene. Shadowlike, the trunks of distant trees appear as faint echoes. Starkly silhouetted foreground trees make powerful vertical statements despite the softening influence of the fog. Flaring gracefully as they meet the earth, they stand in bold contrast with the fine tracery of branches, the shrub layer below, and the curving horizontal lines of the road and embankment. Curiously askew from all the others, a leaning tree is essential to the tension and intrigue of this picture. Its unique angle provides a memorable point of reference that will endure through the coming seasons.

TOP RIGHT The forest presents an entirely different mood in the green glow of early May, with sunstreams and shadows now playing significant roles. The outlines of close trees are crisply defined by the strengthening sun, while leaf-laden branches cloak background trees. The scene's visual depth will continue to diminish as the year's fresh foliage expands and darkens.

BOTTOM RIGHT The landscape is multihued in late October as green leaves mix with others growing gold. The foliage remains full enough to mask distant trees and their lines against the sky. Many tree trunks appear two toned: the combined result of moss accumulated over summer and the darkening effects of a recent rain. Fallen leaves carpet the edge of the road in shades of light brown and amber.

Leaves lingering on beeches and young red oaks are colorful elements in a mid-November drizzle. With most other foliage fallen, the details of forest architecture are again on display into the distance, and the sky has returned as a feature in this muted landscape. Long obscured by summer foliage but now quite evident, evergreen Christmas ferns and shield ferns cover the upper roadbank and wooded slope with their sturdy greens.

Forest Dynamics

Each year the landscape of the eastern deciduous forest undergoes seasonal transformation that is unsurpassed anywhere in the world for its drama or biological complexity. Most vegetation moves from dormancy into vibrant growth and reproduction, then back into dormancy. Compare any two extremes—summer and winter, spring and fall—and the landscape appears so altered it is hardly recognizable. The look, feel, and fragrance of the forest continually change as seasons come and go, and at any point in time there is a distinct quality and mood to the landscape.

The seasonal rhythm is a direct response to cycles of sun energy. Precipitation occurs throughout the year in the temperate climatological zone encompassing the deciduous forest and is the main source of moisture. Though rainfall is a significant secondary influence on the pace of the seasons, the principal factors governing plant growth are the strength of the sun's rays and the length of the day.

Luminous Qualities

The woods are worth watching if for nothing more than the glorious play of light shining through bare branches, streaming through translucent leaves, making silhouettes and shadows of the forest's myriad lines and forms. The luminous qualities of the forest augment and enhance its color, its flowering, and its architecture.

TOP With a little help from the sun, translucent foliage can be more dramatic than the best flowers. In whorls nearly two feet across, leaves of umbrella magnolia, *Magnolia tripetala*, glow in late-day sun on May 23 in Virginia.

BOTTOM Some of the forest's most luminous moments occur among the ferns. Mid-June backlighting accentuates the finely cut outlines of intermediate wood fern, *Dryopteris intermedia*, in Ohio.

Shadows play over the forms, textures, and colors of the forest, revealing and enhancing each for perhaps an hour, perhaps only a moment. Among the most beguiling phenomena of the deciduous woodlands, shadows create visual combinations that are indelibly linked to seasonal events large and small.

ABOVE We typically content ourselves with four main seasons, but within these, why not recognize and celebrate others such as a season of spring shadows? Etched across the dappled surface of a Delaware stream in early April, the graceful lines of the bare woods will soon retreat behind a mask of new leaves.

OPPOSITE LEFT Beech trunks are the forest's best movie screens, shadows its finest actors. In mid May, beech leaves are still new and highly translucent, and in the gentle spring light, their shadows appear soft against the smooth bark. Their outlines will sharpen as the leaves grow more opaque and the sun grows stronger.

OPPOSITE RIGHT Painted black across the gray bark, shadows of beech leaves reveal the sun's lingering intensity on a crisp late-October day.

Deciduous trees present perfect studies in contrast: their leaves the epitome of delicate translucency, their trunks the ultimate in massive opacity. The interplay of these opposites is especially brilliant in spring and fall.

LEFT April 26 in eastern Pennsylvania.

BELOW October 15 in West Virginia.

ABOVE During mid summer, little light reaches ground level in the forest interior, but the high view is often spectacular as sun-streams pierce through windows in the leafy canopy.

LEFT Sun and moon light play even greater roles when winter has reduced the deciduous landscape to its essential architecture. A full moon illuminates the winter night woods on Valentine's Day, February 14, producing a vision that is at once powerful, humbling, and romantically beautiful.

Color Cycles

There are truly two distinct but overlapping cycles of color in a forest year. The first and most obvious cycle revolves around deciduous foliage; the second turns on flowers. In addition to these are the relatively constant colors of evergreens, tree trunks, and the forest hardscape.

FOLIAGE COLOR CYCLES

In broad perspective, the changing hues of foliage have the most profound effect on the color of the woodland landscape. If we consider spring the beginning of the annual cycle, green quickly becomes the dominant color and remains such for many months. This period is hardly monotonous: though

In your mind's eye, can you picture multiple charts representing the colors of your local woodland landscape as they vary from place to place and season to season? The simple exercise of charting woodland colors will develop your ability to distinguish and appreciate a surprising array of natural hues, and will equip you to take a truly painterly approach to landscape design.

On May 11, the sun illuminates unfurling foliage of beeches leaning over White Clay Creek in southeastern Pennsylvania. Within spring, the season of new greens is among the forest's most delightful times. Many hues, such as the honeyed greens of young beech leaves, are both distinct and fleeting, representing special moments to be savored each time they come around in the forest color cycle.

green may be a single color, the green of the deciduous forest is comprised of a seemingly infinite array of hues, tints, and shades. Following the greens, forest color shifts in autumn to the warm end of the spectrum. Although yellows and reds predominate, a suffusion of blue-purple tones is quite apparent, as are lingering greens. In color diversity and overall saturation, the forest's fall foliage exceeds not only its own peak of flower color, but that of virtually any other landscape in the world. Autumn is indeed so riotous that it is easy to dismiss the quieter period that follows as colorless, though this is hardly the case. The leaves of many deciduous trees, shrubs, and herbs persist well into winter and sometimes fully through it, suspended on branches and stalks or carpeting the ground with a richly varied array of earth tones.

The new foliage of many deciduous species is often suffused with amber, bronze, and red before developing its full complement of chlorophyll. Though these tints are secondary to the prevailing new greens, they add significantly to the spring spectrum. In April, the leaflets of bottlebrush buckeye, *Aesculus parviflora*, open amber colored, held by deep red stalks.

TOP The finely dissected leaves of squirrel corn, *Dicentra cucullaria*, are a cool green, especially compared with the bright olive tones of mosses. This image was taken in mid May along the banks of the Susquehanna River in Maryland.

BOTTOM By early May in northeastern Virginia, the foliage of wild ginger, *Asarum canadense*, and Solomon's seal, *Polygonatum biflorum*, have attained the distinct shades of green that they will wear through summer. They complement and contrast with each other in both color and texture.

OPPOSITE TOP Turning in mid October, a sugar maple, *Acer saccharum*, typifies the warm hues most associated with autumn in the deciduous forest. The predominant gold color is interlaced with red and orange, and accented by lingering greens and the near-black of the trunk and branch tracery.

OPPOSITE BOTTOM If asked to name fall foliage colors, few people would readily list blue, pink, and purple, yet these can indeed be part of the autumn forest. In northern Delaware in mid October, mapleleaf viburnum, *Viburnum acerifolium*, is a distinctly cool-hued presence. Its leaves are washed with grayed tones from dark blue-purple to bright pink, picking up on grayed tree trunks contrasting with background greens.

TOP RIGHT The fall color of any given species often varies considerably depending upon its relative exposure to sunlight. Virginia creeper, *Parthenocissus quinquefolia*, takes on rich salmon-pink tones while scrambling over shaded, lichen-covered boulders in a Virginia forest. The same plant would turn scarlet in direct sunlight.

BOTTOM RIGHT Autumn's pageantry isn't over just because leaves have dropped from branches: the forest floor in turn becomes a vibrantly colored carpet. Leaves of sugar maple, *Acer saccharum*, enliven the ground layer in late October in a northern Delaware woodland.

RIGHT Unless we've been trained in art, our color vocabulary is usually so limited it is completely inadequate for describing the subtle hues readily apparent to the eye in the winter landscape. As an aid to developing observation skills, it helps to play with color names while studying the winter landscape. Instead of just tan or brown, try applying others such as straw, salmon, beige, fawn, amber, russet, leather, or parchment. Many beech leaves that began the year in lime green will persist through the dormant season, adding warm tones to the landscape and growing gradually lighter as they are bleached by the winter sun. Such tones are an important part of a late-February day in northern Delaware as a low fog rises from melting snow.

FLOWER COLOR CYCLES

Forest flowering generally follows a recognizable sequence beginning gently with whites and pastel blues, pinks, and yellows, then gradually warming in tone during summer and autumn. The cycle of flowering color is less consistent than the foliage cycle, however, and is occasionally contradicted by the appearance of bright colors including red and scarlet. Though flowers rarely occur in such quantities that they dominate foliage color, they are important overlays, enhancing the elementary forms, textures, layers, and background colors of the forest. Fruits naturally follow flowers, and those that remain past autumn leaf fall are sometimes the most colorful elements in the late-season landscape.

ABOVE In spring, white flowers are common among trees, shrubs, and herbaceous species in the deciduous forest. Though not colorful in a technical sense, they are dramatic in contrast with the predominant greens. In late April in the Smoky Mountains, blossoms of mountain silverbell, *Halesia tetraptera* var. *monticola*, have fallen nearly one hundred feet from the high canopy above. In the cool spring air, they remain clear and white for nearly another week, delicately defining the outlines of mossy rocks in this mountain stream. They are more conspicuous now than when viewed against the sky.

ABOVE RIGHT The spring color cycle includes an abundance of pastel pinks and pink-purples. A rocky streambank near Cades Cove in the Smoky Mountains is beautifully dusted with fallen redbud flowers during the last week of April. Redbuds, *Cercis canadensis*, would be worth growing even if you never looked directly at them while they bloomed.

RIGHT Jacob's ladder, *Polemonium reptans*, spreads to form a solid carpet on a Pennsylvania floodplain in early May. It is one of many beautiful blue blossoms encountered in the spring woods, bringing bits of the sky down to earth.

ABOVE Bright reds make occasional appearances in the forest's summer calendar of bloom. True to its name, fire pink, *Silene virginica*, sets the woods on fire in mid July in West Virginia. Other woodland summer scarlets and reds include cardinal flower, *Lobelia cardinalis*; bee balm, *Monarda didyma*; and red buckeye, *Aesculus pavia*.

TOP RIGHT Blooming in broad drifts in the spring forest, yellow trilliums, *Trillium luteum*, lend their unique color to the Smoky Mountains landscape in late April.

BOTTOM RIGHT Summer flowering is relatively sparse in shaded parts of the forest, but when present, even white flowers make a dramatic impact against the greens. Flowering stalks of black snakeroot, *Cimicifuga racemosa*, are reminiscent of fireworks as they stream upward from a West Virginia woodland floor in early July.

Though less prevalent in the forest than in full sun habitats, members of the sunflower family, Asteraceae, enliven the autumn woods with white, yellow, and various shades of blue and blue-purple.

ABOVE Delicate but profusely flowering, heart-leaved aster, *Aster cordifolius*, adds light blue and lavender tones to the autumn woods.

TOP LEFT White wood aster, *Aster divaricatus*, blooms with great exuberance underneath trees and shrubs beginning in late August and often continuing until the first frost.

BOTTOM LEFT Bright yellow flower wands of blue-stemmed goldenrod, *Solidago caesia*, coincide in color with the fall foliage of pawpaw, *Asimina triloba*, in the West Virginia mountains in early October.

ABOVE Bright red berries of winterberry holly, *Ilex verticillata*, play against a deep blue sky and silver-gray branches in late October in the Pocono Mountains of Pennsylvania. This color combination will repeat on clear sunny days through winter.

ABOVE RIGHT Just when it seems the year's flowering is finished and the last leaves are falling, witch hazel, *Hamamelis virginiana*, bursts into bloom. The shrub's bright yellow is the lone sunny presence on a dark, rainy late-October day in the mountains near High Point, New Jersey.

CONSTANT COLORS

The deciduous landscape doesn't completely remake itself each year: a number of organic and inorganic elements remain relatively constant, their surface hues adding important nuance. Lichens are often overlooked in design analysis of the woodland landscape, probably because they are more suited to serendipitous occurrence than to deliberate cultivation. They are everywhere in the native woods, adding colors sometimes bright as flowers, and they deserve a conscious welcome in the garden.

AN EVERGREEN PRESENCE

Although needled evergreens (conifers) are a major component of transition forests, they are not integral parts of the mixed deciduous forest. With the exception of eastern hemlock, *Tsuga canadensis*, and to a lesser extent, white pine, *Pinus strobus*, native conifers are not able to tolerate the low light levels

beneath the deciduous canopy. Better adapted and much more common are broad-leaved evergreen trees and shrubs, including American holly, *Ilex opaca*; *Rhododendron* species; mountain laurel, *Kalmia latifolia*; and *Leucothoe* species. The evergreen complement of the deciduous forest also includes many ferns, their spore-producing relatives the club mosses, *Lycopodium* species; a number of low-growing perennial forbs such as partridgeberry, *Mitchella repens*, and *Galax urceolata*; and a few sedges, *Carex* species, and woodrushes, *Luzula* species.

The green presence of any of these is usually a welcome sight during the dormant season, but some play more than a color role: evergreen trees and shrubs have the capacity to abridge the line of view. Such visual restriction is often desirable, but in other situations, it simply diminishes the depth and transparency of the winter woodlands and the luminous effects that depend upon that openness.

TOP LEFT Its open form resulting from the low summer light conditions in this northern Delaware woodland, a large mountain laurel, *Kalmia latifolia*, adds its rich glossy green to a late February day while still allowing a glimpse of the distant landscape.

TOP The bark furrows of a mammoth tulip-tree, *Liriodendron tulipifera*, are painted a startling blue by naturally occurring lichens.

BOTTOM Bright yellow lichens coat the cleft surfaces of loose rocks on a West Virginia mountain slope in mid October, extending the golden glow now fading from the forest foliage.

ABOVE A frond of marginal shield fern, *Dryopteris marginalis*, rests on a lichen-covered rock in a West Virginia forest in October. The complementary greens of the lichen and this evergreen fern will remain relatively constant through winter.

ABOVE RIGHT Growing naturally along the edge of a western Pennsylvania woodland stream, rosebay rhododendron, *Rhododendron maximum*, forms a nearly impenetrable visual barrier between the interior woods and the water.

Time and Transition

The native forest is constantly in flux. Popular myth describes the landscape proceeding through an orderly succession, eventually stabilizing in a climax forest; however, modern scientific evidence proves this is hardly the case. Stability is an illusion, believable only within the narrow time scale of human lives. In the long view, forests metamorphose in response to pervasive changes in climate and other environmental influences, including those resulting from human activity. Though sudden change in a critical factor can result in truly catastrophic effects, such as the loss of elms, *Ulmus americana*, or chestnuts, *Castanea dentata*, due to introduced diseases, much apparent chaos in the life of a forest is actually quite healthy, with loss often balanced by opportunity for renewal and adaptation. The regimented aesthetic of traditional formal gardens is usually in conflict with the necessary plasticity of native forests. A garden that seeks to capture the spirit of the forest must welcome change as an inevitable or even desirable part of the aesthetic, as an essential element in ecological stewardship, and as an endearing part of the story of the woodland landscape.

In 1994 a tornado ripped through a section of White Clay Creek Preserve in southeastern Pennsylvania, dramatically altering the landscape. Hundred-foot-tall tuliptrees, oaks, beeches, and sycamores were twisted and torn like matchsticks. This section of the forest was among the more mature parts of the Preserve, beautiful for its tall trees and rich shrub and herbaceous layers, and the effects of the storm were genuinely traumatic to the local community.

In an effort to put this event in perspective, I began reviewing photographs I'd taken to capture the beauty of local woodlands. I was somewhat surprised to find that many of them included unmistakable evidence of past traumas. The mood of these images was neither somber nor filled with regret, but was instead typically filled with wonder at remarkable shapes and forms that told of strength and healing.

ABOVE Late April sunlight plays against the diverse angles and curves of tree trunks. The leaning tuliptree was nearly toppled by an unknown past event; however, a side branch has taken over as leader, and the tree remains a vital part of the forest. Full of imperfect characters, such scenes are rich in story and visual appeal.

Walk the woods with a child and he or she is likely to run past all the straight-trunked trees to stop, transfixed, before a specimen as fantastic as this beech. Improbably beautiful, it invites all manner of contemplation while standing as remarkable testimony to the resilience of *Fagus grandifolia*. Once met, such unique and memorable individuals become repeat destinations in the forest or in the woodland garden.

ABOVE September 22.

OPPOSITE LEFT October 31.

Much of the forest's beauty and intrigue results from the natural fitting of plants to place. Nearly every woodland environment includes a diverse array of habitat niches, some extensive, others quite specialized. The shape, size, color, and texture of plants vary in response to limits and opportunities inherent in the light, soil, and moisture conditions of each niche.

ABOVE CENTER Who can deny the personality in this sycamore, *Platanus occidentalis*? Its startling character has been shaped by at least a century of creek waters that have washed by and over its place at the edge of a wooded Pennsylvania floodplain, and a mossy patina now accentuates its rough-

hewn features. Sometimes it is possible to design a garden around such a venerable specimen; however, it can also be quite rewarding to encourage the development of new, unique and memorable landmarks by allowing natural processes to run their course.

ABOVE RIGHT Looking like a school of fish densely packed in a tiny pond, trout lilies, *Erythronium americanum*, fill a unique niche afforded by a cleft rock outcrop along the bank of the Susquehanna River in Maryland on April 8. Though trout lilies are notoriously fickle in their flowering, this natural scene suggests the powerful imagery or whimsical beauty that may result from mere foliage occurring in an interesting context.

Renewal often depends upon recycling. In late April in North Carolina, a yellow birch, *Betula alleghaniensis*, appears to straddle an ancient tree stump. In fact, the moist organic material of the decaying stump provided an ideal niche in which the birch seed could germinate. The birch's trunks grew upward as its branching roots grew down and over the stump, establishing themselves in the earth. The stump will eventually rot away entirely, leaving the birch perched on stilts over a hollow space. Such stilt trees, as they are commonly known in the Smoky Mountains, are improbable at first sight, but are easily and amusingly explained when process is preserved in the story of the forest.

TOP The graceful, lilting form of this beech evolved as the tree reached out from its shaded position on the bank toward the brighter open space over the creek. Even in winter, when branches are bare, the pattern of this beautifully asymmetrical tree will recall the summer sunlight.

BOTTOM A "nurse" log nurtures a population of dwarf crested iris, *Iris cristata*, blooming in late April in the North Carolina mountains. Naturally moss covered and rich with minerals and nutrients, the rotting log is an ideal germinating bed for the iris, and its form is evident under the new carpet of blue.

ABOVE The line between the native forest and the cultural landscape is often very fine. Now deep within a Pennsylvania woodland, this row of old oaks and tuliptrees once stood in full sun, marking the boundary line between two pastures. In pure abstract, the dark column contrasts stunningly with the light ranks of surrounding young growth. For those who know how to read the forested landscape, the boundary trees are also an important part of the landscape narrative.

RIGHT Play is a key ingredient in the richest experience of both forest and garden, something to be encouraged in children of all ages. Picked up from the forest floor and inserted upside-down in the bark scales of an oak, pawpaw and red maple leaves catch the late-day light on a West Virginia hillside. Such simple, low-impact play can be a delightful means of gaining insight into the nature of forest materials. No one has demonstrated this more beautifully and persuasively than artist Andy Goldsworthy (1990), whose often-ephemeral creations distill and reveal the quintessential patterns and processes at work in the woodland realm.

Forest Architecture

The architecture of the deciduous forest consists of an elaborate framework built around the availability of light, and it is the vertical organization of this framework that is most dramatic and readily apparent. Superficially, forest vegetation may be separated into an overstory of tall trees that meet the sky, creating an arboreal ceiling, and an understory of all things growing in the relatively shady conditions below. A more detailed view recognizes multiple layers: a high canopy of the tallest trees, a mid level of lower-growing trees, a shrub layer, an herbaceous layer, and a ground layer. Vertically unrestrained, vines move freely through these layers.

There is also a horizontal or lateral organization to the composition of the forest, again resulting primarily from the availability of sunlight. The makeup of vegetation in the shaded interior differs significantly from that inhabiting sunnier edges at the periphery of the woods.

Layers

The layered look is the hallmark of the deciduous forest. From an aesthetic perspective, layering packs a maximum amount of visual interest into any one view: an incredible array of lines, forms, textures, and scales from the majestic to the minute. From a biological perspective, layering is an intricate and ingenious means of sharing space, allowing the greatest number of species to make their homes in the forest, each adapted to the unique environmental conditions found at different levels. Forest layers are not finite—the forces of change and renewal result in a constant interlacing and a blurring of the edges between each layer and the next—but layers do define the deciduous forest. Adopting a layered framework in the design of the woodland garden is a sure way to capture one of the most unique visual motifs of the deciduous forest; it also maximizes the number of varied cultural conditions in the garden, providing appropriate niches to support the widest diversity of woodland species.

CANOPY

There is no overstating the grandeur and dignity of the deciduous forest canopy: it is truly awesome. I've always found the top of the woods especially enthralling in mid winter, when trees are completely bare of leaves. Stand still and follow the lines of massive trunks skyward, and you'll observe their graceful splitting into repeatedly finer segments until they become mere threads, barely distinguishable to the naked eye. Then move forward just a step or two, while looking up, and literal millions of angles will shift and change. The canopy is a fabulous study in intricate detail.

Exquisitely displayed in winter's exposed canopy, the signature of a tree is written in its branching patterns and angles. Most trees, including beech, *Fagus grandifolia*, oaks, *Quercus* species, and hickories, *Carya* species, branch in an alternate fashion; others, including ash, *Fraxinus* species, and maple, *Acer* species, produce branches in opposite pairs. With a keen eye, these differences can be appreciated from considerable distance. Individual branch angles also vary among different species; for example, the angles of beech

ABOVE Comprised mostly of red oak, *Quercus rubra*, and beech, *Fagus grandifolia*, the forest canopy brushes the sky nearly one hundred feet from the earth in Pennsylvania in early January. The canopy is the collective summit of the tallest trees in the forest, those capable of growing far above all other vegetation to secure the lion's share of sunlight.

LEFT The deeply furrowed, sinuous branches of burr oak, *Quercus macrocarpa*, play against the late March sky in Wisconsin.

Straight as rules and strictly upright, the trunks of three tuliptrees, *Liriodendron tulipifera*, appear as huge black cylinders, their massive lines accentuated by the delicacy of crossing beech branches, in late March in Delaware.

are relatively narrow, while those of maples are broad. Dormant trees can also be distinguished by the characteristic lines of their branches. The branches of some, including maples, continue along fairly smooth lines. Others such as black gum, *Nyssa sylvatica*, and burr oak, *Quercus macrocarpa*, are noted for their sinuous curves.

Marvelous in detail, the canopy is also visually fascinating in broad perspective: a diverse collection of tree shapes sketched by branches, interrupted occasionally by small patches of open sky. The crowns of canopy trees are shaped by many forces including storms and light competition from other trees; however, they often maintain representative outlines. When growing through the canopy and into the light, the summits of tuliptrees, *Liriodendron tulipifera*, form distinctive spires. Beeches, under the same conditions, become broad, rounded brushes. Breaks in the canopy set off the outlines of the trees, and they also function as literal windows—the forest's fenestration—through which some sunlight will pass to sustain the understory below.

Closer to earth, the great boles of canopy trees contribute mightily to landscape line and texture. The solid vertical lines of tree trunks contrast handsomely with the many horizontal lines often found in the forest, such as delicate crossing branches, flowing streams, or exposed layers of native rock. Bark colors, textures, and patterns add to the visual richness of the woodlands, delightful in their variation and idiosyncrasies. Beeches, *Fagus grandifolia*, are famously gray and smooth; mature ashes, *Fraxinus americana*, are often knobby; chestnut oaks, *Quercus prinus*, are deeply groovy; and shagbark hickories, *Carya ovata*, as might be expected, are shaggy.

Adding to the architectural quality of the forest is the inherent capacity of tree trunks and secondary branches to frame views. As in painting or photography, the foreground interest provided by trees is often a critical point of perspective in the visual composition of the landscape. Whether upright or arching, arranged in a simple pair or in tandem rows, the sturdy lines of trees are wonderfully effective in organizing a scene and directing the eye, and this holds true in the native forest or the woodland garden.

Flowering in the canopy is a relatively subtle event, especially when compared with the vibrancy of the canopy's autumn color. The flowers of most tall trees are quite small and their colors often inconspicuous shades of green, amber, and light brown. Large-flowered exceptions include *Magnolia* species, their relative the tuliptree, *Liriodendron tulipifera*, and most notably, silverbells, *Halesia* species. A number of trees with minute flowers do manage to put on a noticeable show simply because they bloom in such profusion: maples are good examples. Sugar maples, *Acer saccharum*, produce copious quantities of bright yellow-green flowers, suspended in clusters from slender threadlike stalks of the same color. In full bloom, the trees take on a light yellow cast, visible from a great distance. The tiny flowers of red maples, *Acer rubrum*, vary in color from deep red to scarlet. At the peak of spring flowering, trees are enveloped by a noticeable red haze, which intensifies as the

ABOVE Deep furrows and prominent corky ridges distinguish the bark of chestnut oak, *Quercus prinus*, growing on a high rocky outcrop in West Virginia.

BELOW Its horizontal lines intensified by a February snow in Kentucky, an outcrop of stratified limestone beautifully sets off the vertical lines of mixed native hardwood trees.

ABOVE A multitude of minute yellow-green flowers colors the crown of a sugar maple, *Acer saccharum*, in early May in Virginia.

TOP RIGHT Visually and structurally, the forest is about framing. In mid May two trees meet above a Pennsylvania stream to form a continuous arch. This natural frame organizes the view and encourages the contemplation of trees further distant.

BOTTOM RIGHT The flowering and fruiting of red maples, *Acer rubrum*, is one of the truly memorable color events in the spring canopy. Two red maples displaying natural variation in fruiting color are backlit in the early April sun in northern Delaware.

tiny female flowers mature into the winged fruits characteristic of many maple species.

MID-LEVEL OR UNDERSTORY TREES

Lower-growing trees populate the next layer below the canopy. Among them are dogwoods, *Cornus florida* and *Cornus alternifolia*; shadblow, *Amelanchier* species; ironwood, *Carpinus caroliniana*; and pawpaw, *Asimina triloba*. Since the maximum height of true understory trees is usually twenty-five to fifty feet, and canopy trees often grow eighty to one hundred feet or more, there

In full bloom in mid April in the Delaware piedmont, shadblow or serviceberry, *Amelanchier arborea*, is one of the earliest-flowering understory trees. It shares dogwood's habit of producing branches in flat planes. Although typically a modest-sized tree, often with multiple stems, single-trunked specimens of this species can occasionally reach nearly sixty feet in height, mingling with lower canopy trees.

is typically a band of open space between the two layers, contributing to the grandeur and cathedral-like appearance of the forest interior.

Finer in most details than canopy species, understory trees add much to the forest's visual diversity and contrast. Their trunks are always smaller in diameter, and their branches often stretch in broad horizontal planes, seeking light. They also add their own distinct set of bark characters to the array of surface textures, and their own unique autumn hues.

Flowering dogwood, *Cornus florida*, blooms profusely in the understory in late April, taking advantage of increased light from openings in the oak canopy caused by storms in recent years. Decked with blossoms, the dogwood's delicate horizontal planes offer distinct contrast with the vertical lines of the massive oaks.

Flowering in understory trees can be quite spectacular, especially when natural senescence, storms, or other events have created significant openings in the canopy, illuminating lower layers. The high canopy typically takes the brunt of storm forces, acting as a buffer for understory trees. Of course, limbs and large sections of canopy trees may come crashing down on trees in the understory, significantly altering their shapes.

In a healthy forest, true understory trees are intermingled with other species that have the potential to become canopy trees. These may be young plants of the species comprising the current canopy, or they may be different, naturally tall-growing trees which are able to establish footholds in the low light conditions of the understory. These so-called tolerant species will often grow at reduced rates and heights for many years and then quickly move into vigorous growth if the existing canopy opens up. In time, the tolerant species

ABOVE Pawpaw, *Asimina triloba*, typically spreads by underground stems, forming dramatic patches or colonies in the understory. Its huge leaves provide bold, colorful contrast with the dark trunks of canopy trees in mid October in West Virginia.

LEFT In the early May understory, the sinewy bark and delicate branch tracery of ironwoods, *Carpinus caroliniana*, complement the sturdy upright pillars of tuliptrees, *Liriodendron tulipifera*.

Though less powerful than canopy trees in a grand architectural sense, understory trees still serve as significant framing devices, ordering and organizing the woodland landscape at levels closer to human height.

LEFT A casual trail is bordered by naturally occurring ironwoods, *Carpinus caroliniana*, on the edge of a northern Delaware floodplain. This accidental landscape served as direct inspiration for a lakeside woodland walk in the Peirce's Woods garden at Longwood Gardens in nearby Pennsylvania. The design intent was for light-barked trees to line an existing path; however, there was also a desire to use trees that would be more regionally representative and better adapted to local climate than paper birches, *Betula papyrifera*, the classic white-barked tree of New England.

ABOVE Along the same floodplain trail, a shrub layer of mapleleaf viburnum, *Viburnum acerifolium*, adds its rich purple and magenta hues in mid October, in stunning contrast to the muscular gray of the ironwoods.

may eventually overtake and replace the existing canopy species. Such change and evolution is normal in the life of a forest, though it may occur so slowly as to be imperceptible to the casual observer.

SHRUB LAYER

Visually, shrubs are like glue, holding forest trees together, a low horizontal matrix punctuated by vertical pillars. Species diversity in the shrub layer is frequently much greater than in understory or canopy trees, resulting in an exceptionally rich array of shapes, sizes, textures, flowers and fragrances, foliage colors, and fruits.

Though the shrub layer generally occupies a forest layer perhaps three to twelve feet in height, its upper limit often melds with the understory tree layer, since the distinction between trees and shrubs can be ambiguous. By popular definition, shrubs are multistemmed, branching from the ground, and are of relative short stature. Trees are frequently defined as reaching heights of at least fifteen feet, typically with a single stem or trunk and a well-

ABOVE Spicebush, *Lindera benzoin*, is often overlooked as a flowering shrub, though its cheerful yellow blossoms do much to brighten the April woodlands. Many shrubs such as spicebush are tolerant of the low light conditions far below the canopy.

LEFT Dark trunks of tall tuliptrees, *Liriodendron tulipifera*, rise dramatically from a golden matrix of spicebush foliage, *Lindera benzoin*, in the northern Delaware woods in late October.

ABOVE Shrubs are responsible for much of the fall color at lower levels in the forest. Autumn hues linger into late October in the leaves of mapleleaf viburnum, *Viburnum acerifolium*, running in sheets near the forest bottom.

RIGHT Roseshell azalea, *Rhododendron prinophyllum*, adds its spicy-sweet scent to a Virginia forest in mid May. Fragrant-flowering shrubs are a delightful element in the spring forest or woodland garden. Many native azalea species and other shrubs such as sweetshrub, *Calycanthus floridus*, are reliable, fragrant bloomers even in shade conditions.

developed crown. These definitions are satisfactory for categorizing clear examples such as blueberries and oaks, but useless for distinguishing a flowering dogwood and a witch hazel, each of which may grow multistemmed and over fifteen feet tall.

Many shrub species have running natures, growing together to form sweeps and masses that border and define woodland spaces at human level, creating intimacy and enclosure.

HERBACEOUS LAYER

Herbaceous plants are usually the major focus of flower gardens; however, they comprise only one element in the grand scale of the forest environment. Though the herbaceous layer is indeed full of flowers, even the most intense flowering lasts for relatively brief intervals. Foliage, both seasonal and evergreen, is responsible for much of the enduring beauty in this layer.

The herbaceous layer includes many species whose growth requirements are so obscure and exacting that their deliberate cultivation in the garden is impractical or impossible. Among these are hemi-parasites such as beech drops, *Epifagus virginiana*, and saprophytes including Indian pipes, *Monotropa uniflora*. These are integral parts of the forest ecosystem and a joy to be appreciated when present in the woodlands or in the woodland garden.

ABOVE This Maryland floodplain is a classic example of the light- and space-sharing strategies of the deciduous forest. Mayapples, *Podophyllum peltatum*, and bluebells, *Mertensia virginica*, take advantage of the sunlight in early April, blooming while the high canopy of ash, beech, and sycamore and the understory shrubs and trees including pawpaws, *Asimina triloba*, are still leafless. The pawpaws will soon flower, before the large ash leafs out. The bluebells will be past flower and going to seed by the time the trees and shrubs shade the floodplain, and will then go dormant. The large efficient leaves of Mayapples allow the plants to continue growing into the shady season, but they too will die back in summer after their fruits are mature.

LEFT The foliage textures of many woodland herbs equal their flowering interest. *Trillium erectum* boldly contrasts with the fine-cut delicacy of squirrel corn, *Dicentra cucullaria*, in a Maryland forest in mid April. The varied greens of the two plants are set off against the rich red-brown color of the decaying log.

LEFT New leaves of skunk cabbage, *Symplocarpus foetidus*, paint a bright green swatch across the moist forest floor in late April. They'll fade as the woody layers fill in, but at this time of year, nothing is so bold and green.

BELOW Shag carpeting may have vanished along with the 1970s, but the lush green of Pennsylvania sedge, *Carex pensylvanica*, has endured for decades as an elegant forest floor covering beneath beeches in the North Carolina mountains. Though native grasses are a minority in deeply shaded woodland environments, many sedges and woodrushes, *Luzula* species, contribute to the beauty of the herbaceous layer.

True epiphytes are scarce in woodlands, but many herbaceous species will thrive if provided a bit of moist organic matter, whether it be along an old log, on top of a boulder, or in the crevice of a rock ledge.

TOP LEFT Though appearing quite gardenesque, this assemblage is an entirely uncontrived bit of the Delaware woodlands in early August. Organic matter atop a large rock supports a mix of wild ginger, *Asarum canadense*; Christmas fern, *Polystichum acrostichoides*; and white wood aster, *Aster divaricatus*. The canopy overhead consists of beech, *Fagus grandifolia*; oak, *Quercus* species; and tuliptree, *Liriodendron tulipifera*.

TOP RIGHT Perched on a Pennsylvania outcrop in early May, a bright green common polypody fern, *Polypodium virginianum*, complements the dark mossy patina of the rocks. This evergreen fern is a delightful presence through all the seasons of the woodland landscape. When flowers are not the focus, plants with enduringly attractive foliage become key elements in the landscape. In the herbaceous layer of the deciduous forest, ferns are among the finest.

RIGHT Large-flowered bellwort, *Uvularia grandiflora*, is intermingled with maidenhair fern, *Adiantum pedatum*, on a Virginia forest slope in early May. The fern's graceful foliage will persist through the growing season, long after the bellwort flowers have faded.

Ferns often outshine all other plants in the herbaceous layer in autumn. Cinnamon ferns, *Osmunda cinnamonea*, light the Maine woods with reddish-brown hues in late September.

A canopy oak gracefully meets the forest floor in mid March, its mossy covering contrasting with the lighter-colored duff. Root flares of big trees are among the forest's most powerful visual motifs and are worth celebrating in the garden.

GROUND LAYER

Between the tree trunks and the stems and stalks of woodland plants, the forest floor is covered with duff: decaying vegetable matter such as leaves and twigs. Leaf litter, the bulk of which is produced by trees, is key to forest vegetation. As it decomposes, it influences soil chemistry, depth, and nutrient composition. This knowledge alone should be enough to invest fallen leaves with apparent beauty, but in fact, they are quite beautiful simply for the mixture of colors, shapes, and patterns they bring to the forest.

Exposed soil is rarely evident in the forest unless a disturbance causes erosion. Mosses often cover any soil that remains bared. Prevalent at ground level and on the shaded surfaces of trees and rocks, mosses account for a significant percentage of the forest's low-level greens. Mostly evergreen, mosses are especially eye-catching and welcome when encountered in the winter landscape.

ABOVE Leaves of beech, *Fagus grandifolia*, oak, *Quercus* species, and black gum, *Nyssa sylvatica*, adorn the forest floor in late October. Beautiful for its color and pattern, this carpet of fallen foliage is also critically important to forest moisture and nutrient cycles.

LEFT Luminous green mosses clothe rounded rocks in a stream in the Smoky Mountains. Though mosses will grow in much drier sites, the lushness in this late-April scene is dependent upon a steady, high level of moisture.

VINES

 Vines are often a beautiful and intriguing presence in the forest landscape. They link all the layers, traversing the forest vertically from ground level to the upper reaches of the canopy. Forcing a moral filter over the forest, all vines would be judged opportunists at best, parasites at worst. Lacking stems sufficiently strong to support themselves, vines scramble up and over other plants in their quest for sunlight. If vines are too vigorous, they can kill their supports by blocking their light supply; this trait is especially apparent in the rapacious advance of introduced vines including kudzu, *Pueraria lobata*, and oriental bittersweet, *Celastrus orbiculatus*, through North American deciduous forests. Vines and their living supports often coexist indefinitely if conditions are suitable. I know of one instance where a large beech tree leaning over a creek has actually been stayed from toppling by huge grape vines that anchor it from the upper bank, but this is certainly out of the ordinary.

TOP No honor among thieves? In a Virginia forest in early May, pendent seed capsules remain on the dried stems of wild yam, *Dioscorea villosa*, a native herbaceous vining species. The yam had evidently used the grape, *Vitis* species, for support in the previous year.

BOTTOM Sunlight illuminates the rounded leaves of Dutchman's pipe, *Aristolochia macrophylla*, as it climbs the trunk of an understory tree in the North Carolina forest in mid July.

A golden swirl of Dutchman's pipe is set against foliage of red maple, *Acer rubrum*, in the sunlight canopy of a West Virginia forest.

Areas

In addition to its vertical layers, the forest may be segregated into two general areas based roughly on the exposure to light and other environmental influences: the interior and the edge.

INTERIOR

In a pure sense, a forest interior is a sizeable area enclosed by a more or less continuous canopy, undisturbed and uninterrupted by broad watercourses, roads, houses, and other human intrusions. The layers are all intact and the growing environment below the canopy is almost entirely one of shade. Today, few of us experience such places unless we travel some distance from home, although many smaller preserves and most national forests provide the opportunity to explore forest interiors. These places are critical to forest animals, including many bird species, which often require a considerable area of interior woodlands to survive and reproduce. Though the plant diversity and venerable specimens encountered in deep, mature forests are often awe-inspiring, the vegetation and environmental conditions near or at the forest edge are generally more instructive to the woodland gardener.

EDGE

Light is increasingly available nearing the edge of the forest, and it has a significant influence on the composition and behavior of the vegetation. Edge conditions occur wherever the forest is interrupted, by either natural or artificial conditions: where the forest meets a road, a utility right of way, a wet meadow, a rocky promontory, a river, stream, or lake.

At some edges, the species composition remains much the same but plants behave quite differently. They often bloom much more heavily, and their autumn foliage colors are usually accentuated. In other situations interior forest species are joined by sun-loving plants, making for combinations that are frequently quite colorful, especially in autumn.

In the interior or at the edge, woodland waters often reflect and enhance the colors of the forest canopy. They may also bring the reflected colors of the sky into view.

ABOVE LEFT A small pool in the forest interior captures the magnificent greens of a Smoky Mountains springtime. Deeply shaded, this natural woodland water garden is captivating despite the absence of flowers.

ABOVE RIGHT Looking literally like a river of gold, White Clay Creek in southeastern Pennsylvania reflects the late afternoon sky in mid October. The fruiting stalks of Joe-pye weed, *Eupatorium fistulosum*, stand architecturally against the glowing water. This species cannot tolerate the shade of a forest interior, but it thrives in the sun and moisture afforded by this location along the creek.

Favorable light and moisture conditions along forest streams often result in generous flowering and rich autumn coloration in trees and shrubs lining the banks.

OPPOSITE BOTTOM Fringe tree, *Chionanthus virginicus*, flowers freely in the sunny edge bordering a West Virginia river in mid May.

RIGHT Leaves of a flowering dogwood, *Cornus florida*, turn rich red as the tree reaches out into sunlight over a Delaware creek in mid October.

BELOW A moist meadow on a low floodplain interrupts the Pennsylvania forest. In mid August, cut-leaf coneflower, *Rudbeckia laciniata*, blooms gold against the purple flowers of New York ironweed, *Vernonia noveboracensis*. Bordering the meadow are black willows, *Salix nigra*, growing along the creek, and a dense forest of mostly beech and oak begins beyond them.

Out from the canopy and growing in full sun, a mixture of redbud, *Cercis canadensis*, flowering dogwood, *Cornus florida*, and black haw, *Viburnum prunifolium*, blooms profusely on a Virginia slope in early May. The contrasting dark green in the background belongs to red cedars, *Juniperus virginiana*.

ABOVE LEFT Surprisingly enduring combinations are sometimes found in edge locations. Red cedars, *Juniperus virginiana*, are not shade tolerant and would not normally survive long in the company of sugar maples, *Acer saccharum*. For perhaps more than a century, this challenging location at the edge of a West Virginia outcrop has provided the red cedars with plenty of sunlight while keeping the maple forest slightly removed.

ABOVE Staghorn sumac, *Rhus typhina*, adds its brilliant autumn hues to a West Virginia forest edge in mid October.

LEFT The natural spacing of trees growing at a woodland edge is often quite close. Encouraged by sunlight beyond the forest edge, a small grove of *Sassafras albidum* has stems spaced as close as a foot from one another. Thinning of the grove may occur naturally as individuals eventually shade each other, but some of the characteristic curves in the trunks will survive with these trees into maturity.

ROADSIDE WOODLANDS AND FOREST RELICS

As residential and commercial development claims more land each year, roadside rights of way become increasingly important reserves of regional plant diversity and provide opportunities for displaying some of the beauty of the deciduous forest. Many roads cut through woodlands create edge situations conducive to abundant flowering of native trees and shrubs; others present colorful glimpses of forest layers. Forest remnants and individual specimen trees surviving on public and private lands are important links to North America's woodland past and may prove to be unique and necessary repositories of local genetic diversity.

A naturally occurring group of shadblow, *Amelanchier arborea*, flowers profusely along a West Virginia roadside in early May, set off by white pines, *Pinus strobus*.

ABOVE An ancient white oak, *Quercus alba,* is conserved as part of the modern landscape of Winterthur Museum and Gardens in the Delaware piedmont. This great relic of an earlier forest has witnessed many events in the local landscape, including the arrival and demise of the railroad. It is a meaningful link to the natural and cultural history of the region.

TOP LEFT The January sun plays through sugar maples, *Acer saccharum,* closely bordering a narrow Pennsylvania secondary road. Though hardly a forest, these locally native deciduous trees bring a bit of the regional woodlands into the everyday experience of driving.

BOTTOM LEFT A solid shrub layer of sweet pepperbush, *Clethra alnifolia,* glows gold in late October in a moist forest edge bordering a Delaware highway. Canopy trees include sweet-gum, *Liquidambar styraciflua,* and black gum, *Nyssa sylvatica.* American holly, *Ilex opaca,* adds its evergreen hue to the understory.

Diversity and the Beauty of Provenance

The visual richness of the forest is directly dependent on its biological diversity, which resides not only in the number of different species present but also in variations within each species. Variation is a natural result of the sexual reproductive process and is critical to the ability of plants to adapt to changing conditions.

The concept of species is, after all, an artificial means of segregating a complex, constantly evolving living community into a number of discrete and recognizable entities. It's convenient, for example, to define white oak, *Quercus alba*, and swamp white oak, *Quercus bicolor*, as distinct species, each with its own unique combination of traits, but look closely within any population of either and you'll observe considerable variation in characteristics such as time of bloom, leaf shape, or autumn color. In addition, these two oaks naturally hybridize, so if you were to study a forest where the two grow closely together, you're likely to find seedlings that exhibit characteristics from both species. Natural hybrids may never progress beyond infrequent localized occurrences, or they may eventually stabilize to become new oak species. No species is forever, not even one as seemingly timeless as white oak. If we don't respect and conserve the living systems that support adaptive variation, where will tomorrow's forest species come from? Seedlings, and the promise they represent, are a good thing in the forest and in the woodland garden.

While it is neatly convenient to imagine a species as being nearly identical over its native range of occurrence, this is rarely the case. Most species exhibit variation resulting from genetic adaptation to different regional conditions; for example, red maple, *Acer rubrum*, is considered native over much of eastern North America, from Canada south to Florida, but an individual tree from a population in the southern part of the range may be quite different from one that originated in the north. The two plants might differ in cold hardiness, heat tolerance, moisture requirements, disease resistance, habit of growth, flower color, or many other characteristics that could affect their relative suitability in a particular forest or garden. The term *provenance* is used

Distinctly different colors in the winged fruits of red maples, *Acer rubrum*, are an example of variation due to provenance. Though local soil, air, and moisture conditions can also affect attributes such as fruit color, genetic variation resulting from regional adaptation is profound.

TOP In Virginia in early May, the fruits of a red maple are colored salmon pink.

BOTTOM In late April in Delaware, a red maple's fruits turn orange-red.

to describe the origin of plants; for example, one red maple tree may be of Missouri provenance, another of Minnesota provenance.

The importance of plant provenance may have different purposes. From a purely aesthetic standpoint, plants of one provenance may be more visually exciting than those of another. The foliage of alumroot, *Heuchera americana*, tends to be a solid green in plants from northern provenance; plants of southern mountain provenance frequently have leaves that are beautifully marked with silver tones or shades of bronze and purple. Such dramatically marked plants are the obvious choice in a garden inclined toward beauty; however, if the motive is to replicate, conserve, or restore the genetic legacy of one's region, then plants of local provenance should be chosen. Gardens usually offer the opportunity for a reasonable compromise between these two approaches. I delight in growing many marked-leaf heucheras, but when it came to planting black gum, *Nyssa sylvatica*, in our home garden, I looked for plants of

Leaves from six plants growing within ten feet of each other in a native population of alumroot, *Heuchera americana*, along a stream in the Smoky Mountains of North Carolina on May 23.

I'm ambivalent about scenes such as this one. A row of identical maples, genetic replicates of one another, turns evenly scarlet in mid November in northern Delaware. Undoubtedly dramatic in their fall finery, they make me think of a colorful group of revelers arriving too late to a party; everyone else has already had their fun and gone to sleep. Red maples are common in the native woodlands surrounding this landscape, but they color long before mid November. As a means of extending autumn's color, the clonal cultivar trees, selected from distant provenance, are splendidly effective. If the intent is to mirror the timing and the rich variation in reds and oranges that is characteristic of seedling red maples in the regional forest, they are clearly not the best choice.

Pennsylvania provenance in an effort to celebrate some of the unique regional qualities of form and autumn color that I admire in trees in the nearby woodland preserve.

Exotic Questions

The issue of exotic species is an emotional one that has become increasingly contentious. There is no question that the eastern deciduous forest has been profoundly affected by exotics; however, any judgment of these changes as ultimately good or bad is the province of morality, not biology.

What can be said is that, in an alarmingly short frame of time, exotic species have had a destructive effect on the balance of long-evolved forest ecosystems. Some of these introductions have been inadvertent, including the diseases that obliterated the American chestnut, *Castanea dentata*, and are now claiming the eastern hemlock, *Tsuga canadensis*. The majority of exotic plants that plague regional forests have been introduced deliberately in the service of agriculture, horticulture, or soil conservation. In the deciduous forest, the list of troublesome exotics includes familiar names such as Norway maple, *Acer platanoides*; oriental bittersweet, *Celastrus orbiculatus*; autumn olive, *Eleagnus umbellata*; burning bush, *Euonymus alatus*; Japanese honeysuckle, *Lonicera japonica*; kudzu, *Pueraria lobata*; and multiflora rose, *Rosa multiflora*.

In some situations, exotics have only been able to gain a foothold because the forest has already been weakened by other environmental factors such as extended droughts or acid rain. In other cases, exotic species have simply proved more vigorous and competitive, discrediting the frequent claim that native plants should be grown because they are always better adapted. Native plants may be better adapted, but what is most important is that they have proved their ability to co-exist within the balance of a forest community, something that cannot be said for many exotics.

Gardeners contemplating the issue of natives and exotics might gain insight by reviewing the definitions of these relative terms. Though the word *na-*

tive means "indigenous; belonging to by birth," it does not define a time frame. Many of the plants we call native ultimately derive from exotic ancestry: they just happened to have become established here long before the plants that we currently deem exotic. Also, if the issue of provenance is taken into account, how precise is it for a Pennsylvania gardener to confer native status on a black gum, *Nyssa sylvatica*, imported from a Florida forest, although the species may occur naturally in both states? The word *exotic* means "foreign" and "extraneous," but I've always found the second definition most interesting: "having the charm or fascination of the unfamiliar." For those of us gardening with the American woodlands, the challenge is perhaps to adopt an ethic that promotes a healthy balance in the forest community and the designed landscape, and to adopt an aesthetic that recognizes the charm and fascination of the familiar—one that finds both beauty and utility in the common ground.

Though visually arresting and enticing, burning bush, *Euonymus alatus*, overwhelms the native shrub layer in White Clay Creek Preserve in northern Delaware in early November. This shrub is ubiquitous in gardens and public parks, from which it is increasingly spreading through native woodlands.

CHAPTER TWO

Learning from a Woodland Stream

IN MARCH 1983, I began a photographic study of Red Clay Creek as it runs south of Kennett Square in southeastern Pennsylvania. I focused my camera on the view upstream from a small bridge and began a near-daily record of events. In addition to the date and time of each photograph, I recorded my observations about plants, animals, the water, and the sky. I noted the weather and sometimes how it seemed to affect the mood of the scene. As a gardener first inspired by a love of native places in the forested Northeast, I was seeking a deeper understanding of the natural patterns and processes that characterize the woodland landscape. I'd always wanted to make a garden that evoked the spirit of the deciduous forest, and I hoped this study would help me toward my goal. What began as a simple exercise in observation has proved to be one of the most essential elements in my education as a gardener.

In my original plans, the Red Clay Creek site was to be number six in a set of seven places I planned to photograph repeatedly. The other sites I chose were all within the nearby White Clay Creek watershed, and though each of these rivaled the Red Clay location in visual appeal, I found at the end of the first year I had no more than seventeen images of any one of them. Of the Red Clay, I'd accumulated nearly five hundred photographs. The explanation was obvious in retrospect: though the White Clay sites were actually closer to my home, none of them were located along my routine path. In contrast, I crossed the bridge over the Red Clay on my way to work at Longwood Gardens. It was a convenient delight to add a few moments of observation and photography to my necessary journey. I learned more from the Red Clay site simply because I saw more of it; it became a regular influence on my awareness.

I've come to see this as one of the most important revelations of my study, since it relates so directly to the garden and its influence on our perception of the larger landscape. For many of us, our home gardens are the landscapes we experience most often and come to know most intimately. They are a familiar and convenient presence in the daily routines of living. Given good design and sympathetic architecture, they are the first things we view through the bedroom, bath, or kitchen windows. Without even trying, we are alert to landscape events large and small. Though the obvious seasonal cycles of deciduous woodlands are unparalleled in their drama and contrast, a great deal of the delight and intrigue of this landscape is subtly nuanced and is most fully appreciated by a trained eye and a steady gaze. The immersive nature of the garden affords us those opportunities, and so a garden that is truly reflective of the woodlands is perhaps one of our surest means of learning to appreciate the woodlands itself.

I chose March 31 as my starting point in time, selecting what I knew to be the low ebb of color in the local woodland landscape. With spring's drama due, this seemed a good beginning. The air was already warming and again laden with fragrance, something distinctly absent from cold, crisp winter breezes. I set my tripod by the second railpost on the bridge, using it as a fixed point for photography, and captured the scene. Cloudy skies are characteristic of late March in this part of Pennsylvania, and on this overcast afternoon I saw the landscape mostly as a study in grays. The white bark of leaning sycamores, *Platanus occidentalis*, offered the only significant contrast, making up somewhat for the absence of sunny spots and shadows in the diffuse light. Most of the local native plant species still lie dormant, so the only obvious greens belonged to the basal rosettes of two exotic opportunists, garlic mustard, *Alliaria petiolata*, and poison hemlock, *Conium maculatum*.

March 31, 1983, at 4:30 P.M. Upstream view, west-southwest, of Red Clay Creek.

I made a visual inventory of the site to become more fully oriented and to provide a record that would serve as a point of comparison for inevitable change. Undistracted by color, my eye was intrigued first by the basic architecture of the landscape. Two tall trees leaned out from the north and south banks to form an arch over a fallen companion, whose still-sturdy trunk spanned the creek. Together the three created a nearly formal framework, directing my gaze further upstream toward the creek's ultimate vanishing point.

Working from my first photograph, I made a simple pen-and-ink sketch of the upstream view, singling out and assigning numbers to more than a dozen trees I imagined would be the major players in my creekside drama. I used a soft line to depict the tops of distant trees as they met the sky, sloping from the hill above the south bank to the north bank floodplain. The natural bridge at the scene's center (tree number 1) proved to be a tuliptree, *Liriodendron tulipifera*. The right side of the arch was formed by a sycamore, *Platanus occidentalis* (tree number 2) and the left by a double-trunked green ash, *Fraxinus pennsylvanica* (tree number 3). At the base of the ash, a large dogwood, *Cornus florida* (tree number 6), reached out toward the creek, its branches forming broad planes tipped with enlarged buds that would open into May flowers. I noticed a number of other dogwoods growing along the bank upstream from the arch, but most had formed only leaf buds.

I was able to make these winter identifications by using my accumulated knowledge of bark patterns and with the help of William M. Harlow's *Fruit Key and Twig Key to Trees and Shrubs* (1959). Harlow's classic has been in print in various forms for more than half a century, and this modest paperback field guide is still a marvelous tool for anyone interested in putting names on dormant, native, deciduous trees and shrubs.

With my initial inventory complete, I began wondering about past events that had shaped the scene. Searching through my archives, I found I'd taken three casual photographs of the upstream view on earlier travels across the bridge. Though not framed precisely like the photographs in my study, they proved the center tuliptree had stood with two others (trees number 4 and 5) on the south bank as recently as 1978 (see top photo next page) and that it had topped before 1981. I wondered how much time would pass before it would break and be washed downstream and out of sight. (I got my answer thirteen years later, in 1996.)

I watched spring unfold from my vantage point on the bridge. Though changes were slow and subtle at first, by the third week of April I could easily spot a number of plants stirring to life. On the north bank, box elders, *Acer negundo* (tree number 9), were in full bloom, their new leaves lime

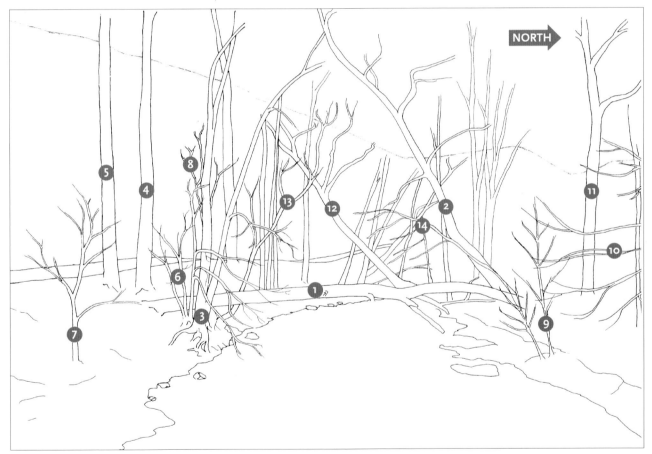

March 31, 1983, at 4:30 P.M. Schematic of upstream view, west-southwest, of Red Clay Creek. Key to trees: (1, 4, 5) tuliptree, *Liriodendron tulipifera*; (2, 12) sycamore, *Platanus occidentalis*; (3) ash, *Fraxinus pennsylvanica*; (6) flowering dogwood, *Cornus florida*; (7) black walnut, *Juglans nigra*; (8) Norway maple, *Acer platanoides*; (9) box elder, *Acer negundo*; (10) American beech, *Fagus grandifolia*; (11) swamp hickory, *Carya cordiformis*; (13, 14): wild cherry, *Prunus serotina*.

TOP LEFT Taken in March 1978, predating my study, this photograph shows three tulip-trees standing close together on the south bank. The leaning tree, already failing at this time, had fallen across the creek by 1981.

BOTTOM LEFT April 18, 1983, at 4:20 P.M. Spring begins to unfold in the deciduous forest.

green. Beyond them, the delicate flowers of spicebush, *Lindera benzoin*, were bright yellow on still-leafless stems. On the floodplain, the strengthening afternoon sun reflected off thousands of Mayapples, *Podophyllum peltatum*, opening like miniature parasols.

I wandered down to the floodplain to observe further details and was surprised to find a population of trout lilies, *Erythronium americanum*, in full bloom among the Mayapples and emerging leaves of wild leeks, *Allium tricoccum*. Though all the trout lilies looked superficially alike, with golden-yellow tepals, I noticed on closer inspection that the flowers of some plants had yellow stamens, others were orange, and still others were deep red. I don't believe it occurred to me to choose a favorite. I was delighted by the obvious variation occurring in this little population within my study site. This discovery and others like it taught me to seek and celebrate the diversity within living populations, both in wild places and in the garden.

ABOVE Variation in the trout lily population on the floodplain includes anthers of yellow, red, and orange.

LEFT Trout lilies, *Erythronium americanum*, Mayapples, *Podophyllum peltatum*, and wild leek, *Allium tricoccum*, begin new growth on the floodplain during the third week of April.

The floodplain was also to home to false hellebore, *Veratrum viride*, the pointed tips of which were rocketing from the soil's surface, unfurling glossy, pleated leaves in dramatic spirals. I'd never seen this plant in a garden before and was perplexed that something so beautifully dramatic was apparently not invited to be part of the repertoire of ornamental horticulture.

As if time were moving backward, the landscape was snow covered when I stopped on the bridge on the morning of April 20: spicebush, box elder, and floodplain flowers were all under a light mantle of white. Though I feared they might be damaged by the sudden chilling, when the snow was melted a day later they all proved to be unharmed. This snow was remarkably late but was well within the limits of historic occurrence in the region. The climate of eastern North America is notoriously uneven in its spring warming and its autumn cooling, unlike that of eastern Asia, which is predictably steady. Genetically accustomed to the vagaries of their native climate, the local creek species were unperturbed by snow that wrought considerable damage on the Asiatic magnolias common in local gardens.

TOP New growth of false hellebore, *Veratrum viride*, erupts from the floodplain.

ABOVE Pleated leaves of false hellebore.

RIGHT April 20, 1983, at 7:45 A.M. A late snowfall blankets the woodlands but does not damage native plants which are adapted to the unpredictable climate.

Slender, sharply pointed, and covered with overlapping amber scales, the dormant buds of the native beech, *Fagus grandifolia*, are among the most distinct and easiest to recognize of all North American deciduous trees. I'd been watching the buds of a large beech (page 73, tree number 10) on the floodplain and was startled by the array of colors displayed as they began opening at the end of April. The outer scales became honey hued as they expanded in the spring light, while some of the inner scales were brushed with rich rose and magenta tones, contrasting sharply with the light greens of the emerging leaves and flower clusters. I'd of course seen beech buds open many times before; this was the first time I'd paid close attention to them, appreciating their color and other traits as if new. Knowing them in detail also explained the subtle but warm wash of color that is characteristic of distant beech trees opening their spring buds, something else I'd appreciated casually but never understood.

The springtime clothing of the forest in new leaves is an event surpassed in drama perhaps only by the colorful falling of those same leaves in autumn. If moisture is plentiful, as it was in 1983, the progression from gray to green

False hellebore, *Veratrum viride*, in a carpet of Mayapple, *Podophyllum peltatum*, on the floodplain.

TOP Amber scales protect dormant buds of American beech, *Fagus grandifolia*.

CENTER A beech bud opens colorfully.

BOTTOM Heavy spring rains encouraged rapid growth of seedlings of touch-me-not, *Impatiens capensis* and *Impatiens pallida*, on the north bank and floodplain. Rain droplets lie as bright jewels on the unwettable leaves, joined by beech bud scales.

can be startlingly rapid. By April 29 the buds of many other trees had started to open, producing a delicate but perceptible green haze of fresh leaves that began blurring distinct lines and softening the hard edges of the scene.

On May 4, just five days later, the scene had been utterly transformed. The arboreal architecture that had stood so stark was now enveloped in billowing green masses of new leaves. The white sycamore bark appeared even more prominent against the verdure and matched the whites of expanding dogwood blossoms on the south bank. On the floodplain, drifts of Jacob's ladder, *Polemonium reptans*, added their cheerful blue hues.

Another five days passed. The spring sun grew steadily stronger, arcing higher and higher each day as it approached the summer solstice, June 21. The morning of May 9 began cloudless, and when I arrived at the bridge at 7:45, the sun had already cleared the south hill. Its rays cut across the creek, illuminating the open downstream area between the fallen tuliptree and the bridge. Covered by over-arching trees now in leaf, the upstream view was cloaked in shade and almost completely obscured. Though dramatic, the scene appeared foreshortened, the depth of view I'd enjoyed suddenly gone,

ABOVE Jacob's ladder, *Polemonium reptans*, blooms on the floodplain in early May.

BELOW LEFT April 29, 1983, at 11:40 A.M.

BELOW RIGHT May 4, 1983, at 7:55 A.M.

and I wondered if this effect would last through the growing season. The day remained clear, however, and when I stopped on my way home early that evening the depth had magically returned. Though my perspective hadn't changed, the sun's shifting over the course of the day now resulted in a glorious golden-green backlighting. I've since learned this distinct green glow is a reliable phenomenon during May evenings in my regional woodlands, when for a week or two the year's new leaves are full but still translucent. Through a bit of simple design choreography, it is easy to bring some of this seasonal magic into the woodland garden.

Though the sunny May days were beautifully appealing, I found considerable intrigue in the rainy interludes. I noticed that each May rainstorm bent branches successively lower as maturing leaves held on to more water and carried more weight: virtually all angles were adjusted downward. The mood of the scene lacked the ebullience of bright days, but there was something serene and satisfying in the plants' sensible response to the rain. By the end of the month, the canopy had completely filled in and the slope of the distant tree line was no longer visible.

ABOVE Dogwood flowers, *Cornus florida*, are held out over the edge of the creek, glowing in the early May sunlight.

BELOW LEFT May 9, 1983, at 7:45 A.M. Strong morning sun foreshortens the scene. Deep shade obscures the upstream portion of the creek.

BELOW RIGHT May 9, 1983, at 6:30 P.M. The depth returns with late-day backlighting.

LEFT May 23, 1983, at 7:50 A.M. Leafy branches are bowed by rain, as the creek runs high and muddy brown.

BELOW June 1, 1983, at 7:50 A.M. The tulip-tree, *Liriodendron tulipifera*, has broken near its end at the floodplain.

I stopped at the bridge on June 1 and was surprised to find the tuliptree broken and lying much closer to the water's surface. The tree had become a fixture in my familiar view, and its breaking was a reminder of how impermanent it truly was. I'd also become accustomed to using it as a walking bridge to the floodplain and was relieved to find it would still serve that purpose as long as I was willing to leap the last few feet.

View north to the floodplain across the newly broken tuliptree.

On June 15, about a week before the summer solstice, I crossed over the tuliptree and walked upstream on the floodplain, passing false hellebores that were now nearly four feet tall and already in fruit. The creek bank was colored amber with catkins fallen from a swamp hickory, *Carya cordiformis*, nearly seventy feet tall (page 73, tree number 11). I walked out on the base of a large leaning sycamore, *Platanus occidentalis* (page 73, tree number 12), and looked back past the tuliptree to the road bridge 250 feet downstream. Although the sun pierced through the canopy to brighten a few small patches, I was mostly immersed in a tunnel of deep shade. It was a curious change in perspective, looking back at my usual vantage point on the sunny bridge through a frame of tall arching trees. The deep shade here under the high,

June 15, 1983. Looking back past the fallen tuliptree to the road bridge, 250 feet downstream.

nearly continuous canopy of tuliptrees, sycamores, oaks, beeches, and hickories explained why dogwoods along this section of the creek produced relatively few flower buds. As I walked back to the bridge and was again surrounded by sunlight, I was acutely aware of the drama of moving quickly between light and dark passages within the woodland landscape, and of being able to contemplate one from the other.

The summer solstice passed uneventfully, as did most of July and August. The days were long and pleasantly alike. As summer's heat became burdensome I found relief by walking upstream into the cooling shade, or out on the tuliptree bridge to sit and watch. Walking the south bank in mid August, I found two tall native perennials blooming in part shade. Eastern figwort, *Scrophularia marilandica*, held its small red-brown flowers nearly seven feet high atop distinctly square stems. Of equal stature, yellow giant hyssop, *Agastache nepetoides*, produced upright spires of tiny light-yellow flowers.

A few times kingfishers and great blue herons flew along the creek and out of range while I fumbled at the bridge with my camera, but on August 18 a snowy egret was much more accommodating, allowing me to capture its graceful arc from the water to a new stance on the fallen tuliptree. I was amused to note that the tree was an attractive destination and perch for others besides me.

Although a few tired leaves begin to turn by summer's official end, they added only small specks of red and gold to an otherwise green mass of foliage. During the last week of September, Virginia creeper, *Parthenocissus quinquefolia*, claimed credit for the first dramatic autumn color, turning scarlet where the sun hit it nearly sixty feet up in the large ash on the south bank (page 73, tree number 3). Black walnut is always one of the last trees to leaf out in spring and among the first to defoliate in fall. In early October a small black walnut, *Juglans nigra* (page 73, tree number 7), on the south bank began shedding its leaves, the individual leaflets floating on the creek's still waters. On the roadbank to the south above the creek, heart-leaved aster, *Aster cordifolius*, and goldenrod, *Solidago rugosa*, were blooming blue and yellow.

June 15, 1983. False hellebores, *Veratrum viride*, are nearly four feet tall and fruiting on the floodplain.

ABOVE August 18, 1983, at 4:15 P.M. A snowy egret begins an arcing flight from the water to a perch on the fallen tuliptree.

RIGHT October 4, 1983, at 4:30 P.M. The scene is still mostly green, except for the brilliant scarlet color of Virginia creeper, *Parthenocissus quinquefolia*, which has climbed nearly sixty feet up in the ash tree, *Fraxinus pennsylvanica*, on the south bank.

Autumn's advance was quite evident on the rainy morning of October 24. A dogwood, *Cornus florida* (page 73, tree number 6), on the south bank had turned bronze-red, the beech, *Fagus grandifolia* (page 73, tree number 10), on the north bank was tinted gold, and ash trees and walnuts close to the bridge were already bare branched. Standing on the fallen tuliptree looking upstream, my eye was drawn to the bright yellow spicebush reaching out from the north bank. I've since come to value this shrub highly for its ability to brighten the shady woodland garden in autumn and for the fact that it is generally ignored by white-tailed deer.

In late October, seeds of wild leek, *Allium tricoccum*, were ripe and jet-black, and the large beech on the floodplain (page 73, tree number 10) turned bright gold, then quickly faded to a ruddy brown after a hard frost on the last day of the month. Some of the most vibrant color along this stretch of Red Clay Creek belongs to the beeches.

The tree canopy had thinned considerably by the beginning of November. The creek banks were fully carpeted with fallen leaves, and the distant tree line was again well defined against the sky. November 2 was clear, and when

I stopped to photograph in the afternoon, the setting sun was directly in my view, illuminating the surface of the creek with deep orange and bronze tones.

A wild cherry, *Prunus serotina*, leaning out from the north bank (page 73, tree number 14) had turned bright orange by November 4; its color rivaled only a Norway maple, *Acer platanoides* (page 73, tree number 8) turning yellow on the south bank. I knew little about this exotic maple species at the time, beyond that it was commonly planted as a shade tree along streets and in parks and gardens. I've since come to know it as a serious threat to the health and diversity of native woodlands, especially in the Northeast. A prolific self-seeder, Norway maple can establish itself and out-compete native hardwood trees, eventually creating near monocultures where virtually no other tree species can be found. Although superficially resembling the native sugar maple, *Acer saccharum*, Norway maple is easy to spot in the late autumn since it holds its leaves and turns color later than any native maples. When I photographed from the bridge on November 16, the only significant color remaining belonged to a Norway maple, brilliantly gold on the south bank. Rain mixed with sleet during the last two weeks of November washed the last leaves

ABOVE Seeds of wild leek, *Allium tricoccum*, are ripe and jet-black on the floodplain in late October.

BELOW LEFT A large beech, *Fagus grandifolia*, reaches its golden color peak around the same time.

BELOW RIGHT November 2, 1983, at 4:20 P.M. The setting sun joins the view upstream.

from trees and shrubs, and by November 30 the landscape was again devoid of any obvious color other than the creek's reflection of the blue sky.

Following a week with little change I decided to walk upstream to look for new developments and to take stock of changes in plants I'd come to know during the growing season. The figwort and giant hyssop had died back to the ground, but their dried stalks were still standing. The hyssop was particularly interesting, its yellow flower spikes having become nearly black in fruit.

November 4, 1983, at 8:05 A.M. Wild cherry, *Prunus serotina*, on the north bank and Norway maple, *Acer platanoides*, on the south bank, provide the only color.

TOP LEFT November 16, 1983, at 10:20 A.M. The last brilliant gold color belongs to a Norway maple, *Acer platanoides*.

BOTTOM LEFT November 30, 1983, at 11:45 A.M. Deciduous trees and shrubs have all shed their leaves.

Beyond them, I noticed the dogwood had set many more flower buds this year than the previous year. Further along, I was pleased to find many small seedling trees of swamp hickory, *Carya cordiformis*. I walked out on the fallen tuliptree, testing its strength, and found it bent more under my weight now than it did in spring. The decaying bark was loose under my feet, and a few small seedlings of one of the woodland goldenrods, *Solidago flexicaulis*, had sprouted in the furrows. A large section of bark had fallen off the trunk near its base on the south bank. Black laces of shoestring fungus crisscrossed the exposed wood. Knowing this fungus can attack both dead and living trees, I wondered if it had been responsible for the tree's demise. Back at my familiar vantage point on the bridge, I could see considerable dieback in the crowns of the two tuliptrees that remain standing near the fallen one at the edge of the road (page 73, trees number 4 and 5). I decided compaction of their roots caused by road construction and traffic had probably weakened the trees, and that the fungus was likely a secondary agent in their decline. Working with woodland gardens large and small in years since, I've taken the utmost precaution in protecting the delicate root zones of existing trees.

ABOVE One of many seedling swamp hickory trees, *Carya cordiformis*, growing along the south bank. In winter, this tree is easily recognized by its fuzzy, deep gold-colored buds.

LEFT The bark has fallen away from the base of the tuliptree, *Liriodendron tulipifera*, revealing the crisscrossing black growth of shoestring fungus.

ABOVE LEFT December 13, 1983, at 12:00 P.M. Light rain lingers from a storm that produced more than four inches of rainfall the day before, swelling the creek completely over the floodplain and repositioning the tuliptree.

ABOVE RIGHT December 21, 1983, at 4:25 P.M. A new island is evident downstream from the tuliptree, built of rock and silt deposited by recent floodwaters.

A fierce storm dropped more than four inches of rain on December 12. I drove to the bridge at 7:30 that evening to find the creek already swollen nearly six feet above normal, indicated by a gauge at the bridge. Though photography was impossible in the rain and darkness, I could see well enough to tell that the floodplain was completely under water. The creek was roiling and rushing past at a furious rate, and the sheer noise of the moving water was powerfully alarming. Almost completely submerged, the tuliptree still stretched across the creek, hit by the full force of the muddy current. I was sure it would be wrenched from the bank and carried off downstream, but when I returned the following morning, it was present, though angled strongly toward the bridge. The flood waters had stripped away most of its bark, exposing the light-colored wood underneath. When the creek returned to its normal level, a new island was visible. It had been built of rock and silt released by the floodwaters as they slowed to make their way past the end of the tuliptree.

The flooding brought many changes. The lower portion of a tree that had been growing nearly half a mile upstream was now lodged upside down against the second leaning sycamore on the north bank (page 73, tree number 12). The trunk of a smaller tree had lodged between the end of the tulip-tree and the north bank, again forming a complete wooden bridge suitable for crossing the creek. The surface of the floodplain was nearly washed clean of its accumulated leaf litter, exposing the blanched growing tips that would produce next spring's Mayapples. The remaining leaves were wrapped almost decoratively around the slender stems of woody plants that strained the flowing floodwaters. Deposits of seed-laden silt were visible in huge patches all over the floodplain.

Temperatures dropped steadily and by December 21 the ground was frozen solid. On the next day, the first day of winter, sudden heavy rain ran quickly over the hard soil and into the creek. The temperature rose from the twenties to nearly fifty degrees Fahrenheit by noon and, standing on the bridge, I was swallowed by a series of mists rolling downstream through the creek valley. Though the day wasn't beautiful in a traditional sense, the landscape this noon was powerfully provocative in mood and raw emotional force. If not for the discipline of my study, I would probably have ignored the creek on such a day and been that much poorer for it. Over time my study taught me to recognize and appreciate beauty that is not fixed or static, but rather dynamic and often ephemeral. Years later I discovered that Ralph Waldo Emerson had much earlier adopted this same perspective, writing in his book *Nature* (1836): "Not the sun or the summer alone but every hour and season yields its tribute of delight; for every hour and change corresponds to and authorizes a different state of mind from breathless moon to grimmest midnight."

Three inches of snow brightened the morning landscape eleven days into the new year. There were no footprints on the road bridge but my own; however, tracks along the fallen tuliptree revealed that it was still the choice of animals wishing to stay dry while crossing the creek. When I stopped again in the afternoon, I found the setting sun perfectly centered in the scene, just left of the leaning sycamore forming the right side of the arch (page 73, tree number 2). Eight days later, with a half foot of additional snow blanketing the ground, the sun had shifted to the north and appeared directly in line with the sycamore's trunk.

OPPOSITE TOP December 22, 1983, at 12:00 P.M. A series of strong mists travels downstream toward the bridge.

RIGHT January 11, 1984, at 10:00 A.M. Footprints in the snow reveal the tuliptree is still used as a bridge by local animals.

OPPOSITE BOTTOM LEFT January 11, 1984, at 4:20 P.M. The setting sun appears just left of the leaning sycamore.

OPPOSITE BOTTOM RIGHT January 19, 1984, at 4:20 P.M. The sun has shifted north (right) and appears directly behind the sycamore.

The temperature plummeted to minus five degrees Fahrenheit overnight on January 19. The next morning I found the creekside landscape covered in hoarfrost. So subtle in summer that they could easily escape notice, the figwort and giant hyssop were now strikingly graceful, outlined by a delicate filigree of frost.

Freezing temperatures continued, and by January 23, the creek was nearly iced over. Stopping in the afternoon, I found the sun now north of the sycamore. I was excited to realize how rapidly the sun's position changed: in just eleven days, it had moved from left to right of the sycamore. My science ed-

January 20, 1984, at 8:00 A.M. Warming up from minus five degrees Fahrenheit overnight, the creek is still frigid in the morning.

ucation had provided an intellectual understanding of this phenomenon, but this was the first time I'd felt the drama it could produce in the physical landscape. In the Northern Hemisphere, the apparent position of the setting sun shifts from south to north along the western horizon as the year progresses from the winter solstice (approximately December 22) to the summer solstice (approximately June 21). It then shifts southward as the year turns toward the winter solstice. The sun follows a corresponding cycle along the eastern horizon, rising at its southernmost point at the winter solstice and moving steadily northward until the arrival of the summer solstice. This pattern is most easily appreciated from a fixed point in place and time of day. The arching sycamore and my 4:20 P.M. photography provided both.

February and March were relatively uneventful. I witnessed a few minor snows, floods, and freezes, but saw no major change in the basic layout of the landscape. The drama to be found was primarily related to the shifting colors of the creek, sun, and sky, set against what had become a very familiar framework. As the days warmed and the last traces of snow and ice dissolved, I

ABOVE Bent over by previous rain and snow, figwort, *Scrophularia marilandica*, is beautifully filigreed by hoarfrost.

LEFT January 23, 1984, at 4:20 P.M. The sun appears right of the leaning sycamore.

ABOVE LEFT March 23, 1984, at 1:00 P.M. Nearly a year has passed since the beginning of my study.

ABOVE RIGHT May 21, 1984, at 4:40 P.M. The nearest dogwood on the south bank is heavily flowered.

noticed a definite but indistinguishable red haze in the distance. Exploring upstream, I found the haze to be myriad tiny flowers of silver maple trees, *Acer saccharinum*, growing along the banks and leaning out over the creek.

The air was again sweetened with spring fragrances when I stopped on the bridge near the end of March, and lingered a while to reflect on the year's changes. The scene was undoubtedly transformed from when I began watching; however, the greatest change had been in my perception of it. I'd come to appreciate the structure and the pace of the landscape and its living community, and knew where to look for the details that set today apart from yesterday or tomorrow.

MY FIRST YEAR on the creek reintroduced me to the full limits and layers of the landscape. Though this perspective had once come naturally to me as a casual observer, my education in woodland wildflowers had unintentionally taught me to focus down toward my feet. In my study, the unbiased view of my camera lens put the herbaceous layer back in perspective with the shrubs, understory trees, and canopy giants, and I was reminded how important the

ABOVE LEFT Reaching out for light, this dogwood is perfectly fit to its niche in the landscape and visually striking in its asymmetry.

ABOVE RIGHT Branches of the same dogwood are pendent when laden with moist snow.

creek itself and the sky were to the visual dynamics of the scene. Aided by my notes and photographs, I was able to describe each season's shifting color spectrum in detail and to chart the cycles of solstice and equinox. Numerous animals encountered during my visits prompted me to compare the vitality of the creekside woodlands with the sometimes inanimate nature of designed gardens. Many daily rhythms became apparent and predictable during the first year, such as the cloaking effects of morning shadows or the luminous depths produced by the sun's late-afternoon backlighting, and I've since learned how to emulate these effects in garden designs.

Though I've stopped less regularly since that first year, I've continued to watch the creek. As four seasons have stretched to more than seventy, I've found continuing inspiration in unfolding events. It's been a delight to follow the lives of individual characters such as the nearest dogwood (page 73, tree number 6) on the south bank. Its flowering in May 1984 far surpassed that of the previous year, and over the long period I've seen the strength of its blooming ebb and flow in response to varying seasonal conditions. I've come to love its form, which is the epitome of asymmetry. The dogwood has no branches on its shaded south side, but reaches north over the creek seeking light with many graceful horizontal branches that become pendent when weighted by snow. Its distinct shape has resulted from a perfect fitting to place and opportunity.

The small island formed during the flooding of December 1983 proved surprisingly enduring, serving as home to a number of plants. Tickseed, *Bidens laevis*, established itself during the first growing season, managing to flower on the island in October 1984. Grasses, including reed canary grass, *Phalaris arundinacea*, arrived the following year, and by 1987 billowing masses of orange and yellow touch-me-not (also known as jewelweed), *Impatiens capensis* and *Impatiens pallida*, spread from the north bank out over the island and the tuliptree bridge. I wondered if woody plants would eventually gain hold, but after flooding removed the sheltering effect of the tuliptree, the island began to decline in size and the assortment of plants it could support. Since 1997, it has persisted only as a small rocky bar, noticeable when the creek's waters are low. Though now a nearly imperceptible feature in the landscape, for me it is a lingering reminder of the fallen tuliptree and its pass-

LEFT October 3, 1984, at 3:00 P.M. Tickseed, *Bidens laevis*, flowers on the new island.

OPPOSITE TOP July 8, 1987, at 12:15 P.M. The island and the tuliptree bridge are nearly obscured by touch-me-not, *Impatiens capensis* and *Impatiens pallida*. Patches of reed canary grass, *Phalaris arundinacea*, are also visible on the island.

OPPOSITE BOTTOM LEFT May 11, 1988, at 7:55 A.M. The plant population on the island has begun to diminish, as the tree bridge begins to disappear and the island is increasingly exposed to currents.

OPPOSITE BOTTOM RIGHT May 3, 1993, at 12:30 P.M. Exposed to the full flow of the creek, the island is barely populated.

May 5, 1997, at 5:30 P.M. The island is
reduced to a small rocky bar, evident only
when the creek's waters are low.

ing influence. Gardens, too, are rich with such benchmarks and cues, and knowing how to read them can be a genuine pleasure, affirming our intimacy with the landscape.

Looking back, I can see how profoundly this continuing study has informed my perspective on both gardens and native places. I've become more accepting of change and transition. Over the years, trout lilies, false hellebore, wild leek, and Jacob's ladder have all persisted on the floodplain, while landmark trees such as the large beech (page 73, tree number 10) are gone, replaced by seedling trees. There have been many transients over the years: newcomers have settled into niches afforded by sun, shade, or moisture.

November 2, 1999, at 11:15 A.M. A multi-trunked swamp hickory, *Carya cordiformis*, forms a new bridge over the creek. It toppled from the north bank in mid September during Hurricane Floyd.

Some have thrived; others have disappeared as conditions shifted, and they've been replaced by others yet. In mid September 1999, Hurricane Floyd dramatically rearranged the creek's woodland landscape. The storm claimed a leaning sycamore (page 73, tree number 12) that had been a stalwart since the beginning of my study, and it felled a multitrunked swamp hickory growing along the north bank; but many sycamore and swamp hickory seedlings are growing along the banks, and the fallen tree is a strong central visual element in the landscape. For me and for local animals, it again provides a natural bridge across the creek. Observing such cycles has led me to welcome the inevitability of change in designed landscapes and to see opportunity in it.

In the realm of deciduous woodlands, I've also come to appreciate and rely upon winter's revelations. No other season is so adept at displaying the essential architecture of the woodland landscape. This is especially true when snow offers a defining cover, reducing color to the barest of distractions and highlighting every true line, every graceful curve. I look forward to winter as a time for taking stock of the garden, contemplating and planning modifications and new features I might make in the coming years.

I've always enjoyed being physically active in the garden, digging, planting, pruning, and propagating, but I've learned that observation and reflection can be among the most pleasurable and rewarding activities. My Red Clay Creek study taught me the value of a notebook and camera as tools for learning about landscape: my notes and photographs were infinitely more revealing of pattern and process than memory alone could ever be. My camera captured myriad details large and small, such as the annual variations in the onset of autumn color or the specific date ranges of plants blooming together.

OPPOSITE BOTTOM January 19, 1984, at 11:50 A.M. The tuliptree is broken but still stretches across the creek. The new island is brightly defined by the snow. In the distant background, the sloping tree line appears dark, contrasting sharply with the sky in this midday light.

TOP RIGHT January 26, 1988, at 8:05 A.M. The sky is warmly rose tinted, still clearing after a storm that dropped four inches of wet snow overnight. The tuliptree has been repositioned by recent high water.

BOTTOM RIGHT January 7, 1991, at 2:05 P.M. Branches are bent under the weight of a heavy snow. Visibility barely extends beyond the arch. The tuliptree has been moved nearly parallel to the south bank.

OPPOSITE TOP February 16, 1993, at 8:00 A.M. A very fine wet snow, still falling, puts a delicate coating on tree trunks and branches, accentuating every exquisite detail in the woodland architecture. Only a small portion of the tuliptree remains along the south bank.

OPPOSITE BOTTOM April 1, 1997, at 7:55 A.M. An overnight snow melts quickly in the strengthening spring sun. The tuliptree has been washed completely from the scene, and the island is barely visible.

RIGHT January 31, 2000, at 12:15 P.M. The island is still evident as snow outlines the multiple trunks of a swamp hickory now spanning the creek under the arch. This tree and another forming a natural bridge further upstream came down during Hurricane Floyd in mid September 1999.

Applying these tools and techniques to my designed landscapes has greatly enhanced my ability and my creative imagination. Recording is becoming ever easier with the advance of digital cameras. Not only can they capture an image of trout lilies blooming on a floodplain: they can simultaneously record the sound of the wind moving through the trees overhead, while noting the date and time to the precise second.

When I began my study, my garden at home was very young and spare. It had little of the substance or subtlety of the incidental landscape I enjoyed from the bridge, and in some ways the natural woodland garden along Red Clay Creek served as a surrogate. Though I still feel a connection to the creek, my garden today has become my most intimate and affecting landscape. It is not a replication of a native woodland, but its design is reflective in ways that continue to enhance my tie to such places. Inspired by woodland colors, patterns, and processes, the garden celebrates the spirit of the deciduous forest, bringing it close, making it an integral part of each day's necessary journey.

CHAPTER THREE

Designing the Woodland Garden

Garden designed to capture the spirit of the deciduous forest need not be a faithful replication of the forest community. The emotional and persuasive power of art results from selection, distillation, and enhancement, and so the most artful, evocative woodland gardens may borrow from any number of patterns and signatures that define the native forest—its lines and framework, its layers, luminous qualities, color cycles, sounds, and scents—melding them into an insightful yet livable landscape. This chapter outlines and describes strategies for celebrating the deciduous forest in the designed landscape, using diverse private and public gardens for illustration.

Abstracting the Forest

The visual complexity of the unedited native forest is sometimes so great that it overwhelms the eye, appearing beautiful but chaotic. In the woodland garden, reducing the complexity and drawing out one or a few distinct motifs can result in a landscape that is powerfully reminiscent of the forest, but is more easily read and more accessible. Three examples come to mind: the woodland room at Scott Amphitheater, a cedar structure in our Pennsylvania garden, and a stream valley garden at Ashland Hollow.

Ever since I first saw it, first sat in it, first felt the power and comfort of its enclosure, the Scott Amphitheater at Swarthmore College in Pennsylvania has seemed to me the ultimate woodland room. Designed by Philadelphia landscape architect Thomas Sears, this stunning space captures the essence of the forest: tall verticals contrasted against the low sweeping lines of the ground plane.

The ampitheater is an inspired example of editing the forest. Prior to construction in autumn of 1941, the naturally sloping site was heavily wooded, with an overstory mostly of tuliptrees, *Liriodendron tulipifera*. The understory layers were removed and the slope was gently terraced to provide level areas for seating within a framework of selected canopy trees. Low retaining walls of Pennsylvania granite schist were built to edge the curving tiers, intensifying their lines. A photograph taken shortly after construction was completed shows the tuliptrees looking nearly like they do today, which is a credit to their durability and to the obvious care that was taken to respect their roots while the amphitheater was being built.

Dedicated in the spring of 1942, the amphitheater has been used since to hold commencement ceremonies. The space is occasionally filled with the sound of music and other gatherings large and small, and it is always a fine place for reading or contemplation while the wind sings quietly in the canopy above.

I've shown these three images in lectures, beginning with the amphitheater covered in a January snow, and asked the audience if they would allow me to call this a garden. Any doubts that are expressed are usually dispelled as the images move from winter's virtual monochrome to the lime light and dappled glow of spring, and on to autumn's warm leafy pointillism. It becomes obvious that this elegant distillation has as much power as any other garden to celebrate the seasons and their colors, shifting light, and moods.

OPPOSITE January. Photo by Claire Sawyers.

ABOVE Mid May

LEFT Mid October

The garden is a wonderful setting for story-telling, and the forest is full of stories. My wife, Melinda, and I frequently walk the nearby woodland preserve for relaxation, to learn about the forest community, and to look for ideas we might use in landscape designs. Years ago we came across two memorable trees, and their story became part of our garden.

A double-trunked tuliptree had fallen and lodged against a triple-trunked oak. When we first came upon the combination, the tuliptree's trunks were still strong and bark-covered, extending at an upward angle through the oak. I sometimes walked up the inclined tree to enjoy the view or to sit quietly listening to forest sounds and observing, unobtrusively, the activities of small animals. In time, I lost my perch to natural processes of decay: the trunks lost their bark and broke at mid point, angling back toward the ground. By this time, however, the two trees had become a familiar destination on our route through this portion of the preserve, and we continued to

stop by this piece of natural sculpture to watch its form evolve and to enjoy its lines silhouetted against the forest sunset.

We eventually decided to abstract the tale of these two trees in our garden. The eastern edge of our property borders an open farm field, with the woods visible in the distance. Sun- and moonrises are superb, and we knew that anything placed along the garden's eastern border would be dramatically silhouetted and would provide a framework for these luminous events. A number of young trees were already planted that would serve this purpose in the future, but for immediate effect and focus we decided to create a wooden sculpture. For materials we used trunks of red cedars, *Juniperus virginiana*, fashioning a simple structure radiating from two points, one at the apex and one on the ground, and held together only by gravity.

Though we originally positioned the sculpture to celebrate the autumn sunrise as viewed from our outdoor dining table, we've come to appreciate it as a reference

point for the shifting arcs of sun and moon as the year moves through the cycles of solstice and equinox. An extension of the garden sundial, it has turned the landscape itself into a solar and lunar timepiece.

Intended as an ephemeral presence, the sculpture has stood, surprisingly, for more than six years at the time of this writing. As the cedar posts have become bowed and weathering has removed most of their bark, we are reminded of similar processes at work on the forest trees that initially inspired our garden art. Both will eventually disappear from their respective landscapes, but the memory of their connection will endure.

BELOW LEFT In early November, a natural sculpture formed by two trees tells the story of woodland process.

BELOW RIGHT Positioned at the eastern edge of the garden, a simple sculptural piece made of red-cedar trunks emulates forest framing and symbolizes the natural process of decline, decay, and renewal on a crisp November morning.

TOP LEFT The sunrise is framed in late October.

TOP RIGHT An early April moon rises through the cedar frame. The notion of celebrating such phenomena in the garden is hardly new. In a *Saturday Evening Post* article in 1930, landscape architect Jens Jensen suggested that a gardener's design palette should include "the changing seasons, the rays of the setting sun and the afterglow, and the light of the moon." Ossian Simonds, in his 1920 book, *Landscape Gardening*, drew an analogy with the landscape painter's approach to composition, suggesting that the sky is the gardener's canvas, and that the "mountains, hills, prairies, or forests" are seen against this background. He recommended that gardeners dedicate space on this canvas to be filled with "clouds and sunshine, with stars and moonlight."

LEFT Five years after creating the cedar sculpture in our garden, I noticed this natural structure one May at the edge of a woods in Delaware. It was completely uncontrived yet the resemblance was uncanny, and it strengthened my belief that garden art can have a profound effect on our ability to see and appreciate natural pattern and process.

The design of Ashland Hollow, a private garden in northern Delaware, includes superb abstractions and echoes of the regional deciduous forest.

ABOVE The house at Ashland Hollow straddles a small woodland stream flowing through a native population of beech trees, *Fagus grandifolia*, and tuliptrees, *Liriodendron tulipifera*. Frequent windows and an open balcony provide an all-seasons intimacy with the landscape. Careful construction ensured the survival of beeches quite close to the house.

OPPOSITE LEFT The balcony looks directly out on the stream valley garden, which is an artful celebration of light and shadow playing through trees and over abstract woodland landforms. The stream is dammed to create four ponds and five small waterfalls, and a mix of native and non-native perennial forbs, ferns, and mosses covers the ground. Visible in the far center is an island covered by mosses and liverworts.

It is especially delightful when the garden and the native landscape offer visual cues to each other. When I first saw the stream valley garden at Ashland Hollow I was greatly moved by the combination of powerful shapes and dynamic green color and light, but unsure of how to relate this artform garden to the natural landscape of regional woodland streams. Then one day while walking along the nearby White Clay Creek I noticed a large rock projecting above the creek's surface, and was struck by how much it evoked the garden at Ashland Hollow. Though the shape of the rock certainly resembled the garden's moss island, it was the combination of this shape and the waters' reflected forest greens that cemented the connection

between the two landscapes. Since that day, whenever I see that rock in the creek I think of the garden at Ashland Hollow, and when I look at the Ashland Hollow moss island I think of the creek. I've learned how powerful subtle abstractions can be in forging a visual and emotional link between the native woodland and the woodland garden. I might never have pondered the rock in the creek were it not for the garden at Ashland Hollow.

OPPOSITE TOP RIGHT The moss island at Ashland Hollow is immersed in the reflected green hues of mid October.

OPPOSITE BOTTOM RIGHT A large rock stands above the surface of White Clay Creek in mid August, silhouetted against the forest's reflected greens.

TOP AND BOTTOM LEFT
Architectural devices both
natural and artificial can
abstract and accentuate
woodland patterns. At Ashland Hollow, the house itself
frames trees in the valley
stream garden, drawing
attention to their contrasting sizes, colors, and lines.
In similar fashion, a natural
arch formed of shale in the
West Virginia mountains
frames the angled trunks
of closely spaced trees.

OPPOSITE LEFT AND
RIGHT The lines, forms,
and colors of the stream
valley garden at Ashland
Hollow are still powerful
in late January. Persistent
beech leaves bring their
color to the edge of the balcony as tree shadows play
across the stucco walls of
the house and the snow-
covered pond and moss
island.

Framing and Enclosing

Whether creating vistas or enclosing and defining garden spaces, the natural architecture of the deciduous forest can be as effective as any made of masonry or steel. Sometimes there is opportunity to frame views or spaces through the selective removal of existing trees. In other situations, tree plantings can be made to define and organize garden vistas and rooms. In most instances, utilizing trees and other natural elements of the forest is considerably less expensive than traditional architectural means.

LEFT Deftly located between two enormous tuliptrees, *Liriodendron tulipifera*, at Patterns, a private garden in Delaware, the bog overlook celebrates the majesty of one of the state's greatest remnant woodlands. The framing forms of the tuliptrees are especially powerful when silhouetted against the bright backlit hues of October foliage, and the overall effect is of a perfect portal into the forest. Projecting just feet beyond the crest of the wooded slope, the overlook gives the effect of being elevated into the grand space below the canopy. The view down is of a woodland bog garden planted to take advantage of naturally moist conditions, and a surrounding sweep of naturally occurring pawpaw, *Asimina triloba*. Though this overlook builds on a unique opportunity, in any garden the simple devices of framing and providing a slight change in elevation often result in a delightful new perspective on the woodland landscape.

In woodland gardens large and small, the transition between wooded and open spaces is especially stirring. Trees and other forest layers can be used to orchestrate space in a variety of ways that enhance the visual or spiritual journey from the interior through the edge and into the light.

In mid October at Mount Cuba Center in Delaware, tall trees create a shaded interior space around the pond (OPPOSITE BOTTOM), opening dramatically to a sunny slope planted in native grasses, mostly little bluestem, *Schizachyrium scoparium*. The mood of the two spaces is entirely different: one reflective and enclosed, the other ebullient and exposed. Later in October, the canopy leaves have begun to drop, and the pond area is much more illuminated (RIGHT). Planted at the sunny edge, a young white oak, *Quercus alba*, is resplendent when backlit by the sun (ABOVE).

An opening onto a restored prairie garden provides the distant focal point of a grand allée cut through native red, white, and burr oak woods at the private Crab Tree Farm in Illinois. This stunning vista has survived more or less intact for nearly seven decades, though the terminal view was originally to field crops. In recent years, a huge white oak, *Quercus alba*, toppled into the prairie grasses. Trimmed of smaller branches, the dead tree has been conserved as a piece of organic sculpture, creating a sense of enclosure around a seating bench placed below. The complete opacity of the oak's great frame magnificently contrasts with the luminous, gossamer stalks of native grasses including Indian grass, *Sorghastrum nutans*, and big bluestem, *Andropogon gerardii*.

Simply called "the keep," this magical garden enclosure was built into an existing copse of trees near the summit of a hill in Delaware's rolling piedmont. Planted mostly by birds, the trees are a beautifully common mix including flowering dogwood, *Cornus florida*, and black cherry, *Prunus serotina*. The center of the space was excavated and large local rocks were used to build a sunken surround with built-in seating and a fire pit at the center. Inspiring in all seasons, this versatile space can accommodate many moods. The trees and rocks together create a great sense of intimacy, inviting hours of quiet contemplation or close conversation. In keeping with a more expansive mood, the surrounding trees frame broad views out over grassy hills, hedgerows, and forest remnants. Whether you're looking in or out, the space amplifies the spirit of sunrises and sunsets, of full moons and winter snows.

It's surprising how rapidly you can define or enclose a garden space or outdoor room solely by planting trees and associated lower layers. When I first moved from a tiny urban garden to one and one-half acres near the edge of suburbia, I was elated by the overall expanded scale but missed the sense of enclosure I'd known. The new landscape consisted mostly of lawn with individual trees scattered about, and none of them worked together to organize the space.

In the rear section of the property, off the south-facing side of the house, a large spreading thornless honey locust, *Gleditsia triacanthos* var. *inermis* 'Moraine', offered the best opportunity to build on existing conditions. Allowing this broad-spreading tree to form the basis for a garden room, I planned a semicircular border at the periphery of its canopy on the south side. Loosely modeling the picturesque hedgerows that edge and define agricultural lands and old farm fields in the local landscape, I planted an irregular mix of trees and shrubs to form the basic architecture of the border. I used small trees so they would acclimate quickly and establish strong root systems that would contribute to long-term health. For trees, I chose three different silverbells, the Carolina silverbell, *Halesia tetraptera*; the mountain silverbell, *Halesia tetraptera* var. *monticola*; and the large-flowered form of two-winged silverbell, *Halesia diptera* var. *magniflora*. Fothergilla, *Fothergilla gardenii*, coast azalea, *Rhododendron atlanticum*, and sweet pepperbush, *Clethra alnifolia*, formed the shrub layer. Initially, the most important complement of the herbaceous layer was a sweep of non-native feather-reed grass, *Calamagrostis* ×*acutiflora* 'Karl Foerster'. The purpose of this seed-sterile grass was to grow quickly and hold the space together until the trees and shrubs grew and developed an enclosing presence of their own: it would eventually diminish and disappear as shade increased. Grasses are often useful in this way, acting as transient agents of change in the evolution of garden spaces from open meadowlike conditions to woodland.

In just a few years, the border grew into a significant wall of vegetation, creating the desired sense of enclosure and privacy, and introducing all-season interest to the landscape. With more than a decade's growth, the border is now a main architectural presence in the rear garden.

LEFT Comprised of an herbaceous layer, a shrub layer, and a tree layer, this enclosing border acts as an architectural framework for an outdoor sitting and dining area, and offers interest throughout the seasons, following the natural color and flowering cycles typical of this part of Pennsylvania. From late April into early May, fothergilla blooms with Carolina silverbell and mountain silverbell. The blossoms of a distant redbud, *Cercis canadensis*, are discernable only as a rose-purple wash of color complementing the spring greens and whites of fothergilla and silverbells, and picking up on the purple foliage of *Heuchera americana* 'Montrose Ruby' in the herbaceous layer.

ABOVE At the back of the garden, redbud blossoms mix with the light lime-yellow flowers of *Sassafras albidum*.

RIGHT Appearing while stems are still nearly leafless, the snow-white blossoms of mountain silverbell are one of the most graceful events in the deciduous woodlands.

FAR RIGHT Silverbells have the delightful habit of dropping their blossoms while they're still pure white. Depending upon temperatures, they'll decorate the ground for nearly a week. We celebrate this spring event in the garden, refraining from any mowing or raking during this brief but beautiful second show.

LEFT The large-flowered form of two-winged silverbell begins blooming just after the others have finished. By integrating different species of silverbell, we enjoy more than three weeks of continuous bloom. Coast azalea blooms in mid May with the later silverbells, infusing the area with its delightful sweet fragrance.

ABOVE The bare branches of the large-flowered form of two-winged silverbell are obscured by a profusion of flowers in mid May.

ABOVE The border is leafy, restful, and green in mid summer, providing a welcome retreat from the heat. The entire space is enlivened in late July and early August by the spicy scent of sweet pepperbush, and by butterflies attracted to its creamy white spires.

BELOW LEFT Leaves turn color and begin to drop by mid October, further opening the view to native Indian grass, *Sorghastrum nutans*, turning tawny and translucent in the sunny meadow garden on the south side of the silverbell border.

BELOW RIGHT A late-January ice storm reveals the elementary architecture of the border's shrub and tree layers, which, though leafless, still create a sense of enclosure and separation from the meadow.

TOP The fruits of large-flowered two-winged silverbell glow in the late-October sunlight. They will remain translucent and chartreuse for a few more weeks, eventually turning a light amber color, and will persist on the tree into winter.

BOTTOM A coating of January ice magnifies the red-brown hues of mountain silverbell fruits. The majority of these pendent ornaments will remain attached to branches throughout the winter season.

TOP By the end of October, the leaves of mountain silverbell have turned golden yellow, contrasting with the tree's own browning four-winged fruits and the rich orange-red hues of fothergilla.

BOTTOM Opaque and brown, the four-winged fruits of Carolina silverbell are silhouetted by the mid-November sunrise.

Entry plantings do a great deal to establish the mood and sense of any garden. In our Pennsylvania garden, the main walk from the drive into the house is simple and direct, but was completely bare of plantings when I first moved to the property. To turn this passage into more of a woodland experience, I cut a new border out of the lawn on the side of the walk away from the house, planting it closely with river birches, *Betula nigra* 'Heritage', fothergilla, *Fothergilla gardenii*, Virginia sweetspire, *Itea virginica* 'Henry's Garnet', and a diverse layer of herbaceous species. Only shrubs were planted between the walk and the house. The border has matured to create an immediate woodsy intimacy, practical and easy to maintain yet inviting and interesting in all seasons.

LEFT The entry walk between garage and house provides a woodsy welcome, enclosed by river birches and fothergilla, flowering in early May.

LEFT The border remains green and cooling through summer, with heart-leaved aster, *Aster cordifolius*, adding its cool blue hues by early October.

RIGHT Planted in an informal drift which emulates spacing often encountered in wild populations, river birches connect the house and garage and create a sense of intimacy along the walk. Before planting, the tree positions were evaluated from inside the house as well as from the garden perspective. This photograph was taken from the glass-doored porch on the south side of the house, looking southeast.

TOP Multiple layers and planting diversity add to the border's all-seasons interest and ease of maintenance. Bluebells, *Mertensia virginica*, planted underneath a fothergilla begin blooming in mid April, while the new foliage of white wood aster, *Aster divaricatus*, is already serving as a weed-reducing ground cover. The bluebells will recede into dormancy during summer, unperturbed by the shade of the overtopping shrub. The asters will put on a floral display in late summer and autumn.

BOTTOM Shade-tolerant white wood aster blooms underneath and through the arching branches of Virginia sweetspire in mid October. The autumn hues of the sweetspire are echoed in the aster flowers.

An elevated view provides a perspective on the relationship of the birches, walk, and house in early November. The presence of two evergreens becomes noticeable as deciduous plants drop their leaves: a native leucothoe, *Leucothoe axillaris*, planted directly under the birches, and a non-native Hinoki cypress, *Chamaecyparis obtusa* 'Nana Gracilis', in the tight space adjacent to the door of the house.

FAR LEFT The bright birch stems dramatically set off the brilliant mid-November foliage of fothergilla.

LEFT The framing and enclosure of the river birches and fothergillas are effective even in mid February when the garden is snow covered.

Passing alternately between sunlit and shaded spaces is among the most stimulating experiences of a walk in the deciduous forest, and a woodland garden that includes such transitions is certain to invite repeated exploration. This design strategy can be very effective even in modest scale. At home, we've been gradually reducing the amount of sunny lawn area, creating enclosures and passages that have a sense of the woods and provide growing conditions suitable for herbaceous woodland species. We planted pawpaws, *Asimina triloba*, to create a transition between the sunny front garden and a woodland room fashioned around an old apple tree.

LEFT Defined by pawpaws, this path still is open and sunny in mid May, as the tree foliage is just beginning to expand. Ferns and spring wildflowers have utilized the available light along the sides of the path.

OPPOSITE TOP LEFT Viewed from inside looking back, the path is cool and shaded in late June. The transition from this intimate woodland space into the sunny area on the north side of the path is stimulating and intriguing.

Well adapted to light conditions at the edge between sun and shade, Culver's root, *Veronicastrum virginicum*, flanks the north end of the pawpaw path in early July.

Seedling beeches, *Fagus grandifolia*, are planted in a group northeast of the pawpaw path. They will mature to overtop the pawpaws and create a shady canopy. In the meantime, the space between these trees is planted with a mix of herbaceous species that are adapted to the intermediate light conditions. New England asters, *Aster novaeangliae*, and prairie dropseed, *Sporobolus heterolepis*, are in full bloom in mid September, and are joined in October by willow-leaved sunflower, *Helianthus salicifolius*, and switch grass, *Panicum virgatum*.
LEFT Mid September
RIGHT Mid October

The glorious gold color of the pawpaws sets off the amber hues of the beeches in early November. Started from seed, the pawpaws are only nine years old and nearly twelve feet tall in this image. Larger-leaved than most deciduous trees, pawpaws have a bold-textured presence in the garden.

TOP The mood inside the pawpaw path has changed dramatically with the turning of the leaves, enveloping strollers in a warm golden glow.

BOTTOM The colorful natural mulch of fallen pawpaw foliage complements *Heuchera americana* 'Dale's Strain' and other herbaceous perennials in early November.

OPPOSITE BOTTOM RIGHT Older, existing deciduous trees, native or non-native, may provide the best immediate opportunity for creating woodland enclosures and developing growing conditions necessary for woodland perennials. In our home garden, a large apple survives from plantings by the original owners. A half-century old, the tree's branches now drape to the ground, creating an enclosure we call our "apple cave." The pawpaw path leads directly into this space, which has become one of the most intimate outdoor rooms in the garden, furnished with seating for a meal, a conversation, or quiet contemplation.

ABOVE The ground slopes gently toward the apple, and the soil under the tree's periphery is moist compared with many areas of the garden. It has proved ideal for many woodland perennials including twinleaf, *Jeffersonia diphylla*, Mayapple, *Podophyllum peltatum*, black snakeroot, *Cimicifuga racemosa*, various heucheras such as *Heuchera macrorhiza*, as well as showy trillium, *Trillium grandiflorum*, and Wherry's foamflower, *Tiarella cordifolia* var. *collina*, which are in bloom in this early May photograph. Rather than pave the entire area under the apple, we created just enough of a walkway to invite visitors into the space, using native stone from a local Pennsylvania quarry.

TOP Showy trillium graces the entry stone with a profusion of flowers in late April.

BOTTOM In September, bouquets of white wood aster, *Aster divaricatus*, spill over the same stones.

Working with Layers

The natural layering of the deciduous forest may be emulated and enhanced through the art of the garden. Working imaginatively with layers will make the most of any garden space, resulting in powerful compositions and rich plant combinations on both large and small scales.

The design of the Peirce's Woods area of Longwood Gardens uses well-defined layers to create stunning, broad-sweeping effects.

ABOVE Planted within an existing canopy that includes mature tuliptrees, *Liriodendron tulipifera*, red oaks, *Quercus rubra*, black birch, *Betula lenta*, hemlocks, *Tsuga canadensis*, and sugar maples, *Acer saccharum*, the garden at Peirce's Woods brings out the drama of the upright tree forms by anchoring them in sweeping masses of herbaceous per-

ennials. The shrub layer and understory trees are placed to enhance the majesty of the canopy trees. At the beginning of May, flowering dogwood, *Cornus florida*, blooms above white sheets of foamflower, *Tiarella cordifolia*, intermingled with Christmas fern, *Polystichum acrostichoides*, and Allegheny pachysandra, *Pachysandra procumbens*.

TOP AND BOTTOM The basal trunk flare of a canopy tuliptree is silhouetted against a vibrant ground layer drift of foamflower, *Tiarella cordifolia*, Allegheny pachysandra, *Pachysandra procumbens*, and creeping phlox, *Phlox stolonifera*, in early May. The space is bordered by evergreen rosebay rhododendron, *Rhododendron maximum*.

TOP The distinctive, irregular lines of a sourwood, *Oxydendrum arboreum*, in the understory layer are an intriguing and delightful departure from the straight trunks of the canopy trees.

BOTTOM The drama of the ground layer in Peirce's Woods comes from planting large drifts of relatively few species, in a simplified idealization of the native woodlands. Here, a near monoculture of foamflower, *Tiarella cordifolia*, arcs around a purple mass of *Heuchera* 'Montrose Ruby' in early May, while pinkshell azalea, *Rhododendron vaseyi*, blooms pink in the distance. Native azaleas are a major feature of the shrub layer in this garden, providing often-fragrant bloom from late April into mid summer.

ABOVE LEFT Plumleaf azalea, *Rhododendron prunifolium*, blooms in early August in dappled light below the canopy in Peirce's Woods.

RIGHT At the edge of the Peirce's Woods area, the strong-tiered effect of pagoda dogwood, *Cornus alternifolia*, is beautifully set against the dark upright trunk of a willow oak, *Quercus phellos*, in early November.

ABOVE RIGHT Vines are an easy tool for bringing foliage or flowering interest into the garden's mid and upper layers. At home, we invited Virginia creeper, *Parthenocissus quinquefolia*, to drape its intense scarlet over the lichen-covered trunks of an old European mountain ash, *Sorbus aucuparia*, enlivening the garden's mid layer in October.

Celebrating and Encouraging Natural Form

Though some amount of pruning and shaping is always necessary in even the most informal, naturalistic gardens, working as much as possible with natural plant forms is usually the most practical and often the most visually interesting approach.

The branches of flowering dogwoods, *Cornus florida*, cascade gracefully over walls enclosing the entrance court at Patterns, a private garden in Delaware. This effect was encouraged by weighting the tree branches with stones when they were young to introduce a downward direction of growth. Especially dramatic during spring flowering and autumn coloring, these dogwood draperies are elegant year-round.

The naturally pendulous lower branches of shrubs such as oakleaf hydrangea, *Hydrangea quercifolia*, offer the perfect solution for softening hard edges in the garden, as demonstrated here on two entirely different scales.

ABOVE LEFT Oakleaf hydrangea clothes the steep banks of a rocky stream bed at the Birmingham Botanical Gardens in Alabama in mid May.

ABOVE RIGHT Oakleaf hydrangeas falling gently over the edges of a wall planter help make this intimate enclosed space in the Idea Garden at Longwood Gardens so comfortable and inviting.

ABOVE Distinctive, irregularly formed trees and shrubs can be especially effective when they occur within an otherwise formal space. A venerable native hawthorn, *Crataegus* species, enlivens a formal courtyard designed by Ellen Shipman at Crab Tree Farm in Illinois. An emblem of the prairie states and a per-sonal favorite of landscape architect Jens Jensen, hawthorns have characteristic broad-spreading, horizontal branches.

BELOW Other hawthorns add their signature shapes to the landscape of Crab Tree Farm in Illinois, in mid October.

ABOVE In mid November, the arching form of arrowwood viburnum, *Viburnum denta-tum*, creates a colorful canopy over a stone stairway and landing at Winterthur Museum and Gardens in northern Delaware. Sensitive placement allows the shrub to achieve its mature natural shape.

OPPOSITE BOTTOM If allowed sufficient space under the canopy, witch hazel, *Hama-melis virginiana*, can grow to an impressive spread, as demonstrated by this twenty-foot-wide specimen in the Barton garden in Penn-sylvania. Even in early April, when the garden is mostly leafless, the strong arching-hori-zontal lines of the witch hazel provide inter-esting contrast with the vertical trunks of canopy trees.

In our Pennsylvania garden, we've deliberately avoided planting shrubs or herbaceous plants that would obscure the graceful trunk flare of this common pin oak, *Quercus palustris*. The moss layer established itself naturally, without any direct planting, and has spread each year aided only by occasional clearing of fallen leaf and twig litter and removal of occasional seedlings.

ABOVE As this May photograph in our front garden at home illustrates, pagoda dogwood, *Cornus alternifolia*, may not be as showy in bloom as flowering dogwood, *Cornus florida*, but its unique form and dramatically tiered branching have their own visual power. We chose this species to repeat the low, horizontal lines of the house.

RIGHT One aspect of celebrating natural form is to welcome seedlings in the garden, allowing plants to fit themselves to place much as they would in their native habitat. Successful naturalization usually results from a match between the cultural requirements of plants, including those necessary to sustain reproductive cycles, and the growing conditions in the garden. It can be greatly rewarding to establish living, changing plant populations, bringing a bit of directed serendipity to your landscape art. You can gently edit as necessary to retain visual order. In this mid-March scene, naturalized blue phlox, *Phlox divaricata*, and autumn alumroot, *Heuchera macrorhiza*, beautifully occupy niches in the native stone steps and retaining wall of Louise Smith's garden in Birmingham, Alabama.

In the forest, life and death are often equally beautiful. In Western human culture, we're usually taught to associate death with loss and sadness, so it may seem curious that in the woodlands, the natural forms of decaying trees are often emblems of vitality. As their materials break down and are reused in the organic cycle of the forest environment, such trees are typically home to myriad living things including fungi, algae, mosses, seedling plants, insects, reptiles, small land mammals, and birds. Look for opportunities to integrate the forms of dead and declining trees with the visual art and story of the woodland garden, as has been done here in the Ward garden in northern Delaware.

Though many shrub and tree species produce distinct individuals, others are colonial, spreading naturally by underground rhizomes to form masses and groves which can add a dramatic presence to the garden whenever space allows. Because they are comprised of uniform material, masses and groves can attractively cover considerable ground in the garden without introducing the disharmony and chaotic appearance that often results from overly diverse plantings.

Bottlebrush buckeye, *Aesculus parviflora*, is a colonial shrub which will grow into a large, domed mass more than ten feet tall if given the opportunity. Flowering in late June in our home garden, this bold display began as five small divisions planted a decade before this photograph was taken. Recognizable in form but now gold-hued in late October, a similar grove acts as a dramatic counterpoint to the opaque, vertical trunks of trees in a wooded section of Longwood Gardens.

Sassafras albidum is capable of becoming a large, single-trunked tree, but is more often encountered in groupings and groves due to its propensity for spreading by rhizomes. In southeastern Pennsylvania, sassafras is a common and beautiful element in old hedgerows and along roadsides and edges of local woodlands. At home, we were looking for a sturdy tree to plant in mass, flanking our driveway as it meets the road. We wanted something locally native to greet visitors, something with multiple-season interest, something quick-growing but reasonably long lived, and something tough enough to withstand the summer droughts and winter road salt spray, so we settled on sassafras.

Instead of buying trees, we saved volunteer seedlings, begged a few more from a friendly neighbor, and transplanted them all in late March of 1996 to begin our entry groves. In just four years, these free trees have grown to form dense masses of foliage that become a kaleidoscope of red, orange, and gold in late October. Five years after planting, the trunks have thickened sufficiently to provide a dark contrast against a January snow, and to create a woodsy sense of enclosure even in winter when branches are bare. There are other sassafras at least a half-century old just down the road from our garden and they're still growing strong, so if we get similar length of service from ours we'll be doing quite well, especially considering the cost.

Gardening at the Edge

Though shaded interior conditions dominate native forests, sunnier settings typical of the woodland edge are common in many private gardens and park landscapes. Some edge areas are more or less permanent, due to clearings which must be maintained for driveways, walks, dwellings, and other utility structures, and these offer opportunities to plant species requiring greater sunlight than the interior environment affords. Many interior, shade-tolerant species flower more freely at the sunny edge, and their fall foliage colors are often richer and more varied.

In suburban gardens, particularly those on land once cleared for agriculture, edge conditions are often temporary, gradually giving way as sunny lawn areas are reduced in favor of woodland plantings. Plants which can make this transition an attractive process are important elements in the evolution of such gardens.

ABOVE Unlike some aster species, smooth aster, *Aster laevis*, will not tolerate densely shaded woodland conditions; however, it will thrive and bloom profusely at the sunnier edge.

RIGHT Pinxter azalea, *Rhododendron periclymenoides*, grows readily but blooms sparingly in deep shade. At the sunny edge, however, it literally covers itself with flowers in early May. Its companion here, foamflower, *Tiarella cordifolia*, behaves similarly.

The running nature and flowing form of cut-leaf smooth sumac, *Rhus glabra* 'Laciniata', make a vertical transition from trees to turf in a south-facing woodland screen in our Pennsylvania garden, adding spectacular autumn hues to the landscape.

ABOVE In mid January, a mix of grasses colorfully covers the sunny ground in front of a paper birch, *Betula papyrifera*, on the Connecticut College campus in New London. The native warm-season grasses seen here are little bluestem, *Schizachyrium scoparium*, and broom sedge, *Andropogon virginicus*.

LEFT Native grasses can be both beautiful and useful choices for planting as transitional elements at the expanding edge of a woodland border. At home, we've used switch grass, *Panicum virgatum*, in the sunny space on the south side of a border filled with mixed shrubs and trees. The opaque, upright forms of two red cedars, *Juniperus virginiana* 'Emerald Sentinel', contrast with the luminous translucence of the grasses. Though not visible in this photograph, two young silverbells are planted among the switch grass. As these mature, they will connect with the existing trees and shade the space now occupied by the sun-loving switch grasses, which will give way to shade-tolerant woodland perennials.

Integrating Exotics

Even among gardeners ardently devoted to growing and conserving North American native plants, few would be so purist as to say that exotics have no place in the designed landscape. The exotic species that is an old family favorite or is a reminder of a visit to a far-away garden is often an innocuous addition even in the native garden. Most importantly, the places in which we make gardens have sometimes been so changed by human influence that certain growing conditions on the site are no longer suitable for the native plants they might once have supported, and in some cases carefully selected exotics may actually be better suited to the design purpose and less consuming of natural resources. For example, for many years I passed a swamp of red maples, *Acer rubrum*, in northern Delaware on my commute to work. The conditions were damp to wet, and the site supported many natural companions of red maple, such as tussock sedge, *Carex stricta*, and skunk cabbage, *Symplocarpus foetidus*. The site now supports suburban tract houses. During construction it was drained to keep basements dry; the surface of the land was reorganized to suit the requirements of driveways, walks, and foundations; topsoil was stripped and removed; and the entire site was compacted by heavy machinery, further altering the soil texture and drainage characteristics. The site will still support red maples, which are broadly adapted, unusually resilient trees; however, tussock sedge and skunk cabbage would not survive unless you stood over them with a watering hose for half the year or took elaborate measures to restore the site's former hydrology. It could be argued that the most practical, conserving approach to planting the toughest places on this modified site would be to choose species naturally adapted to the new conditions, even if that required looking beyond the local native flora. The key qualification of these choices, from a conservation perspective, would be that they have no potential for escaping the garden and naturalizing to the detriment of the local native plant communities.

Late October sunlight streams through Chinese winter hazels, *Corylopsis* species, forming part of the shrub layer under a large pin oak, *Quercus palustris*. Though exotic, these shrubs are visually sympathetic to the scale, texture, and color cycles of local native woodlands. Well adapted to conditions in the garden, they have shown no capacity for naturalizing in the wild.

TOP Even after its bright blue flowers have faded, this ground-covering mass of crested iris, *Iris cristata*, makes for stunning contrast with the dark green, broad leaves of oakleaf hydrangea, *Hydrangea quercifolia*, in early May in the Birmingham Botanical Gardens, Alabama.

BOTTOM Although typically undervalued and neglected by American gardeners, the common Mayapple, *Podophyllum peltatum*, offers some spectacular opportunities for textural combinations in designed landscapes. For many years, we've enjoyed this mix of Mayapples and *Fothergilla gardenii* in a shady section of our April garden.

In our garden, my wife and I have added a few additional constraints to our palette, since we're trying to make a garden reflective and evocative of the regional deciduous forest. We favor native species, but we integrate exotics if they are well adapted to our soil, water, light, and climactic conditions; do not have the potential for introducing pests or diseases harmful to the native flora; are incapable of becoming invasive in the surrounding native landscape; and are visually in sync with the natural scale, textures, and color cycles of our region. We've found, for example, that Japanese ladies'-slipper orchid, *Cypripedium japonicum*, thrives amid native trilliums, asters, and ferns under our old apple tree with no artificial watering, fertilizer, or chemical crutches, in growing conditions that would certainly be fatal to the North American native pink ladies'-slipper, *Cypripedium acaule*. The Japanese species spreads modestly by rhizomes but has no potential for naturalizing in or beyond the garden. Though its pleated leaves are distinct, its flowers very nearly resemble the native species in color and bloom period. We also grow a variety of Chinese winter hazels, *Corylopsis* species, under a large pin oak, *Quercus palustris*. Although we get an occasional seedling in the garden, these plants have been cultivated in our part of North America for more than a century and have shown no capacity for naturalizing in the native environment. These winter hazels bloom in late winter to early spring in a light yellow not unlike that of many native wildflowers and shrubs. Their summer foliage color and texture, golden autumn hues, and bare-branched winter architecture are all similar and complementary to the local native vegetation.

Working with Textures and within the Color Green

The rich diversity of woodland textures and green hues offers myriad opportunities for enduring, eye-catching combinations, and if elements such as rocks, garden structures, and local relics are added to the composition, the design possibilities are virtually limitless.

TOP LEFT A dark green ground cover of Allegheny pachysandra, *Pachysandra procumbens*, provides a highly contrasting backdrop for the lighter green, bold-textured foliage of redbud, *Cercis canadensis*, in late July at Springwood, a private garden in Pennsylvania.

BOTTOM Masses of oakleaf hydrangea, *Hydrangea quercifolia*, cascade gracefully over the banks of a small stream in May, beautifully setting off a rustic bridge in Louise Wrinkle's garden in Birmingham, Alabama.

TOP RIGHT The lacy textural beauty and blue-green color of marginal wood fern, *Dryopteris marginalis*, is accentuated by this sitting stone in early May in the Birmingham Botanical Gardens, Alabama.

ABOVE The native landscape and the cultural landscape are neither mutually exclusive nor incompatible, and in many cases, the juxtaposition of nature and human industry makes for a satisfying visual composition rich in story. The fortunes of Birmingham, Alabama, were once made of steel, and although the great furnaces have ceased operation, the memory of the steel and iron industry is still significant in the city and in its sense of self. Once used to pour molten steel, this furnace crucible now overflows with marginal wood fern, *Dryopteris marginalis*, and Solomon's seal, *Polygonatum biflorum*, in May in the garden of noted conservationist Louise Smith of Birmingham, Alabama.

American hollies, *Ilex opaca*, are integrated carefully in the deciduous woodland gardens of Mount Cuba Center in northern Delaware, creating enclosure and organizing views where desired, but generally leaving the landscape open and luminous.

The Influence of Evergreens

A drive-by evaluation of the landscapes in a typical suburban housing development, even those built on land that was formerly forest, will reveal a heavy reliance on evergreen trees and shrubs. The reasons for using evergreens are varied. The color green, generally taken for granted by many gardeners in spring and summer, takes on greater cachet in the winter landscape. Also, evergreens are often perceived as more "alive" in the winter landscape than deciduous plants. Perhaps most commonly, evergreens are valued for the constant screening effect they can provide. The downside of these evergreen-filled landscapes is that they are relatively static, possessing little of the seasonal drama of a predominantly deciduous landscape. If the purpose of the garden is to evoke the deciduous forest, evergreen trees and shrubs must be used carefully and sparingly, so the garden emulates the open, luminous characteristics of a native woodlands as much as practical. The ground layer is an appropriate place to indulge in native evergreens including ferns, mosses, club mosses, sedges, wood-rushes, and herbaceous perennials, which will add their verdant hues to the winter landscape without diminishing the vistas, as well as the light and shadow play of the woods.

Celebrating Natural Light in the Woodland Garden

To the uninitiated, the woodland garden might seem a place of darkness, but in truth, it can be among the most radiant landscapes on earth. One magical aspect of deciduous woodland plants is that their thin foliage is translucent, particularly in spring and fall, and capable of all manner of incandescent effects.

Many of the most beautifully lit moments in the woodland garden are indeed fleeting, and to welcome this is essential to understanding the nature of the garden's beauty. It is neither fixed nor static but rather dynamic and flowing, built upon the constant flux and innumerable luminous phenomena that characterize the woods. The challenge and opportunity of celebrating natural light in the woodland garden are to match the choreography of a particular design to the natural dance of light through the landscape, and there are

many ways to do this. Though lighting events are frequently ephemeral, they often repeat at predictable times of the day or year. Observe your existing garden landscape and make note of specially lit moments you want to celebrate. Organize pathways, garden seating, or views from inside the dwelling to provide the needed focus at the appropriate time. When creating new parts of the garden, place an emphasis on plants with foliage or flowers that are particularly capable of accentuating the sun's rays, and position them where you are likely to view them glowing against dark-colored backgrounds, shadows, or reflective surfaces.

The Ward garden in northern Delaware is an exceptionally elegant study in greens. Created within the existing forest framework, it relies mostly on mosses and vast sweeps of ferns flowing along a central stream for its considerable drama. Views and perspectives constantly change as you stroll along the garden's subtle but extensive path system.

ABOVE Walking in the garden on the first day of October, I was suddenly transfixed by a group of cinnamon ferns, *Osmunda cinnamonea*, flanking a turn in the stream. The ferns had caught the passing of a sunbeam and were resplendent in the honeyed light of early autumn. The composition lasted only a few minutes, just long enough to capture in photograph and memory.

Returning to the Ward garden just before sundown the following day, I caught a mix of ostrich ferns, *Matteuccia struthiopteris*, and others bathed in the last light. Their shimmering tones shoot down into the water, outlining the course of the stream and highlighting the dark trunks and root flares of oaks and tuliptrees as they meet the ground.

RIGHT Whatever ferns lack in flowers, they more than make up for in luminous potential. Ostrich ferns are lit by late April sunlight in the Ward garden, their glow all the more apparent in contrast with the dark trunks of trees.

In May many years ago I came upon a stand of umbrella trees, *Magnolia tripetala*, in a Virginia mountain forest and was captivated by their thirty-inch leaf clusters glowing in the late-day light. I vowed to one day emulate this effect in a designed landscape. As my wife and I came to understand the paths of natural light in our garden, we realized we had an ideal opportunity under a tall pin oak, *Quercus palustris*, off the south side of our house. We planted two umbrella trees under the high shade of the oak, where they are in the sun's path each morning and late afternoon. Now each year we delight in watching their huge, leafy umbrellas expand into spring's strengthening light until they become glowing green whorls, visible directly from the bedroom.

Could these Wherry's foamflowers, *Tiarella cordifolia* var. *collina*, be more candlelike, naturally sidelit by the sun in late April? For years I enjoyed this phenomenon in a small urban patio garden in northern Delaware.

The delicate, filamentous flowers of *Fothergilla gardenii* are like tiny lightbulbs glowing in late April sunlight against the shadows of river birch trunks.

FAR LEFT By design, sunlight can be employed to enhance and accentuate the colors of translucent fruits, seeds, and flowers. In our garden, I placed this woodland wild oat, *Chasmanthium latifolium*, deliberately in the path of the late-day autumn sun, knowing we would frequently see it sidelit from inside our south-facing glass-walled porch. The golden tones of the grass are further heightened against the blue hues of heart-leaved aster, *Aster cordifolius*, positioned below and behind in the same mixed border.

LEFT Since enjoying many wondrous light effects in the landscape depends on being there at the right moment, it makes sense to create luminous opportunities in view of places frequently visited such as bathroom and kitchen. At home, sweetshrub, *Calycanthus floridus* 'Edith Wilder', is naturally backlit in the late-day view from the bathroom window, its blossoms glowing crimson in early May while their sweet strawberry scent wafts in and through the house.

BOTTOM A mossy lawn is the best stage on which to watch the shadow play and sunlit tracery of the woods. In late January, tree trunks and mountain laurels, *Kalmia latifolia*, make patterns over a carpet of moss in Essex Fells, New Jersey. This scene is little changed from my childhood days in this heavily wooded suburban community, where moss is sometimes welcomed as the naturally occurring, low-maintenance alternative to a grass lawn.

ABOVE Garden walkways can often do double duty as display surfaces for the patterns made by nearby plantings. In early September, the soft dappling of high birch branches melds with the sharp ladderlike shadows of Christmas fern, *Polystichum acrostichoides*, just off the rear door of our house.

ABOVE RIGHT In similar but vertical fashion, a simple stucco wall becomes a literal movie screen as shadows of river birches, *Betula nigra* 'Heritage', are cast against the bare-branched black lines of redbuds, *Cercis canadensis* 'Forest Pansy', in mid November.

RIGHT Among the delights of focusing on natural light in the woodland garden is that its drama continues year-round, as demonstrated by the cinnamon glow of river birch bark on a snow in late December.

ABOVE The woodland garden in the coldest season is replete with remnants of the growing season that take on new life in the winter light. The stems and faded flower clusters of oakleaf hydrangea, *Hydrangea quercifolia*, are aglow in mid January in the Connecticut College Arboretum in New London.

Woodland Walks and Pathways

On more than one occasion I've listened to the suggestions of British gardeners that Americans are too willing to set a few native plants along a path and call it a garden, and there is some truth in these observations. The garden at its best is much more than a random passage through a collection of interesting objects, be they native or not. If it is to be art, and not a mere replication of nature, the garden should make imaginative and confident use of structure to organize the landscape in ways that create richly textured sensual and intellectual experiences. The question is, What qualifies as structure? In the traditional British flower garden, trees are either entirely absent or are minor, peripheral players. The organizing garden structure most often consists of masonry walls and paving, arbors, pergolas, trellises, and clipped ever-

A broad green avenue makes the transition from the more open grassy spaces at the crest of the property to the enveloping structure of the woodland garden below, placing the focus squarely on great vertical trunks, in early October in the Ward garden. The turf becomes increasingly delicate and infused with moss as it extends under the woodland canopy.

greens, with various art objects serving as focal points. While all of this can be stunningly effective, it usually involves considerable expense.

Certainly, the American woodland garden should be more than a simple "walk in the woods," but deciduous trees are among the greatest structural elements in any natural landscapes. If recognized as such in the garden and put to imaginative use, they can play a significant role in organizing artful experiences that are both evocative of the native forest and easier on the budget.

ABOVE In early April, a moss path at Mount Cuba Center in Delaware shows wear where it is most heavily trod but is still beautiful and serviceable. It turns easily and naturally in response to trees and the grade of the land.

LEFT Edged with steel and paved with bark mulch, a subtle, winding path leads visitors on a contemplative journey through the Ward garden in late April. The curves are neither accidental nor arbitrary; each is in response to a tree, tree grouping, fallen log, or landform encountered as the garden unfolds.

ABOVE Fallen leaves enliven a mulched path at Crab Tree Farm in Illinois, leading to a contemplative space enveloped by mature trees. In addition to serving as focal points, garden seats and benches play an important role in providing destinations along woodland garden paths.

TOP RIGHT Crushed stone or gravel may be practical options for paving woodland paths when patterns of use are too heavy for turf or moss. It is usually difficult to maintain a neat edge along these paths, but this may not matter if adjoining plantings are full and sturdy, such as this dense combination of blue phlox, *Phlox divaricata*, and maidenhair fern, *Adiantum pedatum*, at the Leonard J. Buck Garden in northern New Jersey.

A rustic fence separates a crushed stone path from a lower-level planting of bottle-brush buckeye, *Aesculus parviflora*, at Frederic Church's Olana, which overlooks the Hudson River in New York State. The fence materials are sturdy but sympathetic to the look and feel of the local woodlands. Photo by Melinda Zoehrer.

Artfully constructed timber paths can be significant features in the woodland landscape during the dormant months, as exemplified by this arcing path at Ashland Hollow. The timbers read as black against the silver-gray trunks of beech trees, *Fagus grandifolia*.

TOP LEFT Significant changes in grade along woodland pathways require surfaces sturdier and more stable than turf, moss, or crushed stone. At the Birmingham Botanical Gardens in Alabama, weathered railroad ties make an attractive transition to an upper level. The path is edged on the right by yellowroot, *Xanthorhiza simplicissima*, a running woodland shrub ideally suited to such purposes. The path turns as it rises, hinting at destinations further along.

ABOVE Stone may be the best and most beautiful solution for paths with moderate traffic. In early April, the soft texture and lime glow of mosses contrast stunningly with stepping stones in a woodland path at Ashland Hollow.

The path encircling the pond at Mount Cuba Center in Delaware makes use of multiple surfaces from moss to the cut stone that forms the elegant cantilevered bridge over the far spillway. The bridge serves as the far focal point while a mix of blue phlox, *Phlox divaricata*, ostrich ferns, *Matteuccia struthiopteris*, and skunk cabbage, *Symplocarpus foetidus*, provides color and textural interest in the foreground.

ABOVE Stone steps guide garden guests up a mossy slope in a beech copse at the Montgomery Pinetum in Greenwich, Connecticut, in early April, wisely keeping foot traffic off moss and tree roots alike.

TOP LEFT Carefully crafted of stratified limestone, a circular gathering space offers a contemplative destination along a woodland path at Crab Tree Farm in Illinois. The design is an inspired update of the "council ring," an element introduced by midwestern landscape architect Jens Jensen early in the twentieth century.

BOTTOM LEFT Though such things are rare in the native woods, there's no rule that says a woodland garden path can't be straight and true. This bluestone-paved formal walk at Skylands Arboretum in northern New Jersey makes inspired use of sweet bay magnolias, *Magnolia virginiana*, to provide framing and an arching sense of enclosure. The walk is sweetly scented when the trees are in bloom above.

Depending upon personal preference and budget, it is possible to make woodland pathways varying greatly in formality and strength of style while still keeping true to the spirit of the regional forest, as I've observed from visits to two memorable New England landscapes.

LEFT On Maine's Mount Desert Island, the woodland path up Dorr Mountain begins with irregular slabs of local granite forming a stairway through mixed native trees, including paper birch, *Betula papyrifera*, which is perhaps the most-loved deciduous tree in the northern woods. This birch is virtually a New England icon, ubiquitous in everything from the regional landscape, to landscape paintings, to L.L.Bean mail-order catalogs.

RIGHT The overall effect in this section of the path is simple and naturalistic. As the path continues up the mountain, the granite stairway becomes much more tightly ordered and is bordered by huge boulders. Paper birches, from natural seedlings, become the dominant trees, their upright white forms sharply defined against the granite and dark green hemlocks, *Tsuga canadensis*, at the periphery. Though entirely of local materials, the elaborate stonework and the nearly uniform birches make a much stronger design impact.

Go from Dorr Mountain to the famous stairs at Naumkeag in western Massachusetts and you see the same basic pattern notched up many levels in formality and overlaid with what might be called an art nouveau style. Yet for all its artful contrivance, this Fletcher Steele design is still essentially a journey celebrating the beautiful bark and form of one of the region's most notable and characteristic trees.

The Woodland Garden Dwelling

I am often perplexed by talk of "connecting to nature" through the garden when no mention is made of the house. Since woodland nature is so tied to cycles of light, sounds, scents, and other seasonal nuance, it is especially important that connections between a woodland dwelling and garden be made as strong as imagination and resources allow. Given the complexity and hurried pace of contemporary life in North America, with so many stimuli competing for our attention, the phrase "out of sight, out of mind" applies ever more certainly to the great outdoors, including the garden in its quiet but necessary moments. Fortunately, technological advances in modern building materials, particularly those associated with glass, in windows, walls, and skylights, have made it economically and ecologically sound to provide views from all parts of the house into beautiful living phenomena of the woodland landscape.

Set among native beeches and anchored by sweeps of native ferns, the Ward residence in northern Delaware provides a year-round, multifaceted connection with garden and the local woodland landscape.

Built over a waterfall on Bear Run in western Pennsylvania, Frank Lloyd Wright's Fallingwater was undoubtedly designed to invite contemplation of the falls, its sound and cycles. But I've visited the house in all seasons and have found it to be every bit as revealing about the cycles of the forest. Broad terraces are cantilevered far out into the mid level of the woods, their extreme horizontality highlighting the upright forms of forest trees. Step out on any of these terraces in winter or early spring and what is most apparent is the expansive openness of the bare woods, with depth of view at maximum. Come back and enter the same scene in mid summer and the overwhelming experience has become one of enclosure and immersion, with many vistas scaled back to a surprising intimacy. In ways great or small, any imaginatively designed dwelling can provide a connection with the cyclic opening and closing of the forest.

A brilliant model of possibility, not practical-
ity, Philip Johnson's Glass House in New
Canaan provides the ultimate connection
with the surrounding Connecticut woodlands. During a visit in early November, I admired a combination of upright trunks and
low stone walls and the way they directed my
eye to the forest edge below. I was inspired to
hear Mr. Johnson explain his subtle interven-
tions in the landscape, which ranged from
redirecting walls to a gentle editing of the
understory and ground layers. The result is
an artful clarification of forest patterns in
keeping with the spirit of the house.

TOP LEFT Modest in scale and materials but large in imagination, the James Rose House in Ridgewood, New Jersey, offers an intimate connection with the garden.

ABOVE I've learned that a delight of bringing the woods close to the house and providing views from inside-out is having birds become a constant part of the winter experience. A mating pair of cardinals finds food and cover among the berried branches of smooth witherod, *Viburnum nudum* 'Winterthur', in this view from the bathroom window on Christmas day.

BOTTOM LEFT Why not bring the woods close if opportunity permits? A wall of windows invites autumn's woodland glory into the living room of this private home in Mahwah, New Jersey.

Making a connection to a woodland garden isn't dependent on a grand space or budget. My first garden was on an eighth-acre urban lot in Newark, Delaware. We knocked a hole in the back wall, built a patio of local Avondale stone, and planted the tiny space with woodland ferns, wildflowers, and shrubs, using an existing dogwood, *Cornus florida*, as the frame and focal point. A storm door with screen and glass inserts keeps the garden in constant view through the seasons.

ABOVE LEFT A mix of woodland herbaceous plants including Wherry's foamflower, *Tiarella cordifolia* var. *collina*, and maidenhair ferns, *Adiantum pedatum*, thrives in the shade of the dogwood, which is nearly finished flowering in mid May.

ABOVE RIGHT The dogwood greets mid October with rich red and bronze.

In our Pennsylvania home, installing insulated sliding window-doors in a screened interior porch has resulted in a year-round room that provides my wife and I with south-facing views into the garden. We've extended plantings out from the house to incorporate a fifty-year-old sourwood, *Oxydendrum arboreum*, planted by the original owners. This tree has become a favorite focal point and a familiar indicator of seasonal change. In winter, we might enjoy snow on its characteristically twisted branches. The bright chartreuse of its new leaves in mid May is transformed into rich bronze and scarlet by late September, and is especially captivating when viewed from inside the house, backlit by the sun. For a number of years, this tree has been the favorite spring perch for a mating pair of doves that call our garden home.

At home, we've deliberately selected interior furnishings with colors and patterns complementary to those of the local woodland landscape, in the belief that this keeps our eye more attuned to the subtleties of regional color. Our intention is create a graceful segue from house to garden.

ABOVE Myriad greens and pastel blues and pinks are in close view from our glass porch in late April.

ABOVE RIGHT The same room is infused with the warm tones of a late October sunrise, as tree trunks and leaves add their shadow patterns to the stucco wall.

Another way to connect house and garden is to make a habit of cutting garden plants for interior display. In addition to woodland perennials, we've found many native shrubs and trees are excellent choices for cut material, such as this Alabama snow wreath, *Neviusia alabamensis*, decorating our dining table in mid May. Even when long past flower, the autumn foliage of trees and shrubs can make delightful, long-lasting cut material.

Find ways to bring forest fragrances into the house. The entryway at Ashland Hollow is an inspired example of making fragrance a welcoming theme. Sweet bay magnolias, *Magnolia virginiana*, rise through an open arbor, adding their lemon fragrance to the entry space beginning in late spring. In mid June the spicy clove scent of sweet azalea, *Rhododendron arborescens*, drifts gently from a corner niche.

CHAPTER FOUR

Planting and Maintaining the Woodland Garden

OOD DESIGN coupled with appropriate planting and maintenance techniques will result in a woodland garden that is a daily joy and a sustaining inspiration. Perhaps most important to all of this is to work in harmony with the realistic, natural potential of your site and your region. Plan and plant in response to both the opportunities and limitations of your property, and you'll be rewarded by a landscape that is as healthy and enduring as it is beautiful.

Selecting and Acquiring Plants

Whether you're beginning a new woodland garden or planning changes to your current landscape, take time to make a thorough and thoughtful inventory of existing plants. It's especially important to assess large shrubs and trees, since these resources may represent decades or even a lifetime of growth. If they appear to be healthy and well adapted to growing conditions on your property, consider how they might play important roles in the structure and organization of your landscape. Use existing plants to guide your potential plant choices: their presence and relative condition will reveal a lot about the soil, moisture, drainage, light, and overall climatic conditions new plants will encounter on your property.

Conserving existing woodland plants on your property and integrating them into new designs may have additional importance if the plants represent part of the local native vegetation. Whether you're gardening at the edge of a wilderness or in former cornfield suburbia, it's likely that some plants on your property are remnants of earlier forests or seedlings which represent the local genetic pool.

If your desire is to make a woodland garden that truly reflects the spirit and living legacy of the regional forest, it is important to seek plants that not only belong to native species, but that represent the local provenance (see "Diversity and the Beauty of Provenance" in chapter one). These plants are

Just beginning its autumn coloring in mid October, this pagoda dogwood, *Cornus alternifolia*, began as a chance seedling in our garden.

likely to exhibit traits that are unique to the local population including those of practical import such as relative cold hardiness, drought or heat tolerance, and disease resistance, as well as traits of aesthetic value in the garden such as bark and branching characteristics, scent, autumn coloration, and flowering time, color, and abundance.

In our home garden, a number of the plants that represent the local provenance have grown from serendipitous seedlings, including beech, *Fagus grandifolia*, dogwoods, *Cornus alternifolia* and *Cornus florida*, spicebush, *Lindera benzoin*, and sassafras, *Sassafras albidum*. My wife and I have made a habit of looking for seedlings of native woodland plants that show up during the growing season and of seeking ways to use them in our landscape or making gifts of them to local gardening friends. Sometimes a seed germinates in a spot where it may remain and mature in sympathy with our design. Often we transplant found seedlings into a temporary nursery bed, growing them on in our soil until we determine an ultimate placement.

THE ETHICS OF ACQUISITION

As a rule, it is unethical to collect wild plants, seed, or plant parts from parks, preserves, roadsides and other public rights of way, and from the private property of others unless you have specific permission. This rule applies even when the plants in question appear to be threatened by development or other destructive events.

Permission to collect, especially modest quantities of seed or cuttings, may often be obtained through the courtesy of a friendly verbal request or letter. In fact, seed is typically the most practical way of propagating woody plants from wild populations. Larger, established plants rarely survive the trauma of transplanting from native habitats without significant injury. In most cases, "rescue operations," in which plants otherwise destined for destruction are removed from harm's way and relocated to a presumably safe harbor, are best undertaken by conservation organizations or botanical gardens with the knowledge and resources to increase the chances of success.

STARTING PLANTS FROM SEED

Though the range of native woodland species available for purchase as plants is ever expanding, seed is sometimes the only way of acquiring less common or local varieties. In addition to commercial sources, consider botanical gardens, arboreta, and nature societies when seeking special seed.

Details of seed propagation techniques are beyond the scope of this book; however, I'd like to suggest that starting plants from seed can often be done with little fanfare and literally no paraphernalia. The pawpaws, *Asimina triloba*, in our home garden began as seeds simply buried in a row in a temporary nursery area located near our compost pile. The germination rate was astoundingly high, and I enjoyed one-hundred-percent success in transplanting the seedlings to line what we now call our pawpaw path. Notoriously deep rooted and hard to manage in traditional nursery production, pawpaw trees can be difficult to obtain commercially, so the seed-propagation route was not only easy, it was most practical.

PURCHASING PLANTS

In general, whenever pace and patience permit, it is better to buy plants in modest size for the woodland garden, and this is especially true for trees. Small caliper (two inches and under) plants always establish more quickly, require less watering during the process, and usually lead healthier, longer lives than others moved in specimen size. Another factor to consider is that in nursery field production, woody plants are typically acclimated to full sun conditions. Transplanting into a shaded garden setting is much more traumatic for large specimens.

One advantage to field-grown woody plants, particularly if they come from a local nursery, is that the soil they're growing in is likely to be closer to your own soil than is the case with container-grown plants. This factor alone can result in more rapid establishment; however, timing is critically important in digging and transplanting field-grown deciduous plants. They're usually best moved while dormant.

Producing plants in containers allows nurseries to offer plants throughout the growing season, and while this is a benefit to most gardeners, there are a few negative aspects to container-grown woody plants that deserve special attention. The growing medium used is often highly inorganic and extremely porous, designed for rapid drainage during production. If you simply remove one of these plants from the container, place it in a hole dug in your garden, and backfill, you're likely to wind up with a plant that is impossible to keep adequately moist. Your garden soil is likely to be so much heavier, with so much greater potential to attract and retain soil moisture, that it will literally wick dry the porous medium of the container plant. The fix for this is to loosen or cut open the medium to allow for greater contact between your garden soil and the root system.

The most serious side effect of producing woody plants, especially trees, in containers is the likelihood of girdling roots. Though new container types and chemical treatments are being introduced to reduce this phenomenon, in the typical scenario the roots of woody plants often begin growing in circles once they've expanded to the walls of the container. This rarely results in injury when plants are small, but as trees and shrubs grow large in the garden, these encircling roots are capable of completely girdling the main stem, crushing the vital cambium layer and causing death. To avoid purchasing plants with girdling roots, inspect the base of the trunk or main stem and reject the plant if encircling roots can be detected just below the soil level. This precaution is equally valid when buying field-grown stock, since many of these plants may have spent their early years in containers.

A close inspection of form and branching integrity is also warranted when buying trees and large-stemmed shrubs. The asymmetry or other unique character of a particular specimen may be an asset to your garden, but badly crossing main stems or weak crotch angles are most likely to guarantee future headaches.

Though it is a minor point, I've learned the hard way that plants purchased in late fall from heated nursery production houses are especially sus-

Although it may seem like rough treatment, it's important to loosen or open up the overly dense root masses and inorganic potting media typically encountered in container-grown plants. Parting the pot-bound roots of this fothergilla, *Fothergilla gardenii*, before planting will ensure better contact between roots and garden soil, and will make it easier to keep the plant properly moistened once in the ground.

ceptible to browse damage and to winter cold injury. One year in mid November I bought a number of fothergillas, *Fothergilla major* and *Fothergilla gardenii*, for immediate planting. Though all were container grown, some had been exposed to the elements and others had been pulled directly from heated hoop houses. The outdoor plants had begun dropping their leaves and were fairly well hardened to the season's plummeting temperatures, and they all survived the winter without mishap. The others were in full fall color, but their tissues were still quite tender, and they proved the clear preference of rabbits, woodchucks, and other hungry mammals that frequent our garden in winter. By spring, many of these plants were no more than nubs.

A key question when purchasing plants is whether to select seedlings or clonal (vegetatively propagated) cultivars. Genetically identical cultivars offer the comfort of predictable performance, which is often of paramount importance for plants intended to form the cornerstone of a garden design. The down side of such replicated superiority is that too much of it introduces a sameness and predictability to the landscape, and ultimately works against the notion of gardens doing double-duty as conservators of genetic diversity. Seedlings, particularly from unknown sources, can surpass the strength and glory of a cultivar, or they can develop into significant disappointments. A balanced approach is to use clonal cultivars when design dictates, and to favor seed-grown plants with proven lineage elsewhere in the garden, not forgetting the often-beautiful pedigree of local provenance.

Respecting Roots

Sometimes taken for granted as the invisible portion of the garden, the root systems of trees are an extensive and sensitive component of woodland landscapes and must be treated with care and respect. This is particularly important with surface-rooted trees such as beeches, *Fagus grandifolia*.

Make every effort to protect the root systems of significant trees whenever you undertake major construction such as building or modifying a dwelling or outbuildings, digging utility trenches, or installing drives and paved walks.

Mark areas clearly or erect temporary fences to keep heavy equipment and materials out of root zones as much as practical. For large trees, this usually means a minimum of fifteen feet from the trunk and may require a clear zone of thirty feet or more. Keep in mind that the feeding roots of trees typically extend considerably beyond the spread of their aerial branches. Motivate contractors to treat trees respectfully by offering a bonus for good performance or adding a liability clause in the contract tied to the estimated replacement value of trees. Unfortunately, it may take a year or more before damage to tree roots becomes apparent.

When planting within root zones, minimize injury to tree roots by working with hand tools. A rototiller may seem the expedient way to prepare a planting bed under a specimen tree, but the long-term cost may far exceed the immediate benefit. It's also easier and less damaging to install small plants in areas occupied by established root systems.

Healthy tree roots need oxygen, which is generally in greatest supply near the soil surface. If garden design and construction require re-grading the ground, take care to minimize changes in soil level within root zones. Adding as little as four inches of soil on top of a tree's roots can be literally smothering and may result in long-term decline.

Regular, heavy foot traffic over roots can also diminish or destroy a tree's health. If a path must cross over sensitive roots, consider adding paving stones or even a raised boardwalk to take the brunt of the weight.

Matching Plants to Available Light

Spend time learning the daily and seasonal patterns of sunlight on your property, and put these observations to use when planting the woodland garden. Within the forest palette, there are many plants adapted to truly low levels of light; notable among these are the mosses and ferns. Light requirements of the herbaceous ground layer are varied, but most species are adapted to less light on average than typical for open habitats such as prairies; however, though many woodland plants are sometimes referred to as "shade loving," it is often more accurate to call them "shade tolerant." Certainly forest trees grow skyward, competing actively for sunlight, and the majority of woodland flowering shrubs and perennial herbs bloom in spring, when sunlight is still abundant below the deciduous canopy. Framework and foliage interest are basic to woodland beauty, but if flowering is important to your design and desires, plant to take advantage of sunnier edges and of the bright spots that occur in the interior of even the shadiest deciduous landscapes. Keep in mind that the constant shade produced by evergreens and buildings is different in character from the seasonal shade produced by deciduous trees and shrubs.

A frequent challenge of converting a landscape to woodlands is that in early stages, sunlight is often overabundant. If provided adequate moisture, shrubs and young trees can usually tolerate full sun, but the herbaceous ground layer of woodland plants can't abide such conditions. The majority, from *Trillium* species to foamflowers, *Tiarella cordifolia*, do best in the dappled or filtered light typical below a high deciduous canopy. Exposure to full

Showy trilliums, *Trillium grandiflorum*, thrive in the dappled light below the deciduous forest canopy in late April in North Carolina.

afternoon sun is the most stressful, since it is usually hottest and most intense. Often the only practical solution is to plant sun-tolerant species in the ground layer in early stages, with the mix gradually evolving to true woodland species as trees above mature.

Hardiness

Cold hardiness, typically expressed in USDA numbered zones, is still the most common factor limiting the choice of plants in any regional woodland garden. Although plant collectors often enjoy the challenge of growing plants in areas colder than their normal tolerance, when planting a woodland landscape of potentially long-lived woody plants, there's merit in respecting cold-hardiness limits established over decades. The loss of a shrub or herbaceous planting to a frigid winter is usually sustainable, but the loss of a significant tree due to insufficient hardiness can be a genuine setback. Fortunately a wide variety of North American deciduous forest species has significant reserves of cold hardiness and can be grown into the colder regions of the country.

Many factors can affect cold hardiness, including natural genetic variation within a species and stress induced by adverse growing conditions, pests, or diseases. New transplants are often subject to cold damage; however, small woody transplants are often more cold hardy than larger ones. Roots covered in winter by an appropriate mulch are more likely to survive than those under bare soil, and in the coldest zones, a protective cover of snow is the most effective mulch.

Heat tolerance is another critical facet of overall hardiness. Plants may survive the regional winter's worst only to succumb to respiratory failure during long, hot, humid summer nights. I've long admired the distinct bark and autumn color of striped maple, *Acer pensylvanicum*, which is native to my state but not to my particular area. It grows naturally in cool, moist north woods, extending south into Georgia only in the mountains. Beautiful as it

Uniquely dramatic in fall color, striped maple, *Acer pensylvanicum*, grows among rock outcrops along a Virginia mountain stream. The natural range and habitat choices of this species are clues to its need for cool summer night temperatures.

can be, it's unlikely to reach its potential in the summer heat conditions typical in my low-altitude garden, so I've contented myself with enjoying this tree in landscapes where it is truly fit.

Heat stress is increased by lack of air flow and by an excess of pavement or other hard reflective surfaces. It can be reduced to some extent by supplementary watering, but in the long run it is difficult or impossible to counter the effects of climate. The most practical and resource-conserving approach is to select plants naturally adapted to regional climatic conditions and to the cultural niches on your property.

Woodland Soils

In both garden and forest, the woodland ecosystem does not stop at ground level but extends well below the surface to include bacteria, fungi, root systems (of herbs, trees, and shrubs), animals of all sorts and sizes, minerals, water, oxygen, carbon dioxide, and dead organic matter. Those who keep this broad perspective in mind will be rewarded with a woodland garden that is healthier, more manageable, and more alive.

ACIDITY AND ALKALINITY

Soil pH is the standard measure of relative soil acidity and alkalinity, with neutral soils designated pH 7.0. The pH of forest soils typically ranges from very acid, pH 4.0, to slightly acid, pH 6.5. Coniferous forests tend to be most acid, with the majority of deciduous forest soils somewhat less so, measuring between pH 5.5 and 6.5. Soil pH reflects the combined chemical properties of the soil's organic and mineral components, and is heavily influenced by a region's underlying rock. In areas where limestone forms the bedrock, including much of Illinois and Wisconsin, the so-called calcareous soils may have a pH of 7.0 or even 7.5.

Relative acidity effects a plant's ability to take up vital minerals and nutrients, and at extremes can present situations that are toxic to some plants. For example, in highly acid soils some species will suffer from calcium and magnesium deficiencies as well as aluminum, manganese, and iron toxicity. Many deciduous forest species tolerate the full range of soil pH variation normally encountered; however, some such as smooth witherod, *Viburnum nudum*, and many members of the heath family, Ericaceae, which includes rhododendrons and blueberries, *Vaccinium* species, prefer acidic conditions, and others such as southern maidenhair fern, *Adiantum capillus-veneris*, and walking fern, *Asplenium rhizophyllum*, grow best only in neutral to alkaline conditions.

Since the underlying rock is a primary influence on pH, the relative acidity or alkalinity of the soil is difficult or impractical to change on a broad scale. It is possible to influence soil pH on a local basis in the garden by adding lime or gypsum, which increase alkalinity, or by carefully adding aluminum sulfate, which increases alkalinity but can be toxic in excess. Incorporating leaf mold, especially from oak leaves, tends to acidify the soil, as does the addition of pine duff, true peat moss, or muck. It is possible to create specialized niches in the woodland garden by bringing in significant quan-

Southern maidenhair fern, *Adiantum capillus-veneris*, is at home on limestone rock in the Birmingham Botanical Gardens in Alabama.

Forest litter is neither waste nor trash. It is an essential part of woodland soil and nutrient cycles, and an elemental part of the beauty of woodland environments, both wild and designed. Winged fruits of tuliptree, *Liriodendron tulipifera*, commingle with beech leaves, twigs, and other decaying organic matter on the floor of the Pennsylvania winter woods.

tities of rock. I've seen gardens in which alkaline habitats were successfully created on top of an artificial landscape of introduced limestone.

ORGANIC MATTER AND FERTILITY

Most woodland species are accustomed to soils with high organic content. The organic part of the soil is called "humus" and is typically a brown or black substance resulting from the partial decay of fallen leaves and other plant matter. The related term "duff" refers to the decaying vegetable matter on the surface of the forest floor, including leaves and twigs. Often called "litter," a word typically associated with negatives such as disorder, refuse, garbage, and waste, these fallen bits of plants are anything but trash. Forest litter is actually a key asset and an important part of the woodland nutrient cycle. As it decomposes, litter positively influences soil chemistry, depth, and nutrient composition. Keep this in mind and it may appear more beautiful to your eye when observing the ground layer of the woodland garden.

In a natural forest system, minerals and nutrients are available to plants through the breakdown of underlying rock, the decomposition of fallen organic matter, and through rainfall. If you're fortunate enough to begin with garden soil of adequate organic content, woodland species can be sustained indefinitely if the soil is replenished by natural accumulation and breakdown of leaves, twigs, and similar organic material. When beginning a new woodland area with small trees, it usually takes a few years before the trees drop a sufficient quantity of leaves and twigs, and during this time the understory of shrubs and herbaceous species plays the major role in the production and accumulation of organic matter. This is another reason not to remove all the spent and dried material from the garden each fall, but to instead leave at least a portion of it for purposes of renewal.

If the soil is initially lean and lacking in organic matter, add leaf mold (decomposed leaves) to quickly bring the soil up to standard. Leaf mold is best when aged a season or two. At home, we collect leaves in autumn from open areas in the garden and "bank" them in a utility area behind and under an old apple tree. The material from this casual storehouse is an important and often necessary resource in the fortification of soils in our garden, especially as we've continued to trade turf for additional woodland plantings.

Many woodland species are aided in the uptake of nutrients by a symbiotic relationship with various soil fungi, and in some cases these relationships, called "mycorrhizal," are essential to survival. The name is derived from the term "mycorrhiza" which is an integration of plant roots and fungal mycelia. Although poorly understood, these relationships often benefit plants as the fungi break down soil organic matter into compounds that are more accessible. The fungi also seem to grow better in association with plant roots than on their own.

Mycorrhizal fungi are commonly present in mature forest soils rich in organic matter, and are less common in new, highly mineral soils. In keeping with this, mycorrhizal relationships are often unnecessary to pioneer species, but they are especially important to the larger forest species that follow the pioneers. It is possible and sometimes necessary to introduce such beneficial fungi to garden soils by incorporating quantities of forest soil or litter. Conversely, mycorrhizal fungi may be injured or destroyed by the side effects of herbicides and pesticides. Given the critical but little-understood role of these relationships, it seems wise not to jeopardize their health.

MOISTURE AND DRAINAGE

The average rainfall in deciduous forested regions is normally quite adequate to nurture and sustain regional woodland plants. If careful planting, good soil management, and common-sense restraint are practiced in the woodland garden, supplementary watering will be necessary only to establish plantings and occasionally during extreme drought. Sometimes restraint calls for real discipline. I find moist woodland habitats beautiful and alluring, but since my current garden is positioned on a relatively high, dry hillside, I've contented myself with plants adapted to such conditions. Though accepting the limitations of a site is the conserving approach, many techniques can be employed to maximize available resources.

When positioning plants on a relatively dry site, look for low spots and other places where moisture is naturally more plentiful. Especially on a small scale, it's possible to sculpt the ground surface to catch and retain rainfall and surface runoff, and this can make the difference between vigorous growth and decline.

Always consider competition for water among plantings. Grassy turf is notorious for stealing water from the root zones of trees and shrubs. Surface-rooted trees often out-compete underplantings of shrubs and herbaceous plants for scarce water. If the desire is for a full understory beneath trees on a dry site, select deep-rooted trees.

When planting new trees and shrubs, shape the soil to create shallow

Deep-rooted but with wide-spreading branches, black gum, *Nyssa sylvatica*, is an ideal overstory tree since it will not compete too heavily for surface moisture with under-plantings of shrubs and herbs. Its splendid autumn color is in early stages in this mid-October photograph in our Pennsylvania garden.

planting rings or impoundments that will facilitate watering during establishment. These rings should be smoothed over eventually once plants are settled in, since they will otherwise act as barriers to the flow of rainfall over the ground surface, potentially preventing roots from receiving the maximum moisture available.

Take time to match the moisture needs of trees, shrubs, and their associated herbaceous layers. Many trees have been injured by frequent shallow watering of groundcover plantings in their root zones. The root systems of trees are healthiest when watering is deep and intermittent. Constant shallow watering can cause root systems to become concentrated near the surface, leaving the tree less prepared for extreme droughts during which survival may depend partly on a healthy component of deep roots. Constant deep watering may saturate soils, creating conditions low in oxygen which are likely to cause root death and decay.

Sometimes the challenge is a natural excess of water, and it is in such situations that proper drainage becomes critical. The ideal woodland soil is moisture retentive but well drained. This may sound contradictory, but it means the soil includes sufficient organic matter to hold a fair amount of moisture, and that the soil has a means of draining excess moisture when the organic matter becomes saturated. In native forests, deep porous soils and natural slopes are often responsible for good drainage. Garden soils tend to be much shallower, and it is often impractical or impossible to introduce slope where it is naturally absent. In such cases, it may be essential to construct artificial drainage through the installation of drainage tiles or pipes. In a small-scale woodland garden, such as an urban patio or terrace, raised beds may be the best strategy for providing moisture-retentive soil that is also well drained. In all situations, pay particular attention to winter drainage, since this season is often the wettest time of year. The roots of dormant trees are very much alive in winter and are especially vulnerable to injury from low-oxygen, saturated conditions.

Covering the Ground

In a number of conversations with superb British gardeners I've been asked, in effect: "What is it with American gardeners, always so eager to show us their mulch?" Such questions are understandable, since there does seem to be a current vogue in America for setting plants apart from one another in great beds neatly and ostentatiously covered in materials such as shredded bark, licorice root, or crushed stones of any imaginable color. These mulches have grown way beyond the usual purposes of conserving moisture, protecting roots from temperate extremes, and reducing weeds: they have become ornament in their own right. In the best British cottage gardens, profuse flowers and shrubs make any mulch nearly invisible, and I'll say this certainly appeals to my eye. In the American woodland garden, however, mulch is a more complex matter.

As mentioned previously, the natural mulch layer in the forest plays an elemental role in soil and nutrient cycles. It's also easy to observe that few deciduous forests are carpeted with a continuous ground cover of herbaceous plants. Forest litter, a combination of leaves and fallen bits of wood, is often a significant aesthetic component of the woodland floor, occurring in patches between plants. It seems reasonable to me that some emulation of this pattern is appropriate to the naturalistic woodland garden. The varied color and texture of natural woodland mulch is infinitely more interesting than the look of uniform commercial mulches.

Leaf mulch is rarely offered for sale but is often free from municipal and township leaf dumps. If your garden already includes large shrubs and trees, it's easy to produce all the leaf mulch you'll need through appropriate management techniques. In natural woodland habitats, slope is often responsible for keeping leaves from blanketing ground layer plants to the extent that they are smothered over winter, but in the garden, where the ground is often level, raking leaves from low plants may be necessary.

Establish a leaf dump of your own in which to store leaves raked from plantings or lawn areas or collected by mowers. I can't conscience the noise pollution of leaf blowers, especially in residential neighborhoods, but the necessary late-autumn mowing of any lawn areas in the garden can also be a way of corralling leaves into rows or piles for easy pickup. At home, we collect leaves through a combination of raking and autumn mowing. We keep an eight-foot square of very light mesh fabric on which we deposit leaves. The fabric corners are pulled up, gathering the leaves and making it relatively easy to haul them to our storage pile, where they'll age for a season or two. If the leaves that fall in your garden are predominantly oak, you may want to chop them into smaller pieces to facilitate breakdown and reduce their matting tendencies. This can be accomplished with a commercial leaf shredder or less neatly by running a lawn mower over leaf piles.

When planting shrubs and trees, cover their root zones in a layer of mulch. In spring and summer, this will protect against moisture loss, heat stress, and weed growth. Going into winter, a mulch layer will help moderate temperatures, acting as a buffer against too-rapid thawing. In all cases be careful not to allow leaves to accumulate thickly right at the base of the trunk or stems: this invites girdling by small rodents, which can be a serious problem during winter.

New Planting and Transplanting

The optimal time for planting or transplanting herbaceous woodland plants is when they are in vegetative growth or when they're going dormant. Flowering requires much of a plant's energy reserves, and so this is rarely the best time to disturb roots and foliage. As a rule, spring-blooming plants will do well if planted in fall, and fall-blooming plants respond well to spring planting, but container-grown herbaceous plants can often be planted successfully almost any time during the growing season if provided adequate moisture. It's usually best to plant spring ephemerals such as bluebells, *Mertensia*

Given the choice, it's more important to move roots than soil when transplanting plants.

TOP When digging and transplanting this large-flowered two-winged silverbell, *Halesia diptera* var. *magniflora*, in our Pennsylvania garden, I tried to capture as much of the spreading root mass as possible. Since I was moving the tree almost immediately from one spot to another, it was not necessary to have all the roots covered in soil.

BOTTOM The planting hole has been filled with the same garden soil, taking care to position the trunk's root flare slightly above grade to allow for minor settling. The temporary soil ring makes it easier to fully saturate the root zone following transplanting and during the first growing season. Since this photograph, the ring has been smoothed over and this tree is now a vigorous specimen thriving on natural rainfall and soil moisture alone.

virginica, just as they're going dormant. Fall transplanting is physiologically acceptable for the plants, but impractical for the gardener since there is often no above-ground evidence remaining of the plants' exact locations.

Deciduous woody plants are best transplanted in dormancy in either late winter, spring, or autumn. The increasing availability of container-grown woody plants has made it possible to plant trees and shrubs through most of the growing season. Still, it is best to get plants in the ground in early spring so that they can begin establishing new roots before the onset of summer heat and drought, or in autumn so that they can begin establishing new roots before the advent of winter freezes and desiccating winds. Most woody plants will continue to develop roots if soil temperatures are near forty degrees Fahrenheit.

As mentioned previously, it's important to loosen the root masses of container-grown plants to ensure good contact between roots and soil. Proper planting depth is also one of the most important factors effecting long-term health and survival of trees. Observe trees in the native forest and you'll see that their trunks always flare as they meet the ground and the root system begins. This is the normal appearance of a tree whose roots are properly located in relation to the ground plane, and it is established naturally when trees grow in place from seed. When transplanting a tree in the garden, take care to place it at a depth that will permanently position the beginning of the root flare slightly above the soil surface. Keep in mind that some settling usually takes place after planting, and set the tree high enough to anticipate this. Trees planted too deeply look like poles sticking out of the ground: their root flares are not visible. Such trees may survive indefinitely, but rarely will they exhibit the health and vigor of which they are capable.

Though tradition once advised heavily amending planting holes for trees and shrubs with peat moss, fertilizer, and other materials intended to improve drainage, this is no longer deemed desirable. Trees and shrubs usually acclimate fastest, with the least long-term complications, if the soil surrounding their roots is uniform with the local soil characteristics in the garden. It is worthwhile, however, to prepare a planting hole considerably wider than the root system of the plant, to hasten root penetration into surrounding soil. Digging deeper than the root ball is not only a waste of effort, it often results in long-term settling that may eventually place the root zone too deep in the soil.

If you're digging a tree in your garden, try to get as much of the root system as you can safely and comfortably handle. Keep in mind that the roots of most trees extend outward much more than they extend downward. The root balls or container diameters of purchased trees are dictated in part by commercial production techniques and shipping costs: they do not necessarily represent the ideal.

When transforming turf areas into woodland plantings, consider using mechanical methods to remove turf. In late winter or early spring, when soil is moist but not wet, use a sharp spade (or sod cutter if one is available) to shave turf from the planting bed. The removed turf will make an excellent addition to your compost pile. As long as you're not working within a tree root zone, use the rototiller to loosen the soil throughout the bed. A rototiller can also be used to cut turf and incorporate it into the new planting bed simultaneously. A single pass won't be sufficient to kill turf, but two or three passes spaced over the course of a few weeks in early spring are usually sufficient. Whether you choose to use a spade or a rototiller, these methods avoid the use of chemical herbicides and any of their potential negative effects on soil organisms.

Staking and tying may be necessary to stabilize large transplanted trees, but it should be done carefully and removed as soon as it is no longer necessary. Tree trunks must be free to flex if they are to develop strong wood, and many trees have succumbed to the girdling effects of neglected or forgotten ties.

Whenever you have the luxury of planning and planting a completely new area, take advantage of the opportunity to install trees and associated shrubs at the same time. It is much easier to plant this way, and healthier for trees and shrubs if they can simultaneously seek their own root space. If trees are

Transforming the typical suburban lot into a woodland garden usually involves removing lawn. Rather than use toxic chemicals for the job, consider mechanical methods.

planted first and are given time to develop extensive root systems, shrub planting will be difficult, injurious to tree roots, and is likely to require that shrubs be watered for a much longer period of establishment as they compete with enveloping tree roots for moisture.

Design, maintenance, and cultural considerations should all be taken into account when deciding on the proper spacing of trees and shrubs. The usual recommendations for wide spacing may be appropriate in formal gardens; however, it's easy to observe trees in wild populations growing beautifully and healthfully in close proximity to one another. Close spacing usually works well with trees that are narrow and upright in form. Some wide-branching species will shed limbs naturally to accommodate neighbors; others will grow into each other in a conflicting tangle unless heavily pruned. If moisture on the planting site is in particularly short supply, closely planted trees may compete to the detriment of one another unless they are selected for drought tolerance.

Pruning and Cutting Back

The best single strategy regarding pruning is to try to minimize the need by selecting plants whose forms and growth rates are naturally suited to space and cultural conditions. Even if this plan is adopted, regular pruning is inevitable to the maintenance of any designed woodland landscape. A complete treatment of pruning technique is beyond the scope of this book, but there are a few pointers worthy of special mention.

Many woodland trees and shrubs produce flower buds after they bloom, and these remain on plants through winter. The window of opportunity to prune these plants is just after flowering. Fall and winter pruning means the certain loss of next season's bloom.

The most common motivation for pruning is to keep plants at manageable size. Due to inherent variations in the branching patterns of different species, some, such as *Fothergilla* species, can be easily pruned while preserving a graceful shape and winter architecture. Others, such as two-winged silverbell,

Halesia diptera, require great care while pruning to avoid awkward branch angles.

Though less common than it once was, the practice of "topping" trees is generally deplorable, resulting in numerous health problems and often bizarre winter architecture. Since trees planted in utility rights of way and under lines are especially vulnerable to such treatment, it pays to avoid the possibility by appropriate placement when planting.

Many shrubs, however, are amenable to being cut back to the ground. Examples such as spicebush, *Lindera benzoin*, sweet pepperbush, *Clethra alnifolia*, sumac, *Rhus* species, and Virginia summersweet, *Itea virginica*, will sprout readily after cutting, producing vigorous, healthy new shoots. Renewed this way periodically, at intervals of three to ten years, these plants can be indefinitely kept in manageable size, with good form and winter-branch patterns. An important requirement is to ensure adequate moisture during the period following cutback.

Cutting back herbaceous plants is to some extent a matter of personal taste, although the organic litter from the woodland herbaceous layer can play an important role in soil and nutrient cycles. Allowing herbaceous plants to stand during winter can certainly add interest to the seasonal landscape. Depending upon design and plant selections, cutting back herbaceous plants after flowering may be necessary to control unwanted seedlings; however, in other situations volunteer seedlings may be a low-input, desirable way of keeping woodland borders populated.

Although just beginning to expand in mid April, the flower buds on this fothergilla, *Fothergilla gardenii*, were formed the previous summer. Pruning too late in summer or any time over winter would have resulted in little or no spring bloom.

Pests and Diseases

Working with a toxic-chemical-free philosophy, as I do in our home garden, the best defense against pests and diseases is good horticulture: the watchful cultivation of well-chosen naturally adapted plants in optimal growing conditions. It is healthy, from ecological and conservation standpoints, to accept some evidence of insects and other woodland animals as inevitable and relatively innocuous. In other situations, it's sensible to take defensive or precautionary action. Species which are known to be local magnets for pests are best avoided. For example, the native black cherry, *Prunus serotina*, can become a magnificent tree toward the western part of its range, but elsewhere it is smaller and prone to attack by eastern tent caterpillars. A likely result of inviting black cherries into an eastern garden is that you'll have caterpillars defoliating your shadbush, *Amelanchier* species, a rose family relative that can serve as alternate food once the cherries are bare of foliage.

Some factors affecting woodland garden health are difficult or impossible to counter on a local basis, such as the acid rain which is increasingly causing decline and disease in eastern forests, and some large-scale cataclysms will negate the best efforts of individual gardeners, causing uncontrollable, catastrophic damage such as the loss of the original American elms and chestnuts. Such blights are nearly absolute in their effects; however, others, which may appear similar in threat, ultimately prove to be selective and situation-based as is apparently the case with the anthracnose disease of flowering dogwood, *Cornus florida*, caused by *Discula* fungi.

Cultural practices can either protect plants or predispose them to problems. For example, excess fertilizer is likely to promote too-vigorous, soft growth which is especially susceptible to biting and sucking insects as well as multiple diseases.

At present, deer and other browsing animals are among the most frequently encountered pests in woodland gardens. Healthy plants can withstand a reasonable amount of browsing by small mammals, but white-tailed deer are an entirely different matter. The damage they can cause by browsing and rubbing can horribly disfigure and nearly denude the garden. As bad as this is, the damage to native deciduous forests by burgeoning, uncontrolled deer populations is even more tragic, with potentially catastrophic consequences if the situation is not responsibly addressed. Although the clear, open look sometimes witnessed in regional woodlands may at first appear pleasant and parklike, close inspection will often reveal that diversity in the shrub and herbaceous layers has been decimated, and there are almost no small seedlings of canopy trees to be found: they've all been eaten by deer, and the very future of these forests is in jeopardy.

Until the situation is remedied on a larger scale, the alternatives for the woodland gardener plagued by deer are to fence the garden or to shift the plant choices toward less-favorite foods and design to endure a certain amount of damage. When hungry enough, deer will eat an amazing variety of plants, but a few, including white snakeroot, *Eupatorium rugosum*, and spice-

Unpalatable to deer, spicebush, *Lindera benzoin*, is routinely passed by. Here its autumn hues brighten the edge of a woodland path at Mount Cuba Center in Delaware in mid October.

Though it has the potential to be a nuisance in some gardens, at home we've found wild geranium, *Geranium maculatum*, to be a manageable, enduring, flowering filler for woodland borders.

bush, *Lindera benzoin*, are never among these. We live next to a woodland preserve and, despite the frequent nocturnal presence of our dog, we often get as many as twenty deer passing through the garden at night. We've learned that deer are creatures of habit, following established paths over and over again, and we've used this knowledge to minimize damage. We've observed that bucks are especially fond of rubbing antlers on soft-barked, fragrant-wooded trees and shrubs, and accordingly have avoided planting things like sweet bay magnolia, *Magnolia virginiana*, in their path. We've used a different strategy near the back edge of our property, where it meets an open field. There, we've planted various sumacs, *Rhus* species, which regenerate so quickly, they outpace the damage caused by rubbing.

Weeds

There is an arbitrary element to the definition of a weed, which *Webster's Dictionary* says is "any undesired, uncultivated plant that grows in profusion so as to crowd out a desired crop." "Undesired" is the key word: It's obviously possible that one person's weed may be another's workhorse. In our Pennsylvania garden, my wife and I have judged certain native woodland species such as white wood aster, *Aster divaricatus*, and wild geranium, *Geranium maculatum*, to be valuable in part because they self-sow and will fill in empty spots with little effort on our part. Within our design and specific cultural conditions, they are manageable contributors to the landscape, requiring lower resource expenditure than many others which might never renew themselves. We prefer editing minor excesses to purchasing replacements for plants that frequently succumb. In another garden, with different design, sunlight, soil, and moisture conditions, these same two plants might justly be called "weeds."

An important consideration in defining weeds is the effect the species in question may have not only in the garden, but also in the nearby native landscape, if it still exists. It has often been stated that the deciduous forest is capable of re-making itself after disturbance of all kinds. This may have been nearly the truth a century ago, but human influence on the global landscape has forever altered the woodland environment. Beyond trends such as the acidification of rainfall or artificially induced climatic shift such as global warming, the most profound influence on the temperate deciduous forest has been the deliberate and accidental introduction of invasive-displacing exotic species. Any plant, including a local native, may become a weedy nuisance in the garden given the right circumstances; however, exotics may have the additional capacity to grow out of balance and out of control in both the garden and the regional woodlands. The number of exotics plaguing North American deciduous forests is constantly enlarging, but among the recognized worst are Norway maple, *Acer platanoides*; garlic mustard, *Alliaria petiolata*; porcelain berry, *Ampelopsis brevipedunculata*; oriental bittersweet, *Celastrus orbiculatus*; burning bush, *Euonymus alatus*; Japanese honeysuckle, *Lonicera japonica*; stilt grass, *Microstegium vimineum*; kudzu, *Pueraria lobata*; and buckthorn, *Rhamnus cathartica*. I believe it's safe to call any of these weeds.

CHAPTER FIVE

The Forest Palette

THE MAGNIFICENT diversity of the North American deciduous forest is too vast to fit within the covers of any reasonably sized book. This chapter is a deliberately selective account of native trees, shrubs, and herbs worth celebrating in woodland gardens. The general emphasis is on plants which can be grown with relative ease, and I've made a point to include many that are subtly beautiful but unsung. My intention is to offer an inspiring overview of the forest palette, presented as a readable collection of illustrated essays and based upon insights gleaned from direct experience and observation.

Chapter entries are by genus, organized alphabetically for easy reference, with the exception of the ferns, and the grasses, sedges, and wood-rushes, which appear under two entries so-named. Scientific and common names of plant families for each genus are provided as applicable. In the interests of readability, the potential multiplicity of botanical synonyms and common names has been kept to a minimum.

The photographs have been carefully produced and selected to illustrate broad aspects and intimate details that support the design aesthetics outlined in preceding chapters. I've placed special emphasis on the inclusion of seasonal characteristics and qualities not often pictured.

Acer

MAPLE

ACERACEAE, MAPLE FAMILY

I count maples among the best of flowering trees. Each year as my enthusiasm for winter wears thin, I welcome the vibrant red and amber hues of red and silver maples as they suffuse the forest and woodland garden. Silver maple, *Acer saccharinum*, is usually the first to begin flowering, sometimes as early as February during warm winter periods. Though cold hardy to zone 3 and exceptionally fast growing, it tends to be brittle branched and relatively short lived. Its autumn color is usually yellow, never approaching the brilliancy or red hues commonly

TOP LEFT Flowers of red maple, *Acer rubrum*, catch the strengthening rays of the late-March sun outside our kitchen window. Red maple is mostly dioecious, meaning flowers are either male or female and they occur on separate trees. Since our trees are females, I'm able to enjoy lingering red hues as the tiny flowers expand into the familiar "keys" or winged fruits (botanists call them samaras) common to many maples.

The species is native from Canada down through Florida, and not surprisingly, there is considerable variation among populations from different regions. Provenance is particularly important when picking red maples for the woodland garden, so trees should be selected for their performance in your part of the country. Red maples from northern climes are cold hardy to zone 3, but may suf-

fer in the heat of the South. Conversely, southern trees can be exceedingly heat-resistant, but with an attendant lessening cold hardiness.

BOTTOM FAR LEFT Red maples are naturally accompanied by tussock sedge, *Carex stricta*, and skunk cabbage, *Symplocarpus foetidus*, which play interestingly off the smooth tree bark and red flowers in mid April, in a Pennsylvania swamp. *Acer rubrum* is sometimes called swamp maple for obvious reasons; however, the range of variation in the species includes trees genetically adapted to wet soils as well as others evolved to withstand dry upland environments. This is another reason to inquire about the genetic origin of red maples you're considering for the garden. Trees from swamp habitats are usually quite tolerant of moist, soggy, and poorly drained soils in woodland gardens. Though often single-trunked, red maples make superb multistemmed specimens.

LEFT The more-or-less three-lobed leaves of red maples may turn yellow, orange, or brilliant scarlet in autumn, as seen here in branches draping down from a Delaware stream bank, backlit by the mid-October sun. George Longenecker, professor of landscape architecture at West Virginia University, has conducted studies of red maple trees that show a relationship between the amount of red pigmentation in the flowers and the amount in the autumn foliage.

displayed by red maple, *Acer rubrum*, which is generally a better tree for woodland gardens.

Red and silver maples are both "soft" maples, with wood not nearly as hard as the best-known "hard" species, sugar maple, *Acer saccharum*; however, red maple is reasonably sturdy in the landscape and can be quite long lived. All the large maples, including silver, red, and sugar maples, are shallow rooted, with silver maples the most so, but the fast growth, beauty, durability, and multiseason interest of red and sugar maples in particular puts them near the top of my list of trees that might form the framework of the forest garden. Red maples, in particular, are easy to transplant in size.

A common maple on floodplains and along stream valleys is box-elder, *Acer negundo*, also called ash-leaved maple. Its tendency toward brittle wood and pro-

BELOW The intense clear gold of a sugar maple, *Acer saccharum*, against the mid-October sky is an unbeatable combination, as here at Longwood Gardens. Sugar maples may also turn shades of orange and red. Distinct from that of silver and red maples, the mature bark of sugar maples is relatively dark, deeply ridged, and furrowed. Although cold hardy into zone 3, sugar maples are not well adapted to the extreme summer heat in southern climes and are less tolerant of urban air pollution than red or silver maples.

TOP Beloved as the source of maple syrup, sugar maple blooms later than red and silver maples, usually in April or early May. Its light-yellow flowers are pendent on slender filaments that move with the wind.

BOTTOM Sugar maple flowers turn from light yellow to chartreuse as fruits begin to form, and they can brighten the spring landscape for weeks with these cheerful hues, as here in a Virginia woodland garden.

lific self-sowing makes is unsuitable for most garden settings. Lesser known and, I believe, underappreciated are two much smaller maples that hail from cool mountain habitats: mountain maple, *Acer spicatum*, and striped maple or moosewood, *Acer pensylvanicum*. Although they require cool, moist conditions for healthy growth, they offer a unique set of form, flower, bark, and fall color characteristics that can be significant features in the designed landscape.

BELOW Green bark with white stripes easily distinguishes striped maple or moosewood, *Acer pensylvanicum*, another diminutive species native to cool, moist woods and mountains from Canada to North Carolina and Tennessee. Upright to spreading in form and typically fifteen to thirty-five feet tall, it is a bit more heat tolerant than mountain maple. I've seen trees with nearly eight-inch caliper trunks in the Smoky Mountains, but such size is near the limit for this species. This mid-October view shows trees in Pennsylvania's Laurel Highlands.

TOP AND CENTER LEFT The foliage of striped maple is a delight throughout summer and autumn, as seen glowing lime green in Maine in July and light yellow against a dark oak trunk in West Virginia in October.

BOTTOM LEFT The intense scarlet color of striped maple's expanding bud scales is visible from a surprising distance.

OPPOSITE BOTTOM Late-May sunlight illuminates and accentuates the upright flower spikes of mountain maple, *Acer spicatum*, in Virginia. This compact species is usually less than twenty feet tall, occurring as a spreading multistemmed tree or large shrub. It is a northern species, growing naturally in mountain habitats from Canada south, at increasingly high elevations, to North Carolina and Tennessee. Its autumn orange and red hues add to its appeal, and it is worth seeking and growing in garden climates which can provide the cool, moist conditions it requires.

Aconitum

MONK'S-HOOD, WOLF'S-BANE

RANUNCULACEAE, BUTTERCUP FAMILY

The two *Aconitum* species native to North American deciduous forests are subtly colored compared with introduced garden varieties; however, their rambling habits, shade tolerance, and ease of culture make them worthy additions to the woodland garden. They occur naturally from Pennsylvania south to North Carolina, Tennessee, and Georgia, mostly in the mountains, but are durable and long lived at lower altitudes if provided light shade and moist organic soil. The deeply cut lower leaves of both species can be quite attractive when they emerge in spring. As with all monk's-hoods, most parts of the plant are poisonous if ingested, particularly the turniplike roots.

TOP RIGHT White monk's-hood or trailing wolf's-bane, *Aconitum reclinatum,* is occasionally erect and three feet tall, but is more typically lax and rambling, in which case individual stems may be eight feet long. It is content to trail along the ground or can be persuaded to scramble through and over shrubs. The flowers are light yellow or near-white and appear in late spring or early summer, as in this mid-June West Virginia photograph.

BOTTOM RIGHT Viewed through a kitchen window, southern monk's-hood, *Aconitum uncinatum*, climbs nearly six feet into a sweet bay magnolia, *Magnolia virginiana*, in a shaded area off the north side of our house in mid August. It has done this reliably for nearly a decade now with virtually no care, and each summer we look forward to seeing the lower branches of the magnolia draped with purple flowers.

Actaea

BANEBERRY, DOLL'S EYES
RANUNCULACEAE, BUTTERCUP FAMILY

Baneberries are botanical relatives of wolf's-banes, and though their flowers are quite dissimilar in appearance, they too can be toxic if ingested. Indeed the brightly colored fruits seem like they might be alluring to young children; however, their bitter, unpleasant taste makes it extremely unlikely that even the most curious child would consume sufficient quantity to do any harm. Personally, I believe it is good for people to learn at a young age that the entire world is not to be consumed.

The two natives of the eastern deciduous forest hail from rich woods, ranging from Canada quite far south at various elevations, and are long lived and easily grown in the woodland garden. Both bloom in spring, producing white flower clusters held high above the foliage. They differ mostly in fruit. Red baneberry, *Actaea rubra*, has deep scarlet berries. Berries of the aptly named doll's eyes, *Actaea pachypoda* [synonym *Actaea alba*], are porcelain white, each with a dark spot. To confuse matters, white-fruited forms of red baneberry are relatively common, sometimes occurring mixed with red-berried plants, but they lack the prominent dark spot of doll's eyes. The berries of both species usually remain noticeable and attractive through late summer and into early autumn.

TOP LEFT Doll's eyes, *Actaea pachypoda*, flowers in late May in a heavily shaded woodland setting in West Virginia.

BOTTOM FAR LEFT This light blue-leaved form of doll's eyes originated at Mount Cuba Center in Delaware and was noticed by Dick Lighty. Though the foliage character generally comes true from seed, an exemplary form has been named 'Misty Blue' and is intended for asexual propagation.

LEFT Red stalks seem to enhance the eyeball-like appearance of doll's eyes, as here in early August.

Aesculus

BUCKEYE

HIPPOCASTANACEAE, HORSE-CHESTNUT FAMILY

The biggest buckeyes are often magnificent forest giants, but in modest-sized gardens, the shrubby species and smaller trees are most appealing. Of the larger tree species, the Ohio buckeye, *Aesculus glabra*, is most commonly planted, but it is especially susceptible to summer leaf scorch and generally inferior to yellow buckeye, *Aesculus flava* [synonym *Aesculus octandra*], which can reach ninety feet in southern mountain forest coves and is cold hardy to zone 4.

My clear favorite is the bottlebrush buckeye, *Aesculus parviflora*, a suckering shrub that often grows over ten feet tall and can spread indefinitely. A nearly forty-year-old plant in the Olmsted park I played in as a child formed a cavernous mass large enough for me to hide in. As it matures, a mass of bottlebrush buck-eye develops a number of upright stems that form a leafy cover at the periphery and overhead, but these stems are relatively foliage-free below. Low shoots produce leaves up to knee level, so the interior space of a mature mass is very much like a room with a green floor, walls, and ceiling. The design of the Peirce's Woods garden at Longwood Gardens invites visitors to this experience with a subtle path leading into and through an old grove of bottlebrush buckeye.

ABOVE The distinctive silver and red-brown bark plates of an old yellow buckeye, *Aesculus flava*, are among the most memorable patterns in the Appalachian mountain woods. This species occurs from Pennsylvania south to Alabama and Georgia.

LEFT Could someone be hiding inside this twelve-foot-tall bottlebrush buckeye? Among the delights of *Aesculus parviflora* is its habit of blooming in June and July, when little else is flowering in the forested landscape. Though native to Alabama and Georgia, this sturdy species is cold hardy to zone 5 and will grow in a wide range of soil and moisture conditions in deep shade to nearly full sun in the north. This clump in our home garden is approximately ten years old in this late-June photograph. The lower branches at the perimeter of this shrub tend to root as they grow flat along the ground. I've had complete success removing and transplanting these in early spring to start new clumps.

The rich scarlet flowers of this particular tree represent the best red hues of this highly variable species, which may also produce yellow flowers. Native to moist deciduous forests and low woodlands from Virginia south to Texas, this small tree is typically clump-forming and fifteen to twenty-five feet tall. It is cold hardy to zone 4 but requires a moist, partly shaded situation in warmer regions or it will suffer badly from leaf scorch.

TOP RIGHT Typically free of leaf scorch unless subjected to full sun and drought, the foliage of bottlebrush buckeye opens amber, is deep green all summer, and then glows gold in autumn. Leaves are still turning in this mid-October Pennsylvania photograph.

CENTER Gathered fruits of bottlebrush buckeye in our garden in late September.

FAR LEFT Painted buckeye, *Aesculus sylvatica*, blooms light yellow atop rich green leaves in late May in Pennsylvania. Native to alluvial woods and swamp forests in the piedmont from Virginia to Georgia, Tennessee, and Alabama, it is typically a multi-stemmed shrub shorter than ten feet tall. It is not as cold hardy as other buckeyes but is reliable through zone 6.

TOP LEFT Individual flower racemes of bottlebrush buckeye are nearly a foot tall, with white filaments extending one inch out from the flowers, tipped with light pink anthers. The racemes of *Aesculus parviflora* var. *serotina* are even longer and appear nearly three weeks later than typical; however, plants of this variety tend to lose their lower branches and do not have the "clothed-to-the-ground" appearance of the usual form.

TOP CENTER Red buckeye, *Aesculus pavia*, ornaments the mid-May landscape of the Henry Foundation in Gladwyne, Pennsylvania.

Agastache

GIANT HYSSOP

LAMIACEAE, MINT FAMILY

I discovered yellow giant hyssop, *Agastache nepetoides*, when I began my study of Red Clay Creek in Pennsylvania, where it grows seven feet tall in partly sunny spots along the bank. Cold hardy into zone 3, it ranges naturally from Vermont south to Georgia and is interesting primarily for its light yellow flowers in mid to late summer. It has a few relatives with blue-violet to light lavender flowers, including lavender giant hyssop, *Agastache foeniculum*, and purple giant hyssop, *Agastache scrophulariaefolium*. Equally cold hardy, these two prefer full sun to light shade and can be useful at woodland edges and in transitional areas of the garden.

Allium

RAMPS, WILD LEEK, WILD ONION

LILIACEAE, LILY FAMILY

Jet-black seeds of wild leek, *Allium tricoccum*, in late October.

Native in rich, moist deciduous woodlands from Canada south through the southeastern mountains, ramps or wild leeks, *Allium tricoccum*, is a close relative of the cultivated onion. The bulbs have a flavor like leeks, only much stronger, and ramp festivals celebrating the culinary delights of this small bulb have sometimes been held in locales where it grows abundantly. Though slow-growing, ramps are often found in large colonies, thickly and attractively covering the ground with their light green leaves in spring. The foliage dies down by July, when white flowers appear. These are followed by clusters of jet-black fruits that often remain standing through winter. Hardy into zone 3, ramps are an interesting addition to moist, shady spots in the woodland garden (see pages 75 and 86).

Alnus

ALDER

BETULACEAE, BIRCH FAMILY

Male catkins of hazel alder, *Alnus serrulata*, catch the wind and strengthening sun in mid April in northern Delaware.

The native alders are multistemmed shrubs with strong, suckering growth habits. They typically grow on wet or damp soil in swamps and along streams, in full sun or partial shade, and can play an important role in soil and streambank stabilization in the wild and in the woodland garden. The two most often encountered, hazel alder, *Alnus serrulata*, which is cold hardy through zone 5, and speckled alder, *Alnus incana* [synonym *Alnus rugosa*], hardy into zone 3, are nearly identical in appearance. Though neither has significant fall color, they are both quite attractive in late winter and early spring, when the male catkins dangle in sunlight.

Amelanchier

SERVICEBERRY, JUNEBERRY, SHADBUSH
ROSACEAE, ROSE FAMILY

Because *Amelanchier* species tend to hybridize in the wild and in cultivation, their taxonomy is quite messy. Fortunately, this has no bearing on the certain fact that serviceberries of all sorts are among the earliest to welcome spring, and there is hardly a bad one in the lot. They bloom in March or April, long before

ABOVE Flowers of downy serviceberry, *Amelanchier arborea*, are pure white in mid April. The obviously downy leaves vouch for the common name. Although the flowers of serviceberries and shadbushes are ephemeral, often lasting only a week, their early appearance is particularly welcome in the woodland garden. The flowers mature into small fleshy fruits that turn gradually from green to red to purple-black. They are often ripe by June, hence the alternate name Juneberry. The fruits are sweet and edible, and are a favorite of woodland birds.

RIGHT Shadbush or eastern serviceberry, *Amelanchier canadensis*, blooms in mid April below tall trees in moist woods on the Maryland coastal plain. This species is typically shrubby. One delight of all *Amelanchier* species is their willingness to bloom strongly even when deep within the spring understory.

flowering dogwood, *Cornus florida*, with which they commonly associate, and are followed closely in bloom by redbud, *Cercis canadensis*. They range naturally from Canada into the southern United States on a wide range of soils, and the tree species are often observed leaning out from the edges of mountain woods and streambanks. All serviceberries are easy to grow in the woodland garden, preferring slightly acid conditions, and will tolerate dense shade or full sun if provided adequate moisture. All are cold hardy to zone 4, with shadbush, *Amelanchier canadensis*, hardy into zone 3.

Serviceberries tend to be small understory trees or multistemmed shrubs, though both downy serviceberry, *Amelanchier arborea*, and smooth serviceberry, *Amelanchier laevis*, can grow over forty feet tall if conditions are right, as they sometimes are in the rich, moist southeastern mountains. There are also low-running types including coastal plain serviceberry, *Amelanchier obovalis*, and running shadbush, *Amelanchier stolonifera*, which grow only three to six feet tall.

Many commercial serviceberries belong to *Amelanchier* ×*grandiflora*, the apple serviceberry, which is a hybrid between *Amelanchier arborea* and *Amelanchier laevis*. The clonal cultivar 'Autumn Brilliance', shown here in late October, is among the best for red-orange autumn color. Fall color on serviceberries is typically orange but can range to bronze and bronze-purple.

Serviceberries are especially stunning in spring and autumn. Growing at a woodland edge in northern Delaware, downy serviceberry produces a profusion of white blossoms against the deep blue mid-April sky, then turns brilliant orange in mid October.

ABOVE The non-running wood anemones tend to be larger and taller, as is the case with thimbleweed, *Anemone virginiana*, which is typically two feet in height. The subtle flowers are white strongly suffused with green, but I like this plant for its thimblelike seedheads which last nearly through winter. In fact, this is one of those wild plants that caught my eye before I began gardening. The little thimbles come apart gradually as the cold season progresses, dispersing fuzz-covered seeds into the winter wind and sunlight. It is easily grown in deep shade or at a woodland edge, into zone 2.

RIGHT Wood anemone, *Anemone quinquefolia*, runs through the foliage of twin-leaf toothwort, *Dentaria diphylla*, and up the moss-covered trunk of a yellow birch, *Betula alleghaniensis*, in the Smoky Mountains in late April. Attractive in flower and foliage, this diminutive anemone sometimes forms spreading colonies on the woods floor. It goes dormant by late spring, so it is best in the garden when intermingled with other, more-lasting companions, such as the evergreen twin-leaf toothwort. Wood anemone is cold hardy to zone 3.

Anemone
WOOD ANEMONE, THIMBLEWEED
RANUNCULACEAE, BUTTERCUP FAMILY

Woodland anemones are delicate but appealing parts of the spring landscape. Most occur naturally in moist woods on rich organic soils, and they require these conditions to grow their best. Though there are many species, they can be separated into two groups: those that run by rhizomes and those that stay put, growing from a thickened stem or tuber.

Anemonella
RUE ANEMONE
RANUNCULACEAE, BUTTERCUP FAMILY

The botanical ending *oides* means "resembling," and certainly the foliage of rue anemone, *Anemonella thalictroides*, looks like that of the true rue, *Thalictrum*. The genus name of this delicate spring ephemeral also recognizes it as a close but diminutive relative of *Anemone*. Tiny but tough, rue anemone is cold hardy to zone 4 and will thrive in a variety of light conditions if provided moist, well-

drained organic soil. It grows from a cluster of small tubers, which can be divided to make more plants in the garden. In its native habitat, from New England south to Florida, it is often found on sloping ground.

Aquilegia

WILD COLUMBINE
RANUNCULACEAE, BUTTERCUP FAMILY

It's inspiring to see how many wild nooks and crannies wild columbine, *Aquilegia canadensis*, calls home. I've seen it naturalized in vast sweeps through clearings in northern woodlands, tumbling over limestone outcrops and peeking out in full bloom from the shards of a West Virginia mountain shale barrens. It ranges from Canada south to Texas and Florida, and its tendency to self-sow into certain spots when conditions are right, and then move on, is a clue to how it is best treated in the woodland garden. Though individual plants may be short lived, populations of wild columbine can be enduring. It is often best to sow seed *in situ* or to place plants in several spots in the garden and allow them to self-sow where they prove best adapted.

ABOVE I know of few more graceful, crisply elegant spring flowers than rue anemone, *Anemonella thalictroides*, here flowering in late April in the Pennsylvania woods. There are also pink and double forms in cultivation.

BELOW Wild columbine, *Aquilegia canadensis*, is at its best when naturalized in the woodland garden, as seen in this early May view at Ashland Hollow in northern Delaware.

Though tolerant of somewhat alkaline conditions, wild columbine will grow on a variety of soil types and pH conditions. It is most persistent and flowers best with some direct sunlight. Since it goes dormant in summer, it's best to plant it with other more-enduring low companions such as ferns. Cold hardy to zone 3, wild columbine is also surprisingly heat resistant.

Aralia

SPIKENARD, WILD SARSPARILLA
ARALIACEAE, GINSENG FAMILY

On the one hand, it is easy to understand why wild sarsparilla, *Aralia nudicaulis*, has been overlooked by most gardeners and nurseries. Though slightly similar in appearance to its close relative ginseng, *Panax quinquefolius*, its fruits are black rather than bright red, and its flowers are grouped in small green globes held near the ground in late May. On the other hand, there is nothing subtle about spikenard, *Aralia racemosa*, which is equally neglected in gardens. Growing up to six feet tall in rich woods from Canada south to North Carolina and New Mexico, it is one of the boldest, most architectural woodland herbs. It can be easily grown from seed and is cold hardy to zone 4.

TOP If conditions are consistently moist through summer, the leaves of spikenard, *Aralia racemosa*, will turn a pleasing light yellow by early October.

CENTER Initially light green, the berries of spikenard are wine-red in late August, turning dark purple by fall.

RIGHT Spikenard grows six feet tall at a woodland edge along Virginia's Blue Ridge Parkway in late July. The terminal flower clusters are just beginning to develop atop the foliage and will eventually develop into large clusters of berries. The ebony-black stems and bold foliage of this little-grown plant can make an unbeatable textural addition to the herbaceous layer of the woodland garden.

Arisaema

JACK-IN-THE-PULPIT, GREEN DRAGON
ARACEAE, ARUM FAMILY

If you peer inside the leafy spathe of a Jack-in-the-pulpit and look down at the bottom of the upright spadix, where the individual flowers are located, you may find Jack or you may find Jill. My friend, mentor, and former supervisor at Longwood Gardens, "Dutch" Huttleston had done his doctoral dissertation on *Arisaema triphyllum* and was fond of suggesting this common woodland plant be adopted as the banner of the women's movement. He'd explain that young plants of this species start out masculine, with only male flowers present or functional. As they grow stronger and more capable, they switch to feminine gender and produce only female flowers. If for some reason a plant becomes weakened, it reverts to masculine gender, since it takes a lot less energy to produce pollen than it does to produce a cluster of big red berries.

Beloved of children but often taken for granted by adult gardeners, the common Jack-in-the-pulpit deserves to be considered for the woodland garden. Though perhaps not as showy in bloom as the Asian *Arisaema* species, it is much easier to grow and more tolerant of the orange rust disease found in North American forest environments.

ABOVE Jack-in-the-pulpit, *Arisaema triphyllum*, blooms above spring beauties, *Claytonia virginica*, in the Delaware woods in late April. Taxonomic botanists have named several varieties of this species differing in foliage characteristics and in the coloration of the spathe. Plants with spathes richly striped in dark purple have been recognized as *Arisaema triphyllum* var. *stewardsonii*. A dizzying mix of spathe colors and patterns is often found in any large population.

FAR LEFT Inflorescences from two plants of Jack-in-the-pulpit have been opened to display flower characteristics. The smaller plant at left has only pollen-producing male plants at the base of the clublike spadix. Green female flowers are visible in the larger plant at right.

LEFT Though the foliage has died down in this late-August photograph, a bright scarlet berry cluster of a Jack-in-the-pulpit remains as a splendid highlight within a flowering ground cover of white wood aster, *Aster divaricatus*. These two are sometimes companions in their native habitat, and we've found this combination durable in our Pennsylvania garden.

Growing from a flattened corm that is renewed each season, Jack-in-the-pulpit prefers rich, moist organic soil. It ranges naturally from Canada south to Texas and Florida, and is cold hardy to zone 3. Its close relative, the green dragon, *Arisaema dracontium*, is an interesting though somewhat subtler plant found in moist woods and floodplains from Canada south to Texas.

Aristolochia
DUTCHMAN'S PIPE, PIPE VINE
ARISTOLOCHIACEAE, BIRTHWORT FAMILY

John Bartram introduced Dutchman's pipe, *Aristolochia macrophylla* [synonym *Aristolochia durior*], to cultivation in 1783, and since then it has been used as a summer screen on countless American front porches. This deciduous woody twiner can still be quite impressive when used in this way, but it is also an inspired choice for bringing bold foliage up and over shrubs and into tall trees in the woodland garden. Tolerant of dense shade or nearly full sun, Dutchman's pipe occurs naturally throughout the Appalachian region, in rich mountain woods from southern Pennsylvania to northern Georgia, and is cold hardy to zone 4. It will grow on a variety of soils and is quite drought tolerant, though growth will be much lusher with steady moisture. It is capable of ascending more than thirty feet into supporting trees or other structures. The bold foliage is its main attraction, often turning bright gold in autumn; however, the curious

pipelike flowers are worth close inspection and are sure to delight children and others still young at heart.

Similar but smaller-leaved and less commonly available is pipe vine, *Aristolochia tomentosa*, which is densely hairy where Dutchman's pipe is smooth surfaced. It grows natively on alluvial soils from Indiana south to Florida and is cold hardy to zone 5.

Aronia
CHOKEBERRY
ROSACEAE, ROSE FAMILY

Closely related to serviceberries, *Amelanchier*, are chokeberries, *Aronia*, often-overlooked spreading shrubs that offer four-season interest for the woodland garden. Both red chokeberry, *Aronia arbutifolia*, and black chokeberry, *Aronia melanocarpa*, have clear-white spring flowers, dark green summer foliage, brilliant red or wine-red autumn color complemented by attractive fruits, and fine winter architecture. The highly glossy fruits (botanically they are pomes, like apples) are bright red on *Aronia arbutifolia* and purple-black on *Aronia melanocarpa*. Both species are wide-ranging, especially in bogs, swamps, and wet woods, and are tolerant of poorly drained soils. Adaptable to sun or shade and wet or dry conditions, they are easy to transplant and long lived. Red chokeberry is cold hardy to zone 4, black chokeberry to zone 3.

An age-old but still-winning use of Dutchman's pipe is as deciduous screening on porches, seen here in Maine in late June.

OPPOSITE TOP Green dragon, *Arisaema dracontium*, is noted for its extended spadix.

OPPOSITE BOTTOM LEFT The late-May foliage of Dutchman's pipe, *Aristolochia macrophylla*, is a cheerful green as it climbs into deciduous trees in a West Virginia mountain woodlands.

OPPOSITE RIGHT The pipelike flowers of Dutchman's pipe are green with a broad, flat limb at the top. The limb begins brown speckled and darkens to deep brown-purple with age, setting off the bright yellow throat.

RIGHT Red chokeberry, *Aronia arbutifolia*, flowers in mid May on the New Jersey coastal plain and displays glossy red fruits in late September.

Goat's beard, *Aruncus dioicus*, blooms in late May in a shaded section of our Pennsylvania garden, its flowers set off against the dark evergreen foliage of Christmas fern, *Polystichum acrostichoides*.

ABOVE LEFT Autumn fruit and foliage color on *Aronia arbutifolia* 'Brilliantissima' are spectacular in early November in northern Delaware. This clonal cultivar is reliable and widely adapted, though the variation exhibited by seedlings may be equally charming.

ABOVE RIGHT Winter stems of *Aronia arbutifolia* 'Brilliantissima' are dramatic against a January snow cover in the Connecticut College Arboretum. The multistemmed habit and spreading nature of chokeberries make them ideal for massed plantings.

Aruncus

GOAT'S BEARD
ROSACEAE, ROSE FAMILY

My fondest memories of goat's beard, *Aruncus dioicus*, are of coming upon it in full bloom in June in the Virginia mountains, as its large creamy-white flower clusters reach out from forest edges toward the sun. I've also admired it growing from crevices in nearly vertical rock faces, sustained along with wild ginger, *Asarum canadense*, by water seeping down the surface. Goat's beard is dioecious, and though male plants are slightly showier in bloom, both male and female plants can be quite spectacular, even in dense shade where flowering is not quite as exuberant. This large herbaceous perennial can be used in sweeps and masses to define woodland spaces in summer, much the way woody shrubs might be used.

Ranging in moist woodlands from Pennsylvania south to North Carolina and west to Oregon and California, goat's beard adapts to a wide range of soil conditions and is cold hardy to zone 4. It can withstand dry summer conditions, but the foliage is best when moisture is constant through the growing season. In warm regions it prefers the filtered light of the forest, but it grows well in full sun at mountain elevations.

Asarum

WILD GINGER

ARISTOLOCHIACEAE, BIRTHWORT FAMILY

Wild ginger, *Asarum canadense*, is among the most adaptable and useful woodland ground covers. Occurring naturally in rich woods from Canada south to Alabama and Louisiana, this vigorous spreader is cold hardy into zone 3 and easily grown in dense shade or at sunny woodland edges if provided adequate moisture. The flowers, appearing inconspicuously low to the ground in spring, are deep ruddy brown in color and more curious than attractive. The evergreen wild gingers were once grouped in *Asarum* but are now listed separately as *Hexastylis*.

TOP RIGHT Growing naturally in the Virginia mountains, wild ginger, *Asarum canadense*, covers the ground even in this densely shaded setting. Its spreading root mass is useful for stabilizing woodland slopes. Since the foliage is deciduous, consider interplanting with sturdy evergreen ferns such as Christmas fern, *Polystichum acrostichoides*, to provide winter interest.

BOTTOM RIGHT The heart-shaped leaves of wild ginger are among the bolder-textured native woodland ground covers. Wild ginger is quite capable of growing in thin soil layers atop rocks if conditions are moist as seen in this early August scene from Pennsylvania.

Asclepias

MILKWEED

ASCLEPIADACEAE, MILKWEED FAMILY

Although milkweeds are most commonly associated with sunny fields and meadows, at least two species, tall milkweed, *Asclepias exaltata*, and four-leaved milkweed, *Asclepias quadrifolia*, are true forest denizens, worthy of including in the woodland garden.

Pawpaw flowers appear in early May, beginning when branches are bare. Their red-purple hues can be accentuated by side- and backlighting.

TOP LEFT Tall milkweed, *Asclepias exaltata*, is also sometimes called poke milkweed, but I see nothing pokey about it: the flowers remind me of rocket ships shooting out into space. If I were inclined to name a selection of this plant, 'Buck Rogers' might be appropriate. Native to moist upland woods from Maine to Virginia, southward in the mountains, and west to Minnesota, this species may grow five feet tall and is cold hardy into zone 3. It is flowering in late July in this North Carolina image.

LEFT Tall milkweed turns a pleasing gold in early October in a shaded West Virginia woodlands.

TOP CENTER Silky threads catch the mid-October sunlight and carry tall milkweed seeds to new destinations on the autumn breeze.

TOP RIGHT Delicately attractive in whorls of four, the flowers of four-leaved milkweed, *Asclepias quadrifolia*, open in spring, as shown in this late-May photograph from Virginia. This species will tolerate dry conditions and is cold hardy through zone 4.

Asimina

PAWPAW
ANNONACEAE, CUSTARD APPLE FAMILY

Pawpaw, *Asimina triloba*, is the northernmost and most cold-hardy species in the Annonaceae, a mostly tropical plant family known for a number of prized tropical fruit trees such as *Annona cherimola*, called cherimoya or custard apple, and *Annona muricata*, the soursop or guanabana. This helps explain the nearly tropical appearance of pawpaw, which sports some of the largest simple leaves in the north temperate deciduous forest. The most common pawpaw species, *Asimina triloba*, is native to rich damp woods from Michigan to New York and south to Florida and Texas, and is hardy through zone 5. The extreme southeastern natives, slimleaf pawpaw, *Asimina angustifolia*, and bigflower pawpaw, *Asimina obovata*, have even showier flowers but are limited to zones 8 and 9.

TOP The proverbial pawpaw patch, in early May in Virginia, with the spring sun playing off the smooth, gray bark. Though strongly suckering and typically colonial, pawpaw, *Asimina triloba*, can be easily grown as a single-stemmed or multistemmed tree by removing suckers until plants gain some maturity.

BOTTOM Rising up from the floodplain and contrasting dramatically with the texture and horizontal lines of this West Virginia limestone outcrop, these pawpaws are just beginning to turn color in early October.

TOP Few trees rival the clear autumn color and huge pendent leaves of pawpaws, seen here in our Pennsylvania garden in early November.

BOTTOM Though the familiar poem tells of picking up pawpaws and putting them in your pocket, this is not truly advisable, since ripe pawpaw fruits are quite soft and break open easily. The light yellow flesh is edible and sweet, slightly reminiscent of bananas but more custardlike in texture. The shiny amber-brown seeds are not edible. Pawpaw trees need to be cross-pollinated by others for good fruit set. If pawpaws could be bred to have the indestructibly plasticlike skins of supermarket tomatoes, they'd probably be sold commercially.

TOP White wood aster, *Aster divaricatus*, is a prolific bloomer, beginning in late August and lasting through September and well into October. It is an abundant self-seeder and not a good companion for delicate species; however, its self-renewing nature makes it an ideal flowering ground cover.

BOTTOM Though adaptable enough to withstand nearly full sun if conditions are moist, white wood aster is also able to grow in the dry shade below shrubs, as shown here blooming through Virginia summersweet, *Itea virginica* 'Henry's Garnet', in late October.

RIGHT The woodland asters have a nearly year-round presence in the garden. By early May, new foliage of white wood aster attractively covers the ground. It has shared space with shrubs and other durable plants such as Christmas fern, *Polystichum acrostichoides*, for many years in our garden. In some populations, the stems are nearly ebony black, and this character typically comes true from seed.

Aster

ASTERACEAE, ASTER FAMILY

The most commonly cultivated native asters, such as New England aster, *Aster novae-angliae*, and smooth aster, *Aster laevis*, are plants of mostly sunny environments. They're often useful in transition areas and along sunnier woodland edges, but they really don't like heavy shade. Well deserving of attention are three true shade species that can be stars in the woodland garden from late summer through autumn: white wood aster, *Aster divaricatus*, large-leaved aster, *Aster macrophyllus*, and heart-leaved aster, *Aster cordifolius*. These are tough, widely adaptable, and durable plants, valuable for the groundcovering qualities of their foliage as well as for their flowers. Though plants are inclined to self-sowing, with appropriate design this aspect can be an asset in the woodland garden. All are cold hardy to zone 3.

Another uncommonly grown species worth mentioning is zigzag aster, *Aster prenanthoides*. It is a rhizomatous spreader, sometimes forming colonies, and is native to streambanks and other very moist, partly sunny woodland habitats. The flowers are light blue, larger than those of heart-leaved aster but not as prolific. It is hardy through zone 5. I've admired it tumbling around rocks bordering my local White Clay Creek, in full bloom by early September, and I would certainly have it in our home garden if we had a stream running through.

Dry seed stalks of white wood aster set off the early November color of *Fothergilla gardenii*. Though deadheading to reduce self-sowing is sometimes recommended, I find such work tedious and impractical, and prefer to enjoy the winter presence of the dried stalks, planting this enthusiastic aster in spots where it can be savored with abandon.

TOP The foliage of large-leaved aster, *Aster macrophyllus*, forms a neat green carpet in the dense shade of a western Pennsylvania woodlands in late July. This rhizomatous species would be valuable in the woodland garden even if it never bloomed.

BOTTOM Flowers of large-leaved aster may be light blue but are frequently white, as seen in this late-July photograph from the Tennessee mountains. This colony was intermingled with spikenard, *Aralia racemosa*, and wild ginger, *Asarum canadense*.

ABOVE Often reaching three feet in height, heart-leaved aster, *Aster cordifolius*, can easily hold its own when interplanted with shrubs. In this early October view its light blue hues are highlighted against a ground cover of Allegheny spurge, *Pachysandra procumbens*. Drought tolerant and durable, this aster has persisted for many years within the competing roots of trees and shrubs.

TOP RIGHT Flowers of heart-leaved aster may be light lavender-blue to near-white and are particularly appealing when they catch the late-season sun. This is one of the last things blooming in the autumn garden, typically continuing past the first frosts, often well into November in our Pennsylvania garden.

Native to moist, north-facing woods in the southeastern mountains, false goat's beard, *Astilbe biternata*, is extremely shade tolerant and is cold hardy through zone 5. It grows best in richly organic, moisture-retentive soils. The bold-textured foliage often turns rich golden yellow in autumn.

Astilbe
FALSE GOAT'S BEARD
SAXIFRAGACEAE, SAXIFRAGE FAMILY

No wonder it's called false goat's beard. It takes a trained eye to quickly distinguish *Astilbe biternata* from goat's beard, *Aruncus dioicus*. Though they belong to different families (*Aruncus* is in the rose family), both produce bold-textured compound leaves topped by creamy-white flower clusters, and both bloom from late spring to early summer. The clusters of *Astilbe biternata* tend to be a bit more tapered and spirelike.

Betula
BIRCH
BETULACEAE, BIRCH FAMILY

North American native birches can be some of the most magnificent, enduring trees in the woodland garden if properly selected and sited. The garden reputation of birches as relatively small, short-lived trees has developed from the overuse and inappropriate use of the European white birch, *Betula pendula*, which is extremely susceptible to the bronze birch borer and poorly adapted to most of the United States from zone 5 south. The North American native birches are much less vulnerable to this pest, and in fact, river birch, *Betula nigra*, is fully resistant.

TOP RIGHT In winter, sweet birch or cherry birch, *Betula lenta*, might be mistaken for a black cherry. Its bark is silver to dark gray, with prominent horizontal markings called "lenticels." The bark occasionally splits and folds back slightly, but it never peels in big sheets. This large tree grows fifty to seventy-five feet tall and often forms part of the canopy. Native primarily to northern regions but extending south at cooler, higher elevations, it is fairly free from bronze birch borer unless stressed by excessive summer heat and drought. Back when birch beer was made from natural ingredients, this tree was the primary source of flavoring. The inner bark, even of small branches, is sweet to the taste and strongly wintergreen scented. At one time this tree was also used in the commercial production of oil of wintergreen. In forest and garden alike, I enjoy chewing on a small twig or just stripping the bark back to enjoy the fragrance. Most birches have yellow fall color, but the clear gold autumn tones of sweet birch are the best of all.

RIGHT At its best, yellow birch, *Betula alleghaniensis*, has shimmering brassy-brown bark that peels delicately in fine, translucent streamers. This is the most shade tolerant of the birches, and it has the vigor and longevity to become a one-hundred-foot-tall canopy tree in ideal circumstances. Like sweet birch, it is mostly a northern tree of moist woods, extending south only in the mountains. It requires an even cooler summer climate for health than sweet birch does, but can be a real jewel in the woodland garden whenever conditions will support it. The inner bark and twigs are wintergreen scented but not as strongly as those of sweet birch.

Birches are frequently pioneer trees—the first to become established in forest clearings, old fields, and roadside rights of way—however, many of them can be surprisingly long lived, lasting more than a century. The best of them provide four-season interest in the woodland garden. All are cold hardy to zone 3.

LEFT This late-July image from Mount Desert Island in Maine speaks of the cool, moist conditions preferred by white birch, *Betula papyrifera*. I'm sure many a child has written notes on a scrap of the peeling bark of this tree, which is also called paper birch; and another name, canoe birch, suggests the tree's use in canoe-making. It also prefers cool, moist conditions for best growth but has proved superior to European white birch in its resistance to birch borer. The whiteness of its bark is unsurpassed.

White birch is especially dramatic when highlighted against shadow or other dark backgrounds. In Grover Cleveland Park in northern New Jersey, my brother and I were well acquainted with "ghost canyon," the name we'd learned from older kids for a natural hollow, darkly rimmed by hemlocks and punctuated by the ghostly white birch trunks. The visual excitement and mood of this landscape was strongly felt by impressionable youth. I was delighted years later, studying records from the Olmsted Center at Fairsted, to learn the hemlocks were native to the site, but the white birches were the deliberate artistry of the Olmsted office, the nation's first landscape architecture firm, which was responsible for the park's design.

BOTTOM LEFT The bark of white birch is sunlit against background shadows.

BELOW The recent popularity of river birch in North American gardens is due in large part to the introduction of especially light-barked cultivars including *Betula nigra* 'Heritage'. The spacing of these trees in our garden at home directly emulates the close spacing often encountered in native populations.

ABOVE LEFT Pink and salmon hues in the bark of this river birch, *Betula nigra*, resonate with a native pinxter azalea, *Rhododendron periclymenoides*, growing below and behind. This is not a cultivar but merely a colorful example of this species, which is nearly invulnerable to borer attack and is unquestionably the best birch for regions with high summer temperatures. Beautiful as a single-stemmed or multistemmed tree, river birch has the capacity to live well over a century and to exceed one hundred feet in height. It is sometimes called red birch.

ABOVE RIGHT Though river birch is rarely included in discussions of flowering trees, we are well aware of the bright yellow of its pendent catkins each April as they dance in the spring breeze before a background of redbud, *Cercis canadensis*, in flower.

LEFT Gray birch, *Betula populifolia*, is a small tree, usually only fifteen to twenty feet tall and typically multistemmed. It is a relatively short-lived pioneer species, most common on infertile soils including the sterile, acid sands of the New Jersey Pine Barrens. Its bark is chalky white but remains tight and rarely peels. Though more heat tolerant than white birch, gray birch may suffer from borer attack and leaf miners when stressed.

Caltha

MARSH MARIGOLD
RANUNCULACEAE, BUTTERCUP FAMILY

Here's one for the woodland water garden. The bright golden yellow of marsh marigold, *Caltha palustris*, is especially welcome in early spring as it blooms naturally in wet woods, meadows, swamps, and bogs, often in shallow water. This species is circumboreal, ranging south in the United States to Virginia, West Virginia, Illinois, Iowa, and in the mountains to North Carolina and Tennessee, and is cold hardy through zone 2. It is easy to grow in soils that are damp or wet at least during the early part of the year, and is a natural choice for massing in low soggy spots, at the edges of slow streams, or in shallow water at pond margins. Though tolerant of dense shade, it blooms more enthusiastically in the spring sun of fully deciduous woodlands.

TOP LEFT Marsh marigold, *Caltha palustris*, blooms at the beginning of May in a soggy section of the deciduous woods in West Virginia, along with skunk cabbage, *Symplocarpus foetidus*, a frequent companion.

BOTTOM LEFT Flowering in mid April in Maryland, marsh marigold is appealing up close as well as in distant drifts. It is a spring phenomenon, going dormant during summer.

Calycanthus

SWEETSHRUB, CAROLINA ALLSPICE, STRAWBERRY SWEETSHRUB
CALYCANTHACEAE, CALYCANTHUS FAMILY

There's a large patch of sweetshrub growing on the nineteenth-century Quaker farm just down the road from me, and it's been there longer than anyone in the neighborhood can remember. *Calycanthus floridus* seems once again to be coming into vogue, but the frequency with which it is found in old farm landscapes is evidence it was a favorite many years ago when fragrance and ease of culture were deemed more important than novelty.

Native from Virginia to Florida, in moist woods and streambanks, sweetshrub is among the most delightful shrubs for the woodland garden. Hardy to zone 4, it adapts to an extraordinarily wide range of soil and moisture conditions, and though it blooms best with some sun, I've encountered it flowering in the dense shade of southern mountain forests.

I don't know of another shrub capable of scenting the garden for more than nearly two months in spring. At best the fragrance of sweetshrub is deliciously fruity, reminiscent of apple, banana, or strawberry, as recognized by the alternate

The dark red to maroon flowers of *Calycanthus floridus* 'Edith Wilder', blooming here in mid May, are typical of the species. This cultivar is my favorite, with a strong strawberry-apple scent. The fragrance of sweetshrub varies in intensity during different times of day and often seems strongest when temperatures are warm or warming. Individual flowers are typically most fragrant when newly open. 'Edith Wilder' is a vigorous grower, capable of reaching ten feet.

The chartreuse to banana-yellow blooms of *Calycanthus floridus* 'Athens' are distinct, and this cultivar is among the most reliably fragrant. I'd say it is one of the most apple scented, but part of the fun of growing sweetshrub is inviting conjecture on its fragrance. 'Athens' is a fine design complement to 'Edith Wilder', since it grows only six feet tall and fits well in smaller spaces. This photograph shows it blooming on the first day of summer in southern New Jersey.

Even in years when we've been afflicted by withering droughts, *Calycanthus floridus* 'Edith Wilder' has finished the season with a golden flourish, as here in early November. It is among the best selections for fall color.

names strawberry sweetshrub and Carolina allspice. Seedlings can be quite variable, however, and the worst can smell like vinegar, so it is important to sniff-test seed-grown plants before affording them a prominent position in the garden. The other approach is to play it safe by acquiring a proven clonal cultivar such as 'Athens', 'Edith Wilder', or 'Michael Lindsey'.

Sweetshrub spreads by suckers and can form extensive patches if uncontrolled. Its growth can easily be checked by removing sucker growth at the periphery of the plant and by selectively removing older stems from the center and allowing young suckers to take their place.

Campanula

TALL BELLFLOWER
CAMPANULACEAE, BELLFLOWER FAMILY

Tall bellflower, *Campanula americana*, is a winter annual or biennial and distinct enough from other North American *Campanula* species that it is often distinguished as *Campanulastrum americanum*. It is worth considering in the woodland garden, because when conditions are right, it grows in self-perpetuating

profusion, adding its deep purple blue to forest greens. Occurring naturally in open, occasionally dry woods and moist edges from Ontario to Minnesota south to Florida and Oklahoma, it is cold hardy to zone 3.

LEFT The blue-purple spikes of tall bell-flower, *Campanula americana*, are nearly five feet high at the edge of a North Carolina deciduous forest in late July. I've also observed it growing in a native habitat with bottlebrush grass, *Hystrix patula*, a combination worth repeating in the woodland garden.

Carpinus
IRONWOOD, BLUE BEECH, MUSCLEWOOD, HORNBEAM
BETULACEAE, BIRCH FAMILY

Despite the insignificance of its flowers, ironwood, *Carpinus caroliniana*, is among the best small trees with four-season interest in the woodland landscape. Its common name ironwood refers to the incredible density of the wood, which was used to make machinery gears in the Colonial era. Even in modern times, this tree is a challenge to the sharpest or most powerful saw. Musclewood is also a quite descriptive name, since the light gray bark appears to be covering lean, sinewy, muscular tissue.

In many ways ironwood resembles a small beech, *Fagus grandifolia*, and its foliage is a close second. In spring, new leaves emerge chartreuse and translucent, enlivening the gray bark with dappled patterns. Summer foliage is rich dark

green, accompanied by the pendent, hoplike fruit clusters. Autumn color is a kaleidoscope of orange, red, and burnished gold, and the horizontal layering in the branch tracery continues as a delight through winter snows.

Carpinus caroliniana ranges from Nova Scotia to Minnesota and south to Florida and Texas, typically in moist woods and on floodplains. It is cold hardy to zone 3. A very slow grower, ironwood may take a decade to reach ten feet in height, but has the capacity to grow over fifty feet tall with time and ideal conditions. It is quite shade tolerant and will endure beneath a high deciduous canopy. I've seen it used to superb effect framing patios and other shady spaces in woodland gardens.

OPPOSITE BOTTOM The fine-textured horizontal tracery of ironwood, *Carpinus caroliniana*, is a delight in all seasons, as seen covered in mid-October hues or with a mantle of snow in January.

TOP RIGHT Late November sunlight caresses an ironwood in a Delaware deciduous woodland. Since the mottled bark is a unique facet of this tree's appeal, ironwood is most effective when growing as a multistemmed specimen, something it is inclined toward naturally.

BOTTOM RIGHT The fall foliage of ironwood is especially photosensitive, with distinct patterns of gold and orange revealing how leaves have rested against one another while the autumn sun has worked its magic.

Carya

HICKORY

JUGLANDACEAE, WALNUT FAMILY

Hickories would no doubt be more widely planted if not for their truly tap-rooted nature, which makes them difficult to transplant or to grow to size in a container. They can be grown from seed planted on site and should certainly be conserved and appreciated whenever they occur in the woodland wild landscape and garden.

RIGHT As Ralph Emerson and Henry Thoreau noted, the beauty of Nature is often in the details. Among these details are the unique, fuzzy, golden winter buds of swamp hickory, *Carya cordiformis*; in addition to their coloration, they are naked in botanical terms, meaning not covered by bud scales. I always enjoy seeing them, whether on trees growing in their typical low woodland habitat or in the garden. Ranging from Quebec to Minnesota and south to Florida and Texas, swamp hickory is hardy to zone 4.

TOP LEFT Most hickories have attractive yellow to golden-brown autumn color. Pignut hickory, *Carya glabra*, is about the brightest golds, as seen here intermingled with flowering dogwood, *Cornus florida*, in Virginia. Pignut hickory has relatively smooth gray bark and is cold hardy to zone 4.

TOP RIGHT Soft light near dusk in early May in a Virginia mountain valley plays off the exfoliating trunks of shagbark hickory, *Carya ovata*. Though the tree most often occurs on moist soils, from Maine to Minnesota and south to Texas, I've seen it grow over eighty feet tall in relatively dry upland woods. It's cold hardy to zone 4 and beautiful when grown in a grove.

OPPOSITE TOP LEFT The sloping floor of a Virginia deciduous forest is carpeted by blue cohosh, *Caulophyllum thalictrioides*, in early May, hinting at what this plant might do in the woodland garden.

OPPOSITE TOP RIGHT A rich mosaic of blue cohosh and *Trillium erectum* covers the ground under a high deciduous canopy along the banks of the Susquehanna River in Maryland in late April.

Caulophyllum

BLUE COHOSH
BERBERIDACEAE, BARBERRY FAMILY

The ruelike foliage of blue cohosh, *Caulophyllum thalictrioides*, is among the prettiest of all woodland herbs, delicate yet full enough to create a knee-level carpet over the forest floor. Though it is often found in vast self-sown populations in the wild, its artificial propagation by division or seed is slow, and this has resulted in relatively low commercial availability.

Blue cohosh prefers moist, often sloping woodland habitats, and ranges from Canada south to the Carolinas. It is often associated with calcareous soils and limestone outcrops, though it will grow satisfactorily in slightly acid conditions. It is cold hardy to zone 3.

Ceanothus

NEW JERSEY TEA, MOUNTAIN SNOWBALL
RHAMNACEAE, BUCKTHORN FAMILY

Though white-flowered *Ceanothus americanus* pales in comparison with the unbelievably blue California native species, it is an attractive part of the central and eastern deciduous forests, easy to grow, and worth considering in the wood-

CENTER LEFT New foliage and flowers of blue cohosh emerge a fantastic dark purple, lightly covered by a waxy bloom.

CENTER RIGHT Berrylike seeds of blue cohosh are typically displayed on leafless stalks by mid October, as seen in this image at Mount Cuba Center in Delaware. The seeds often remain evident and colorful into winter.

LEFT Though this photograph was taken in late July in the Virginia mountains, it explains why *Ceanothus americanus* is sometimes called mountain snowball.

land garden. It is the most cold-hardy *Ceanothus* species, adaptable to zone 4. Despite its common name, it is native to mixed deciduous forests and forest margins from Canada to South Carolina and Texas. It seems to demand a well-drained soil but is otherwise exceptionally tough and durable, able to thrive on dry hillside conditions that would be impossible for many other shrubs and herbaceous plants. I've seen it blooming profusely from piles of shale deposited at the base of mountain roadcuts in nearly full sun.

Cercis

REDBUD

FABACEAE, PEA FAMILY

Redbud, *Cercis canadensis*, is particularly important from a color design perspective, since it is one of the few spring-flowering native trees whose blossoms are not white. Quite happily for gardeners, it is a naturally wide-ranging species occurring in moist woods and forest openings from Connecticut to Michigan, Iowa, and Nebraska, south to Florida and northern Mexico. Redbud is cold hardy through zone 4 if proper attention is paid to selecting trees of regional prove-

ABOVE In southeastern Pennsylvania, redbuds, *Cercis canadensis*, typically live a long time but frequently lose stems and large branches to cold injury or canker diseases. For this reason, I'm always reluctant to place them front and center in a design that calls for symmetry or uniform appearance. My best results with redbud at home have been from trees planted at the periphery of our property, at a back edge facing a small meadow section, keeping company with a 1930s tractor, sumacs, and other relics of the true "county casual" landscape. The wash of color from the redbuds is enjoyed from great distances in the spring garden.

RIGHT Redbud can grow to thirty feet tall, especially toward the southern end of its range, as exemplified by this specimen in the Birmingham Botanical Gardens in Alabama.

nance. As with many woody species, relative cold hardiness and heat resistance vary considerably between populations in cold, northern climes and those in the extreme south.

Beyond flowers, the foliage of redbuds is a bold-textured presence in the landscape. Autumn color is sometimes a pleasant gold but often unremarkable. The unusual clonal cultivar 'Forest Pansy' has new leaves that open like purple patent leather, turning deep wine colored and then bronze-green as the season progresses. Though quite handsome in the garden, it is one of the least cold-hardy cultivars, reliable only in zones 7 and warmer.

TOP RIGHT I'm a member of the camp that is inclined to ask plant introducers: "But why do you want a white form of something which is normally so rich in color?" In the case of *Cercis canadensis* var. *alba*, I'll admit this white form, at its clear best, can be quite elegant despite the awkward common name of white redbud. Redbuds, like many woody members of the pea family, are virtually impossible to root from cuttings, so the white form must be grafted or grown from seed, which yields variable results.

Chionanthus
FRINGE TREE
OLEACEAE, OLIVE FAMILY

The genus name is derived from *chio* meaning "snow" and *anthos* meaning "flower," so in a completely orderly world this tree might be called snowflower. Still, fringe tree is an apt moniker for this delightful small flowering tree, whose white blossoms do resemble a fanciful white fringe suspended in the spring sunlight.

Native from southeastern Pennsylvania and southern New Jersey to Florida and Texas, usually in rich woods and along rivers and streams, fringe tree, *Chionanthus virginicus*, is cold hardy to zone 4. It is one of the last trees to leaf out in spring, and its autumn color is a pleasant but unremarkable lime-yellow. This species is mostly dioecious, and though male trees have showier flowers, female trees offer the added interest of blue fruits in summer and autumn. It is easy to transplant and adaptable to a wide range of soil types and moisture conditions. It flowers best with plenty of sun but puts on a good show even under a high deciduous canopy.

CENTER RIGHT Mid-May sun illuminates the flowers of fringe tree in a Pennsylvania garden.

BOTTOM RIGHT The blue fruits of female fringe trees are appealing details in the summer and autumn landscape.

ABOVE LEFT AND RIGHT Often growing as a large shrub or small tree to twenty feet tall, fringe tree, *Chionanthus virginicus*, is a fine choice for any intimate space in the woodland garden. It is a main feature of this terrace at Ashland Hollow in northern Delaware, helping to define the space whether bare branched in March or just finished flowering in late May.

OPPOSITE TOP RIGHT No wonder it's called golden-star. *Chrysogonum virginianum* throws bright yellow blooms across a low carpet of deep green, seen here in mid May.

OPPOSITE BOTTOM RIGHT Black snakeroot, *Cimicifuga racemosa*, blooms strongly in the late-July sunlight at the edge of a northern Pennsylvania forest. Truly one of summer's best bloomers, this graceful perennial is long lived in the woodland garden.

Chrysogonum

GOLDEN-STAR
ASTERACEAE, ASTER FAMILY

In my earlier life in plant taxonomy, I learned how difficult composites (another term for members of the Asteraceae) could be to identify, especially yellow ones. In taxonomic lingo they are referred to as DYCs (meaning damned yellow composites). Later, thinking more like a gardener, it occurred to me that this acronym might still be useful for referring to the preponderance of yellow composites found in perennial borders; however, golden-star, *Chrysogonum virginianum*, which scatters its bright yellow flowers across a low surface of dark green, is too elegant to lump with the DYC crowd.

Though the species *Chrysogonum virginianum* is native to woodlands from Pennsylvania and Ohio south to Florida and Mississippi, there are two botanical varieties found within this range. Both are strongly rhizomatous spreaders. The typical variety, *Chrysogonum virginianum* var. *virginianum*, is more northern in distribution, cold hardy into zone 4, and may be distinguished by its upright-flowering stems, which are sometimes a foot tall. More southern in its range and somewhat less cold hardy is *Chrysogonum virginianum* var. *australe*. It is also lower-growing, often darker green in foliage, and spreads by aboveground stolons. In cultivation the two varieties easily cross and much of the material in commerce is mixed.

Both varieties are extremely useful woodland ground covers and are evergreen in warmer regions. They flower most feverishly in spring, slow in summer, and then resume their blooming as temperatures drop toward autumn. Though best in moist organic soils, golden-star is quite adaptable. It survived in some awful clay soil in my old urban Delaware garden.

Cimicifuga

BLACK COHOSH, BUGBANE, BLACK SNAKEROOT
RANUNCULACEAE, BUTTERCUP FAMILY

Three *Cimicifuga* species are native to eastern deciduous forests, and though only one is commonly available commercially, all are beautiful plants for woodland gardens.

Variously called black snakeroot, black cohosh, bugbane, and rattletop, *Cimicifuga racemosa* is most common in the wild and in commerce. A stately plant sometimes nearly seven feet tall, it is native to moist and dry woods on the piedmont and in the mountains from Massachusetts to Indiana, south to Missouri and Georgia, blooming from May to July depending upon elevation. It is cold hardy to zone 3. As its range might suggest, it is widely adaptable in the garden, and though it is most impressive when provided moist organic soil, it does surprisingly well in poor dry conditions if shaded. Travel the Blue Ridge Parkway in summer and your driving skills may be impaired as your eyes become glued to the white spires of black snakeroot rocketing out from the woods edge, sometimes commingled with Turk's cap lily, *Lilium superbum*. The large, compound leaves of black snakeroot are a significant presence in the garden even when plants are not in flower.

The remaining two species are later-blooming and are cold hardy to zone 4. Shorter but similar in appearance to *Cimicifuga racemosa*, mountain bugbane, *Cimicifuga americana*, occurs only in rich mountain woods in Virginia and West

TOP Though pretty to look at up close, the flowers of black snakeroot, *Cimicifuga racemosa,* have a musky odor. Long after the flowers have faded, the dried seed stalks sometimes make a rattling sound, vibrating in autumn and winter winds.

BOTTOM If moisture is consistent through summer and plants are grown in part sun, the foliage of black snakeroot may turn a burnished gold, as pictured here in early October in West Virginia.

Virginia, Kentucky, Tennessee, North Carolina, and Georgia. It flowers from July to September. Least common is Appalachian bugbane, *Cimicifuga rubifolia,* which occurs only in cool mountain woods from southwestern Virginia to North Carolina, Tennessee, and Alabama, with disjunct populations in western Kentucky and southern Illinois. In its native habitat it grows almost exclusively on limestone, though it will tolerate slightly acid soil in the garden. It is an August-to-September bloomer, with distinctive foliage resembling that of fragrant blackberry, *Rubus odoratus,* growing three feet tall in flower.

Claytonia
SPRING BEAUTY
PORTULACACEAE, PURSLANE FAMILY

Individually, spring beauties, *Claytonia virginica,* are easily taken for granted amid the excitement of spring, but when they occur as a flowering carpet, cheering the forest floor, they are among the mating season's best events.

Most *Claytonia* species grow from rounded corms and can be increased by separating the offsets. They are true spring ephemerals, going fully dormant in summer. The most common spring beauty, *Claytonia virginica,* is found in rich woods from Canada to Georgia and is cold hardy to zone 3. Its leaves are narrow and strap shaped, and the flowers are white with pink-striped petals. Carolina spring beauty, *Claytonia caroliniana,* is more of a mountain species, with noticeably wider leaves and often, though not always, deeper pink flowers. The two sometimes grow together in the wild. Both are fine candidates for naturalizing in the woodland garden.

Clethra
SWEET PEPPERBUSH, MOUNTAIN CLETHRA, CINNAMON CLETHRA
CLETHRACEAE, CLETHRA FAMILY

The two North American native *Clethra* species are quite distinct from one another in all aspects except their flowers, but both are superb woodland garden plants. Sweet pepperbush, *Clethra alnifolia,* is native to moist woods and swamps, mostly near the coast, from Nova Scotia and Maine to Florida and Texas, and is cold hardy to zone 4. It is among the most fragrant native shrubs, capable of filling a large area of the summer garden with its sweet spicy scent. The flowers continue for weeks in July and August, and though typically white, many

ABOVE In late April at Winterthur Museum and Gardens in northern Delaware, a sea of spring beauties, *Claytonia* species, ties together tall trees and Mayapples, *Podophyllum peltatum*, in an inspired alternative to the chemical-intensive forest lawn.

TOP RIGHT Sweet pepperbush, *Clethra alnifolia*, has been an enduring part of a mixed woody border in our garden for more than a decade, easily enduring the transition from sun to shade as the trees have matured. Though native to moist or wet soils and very tolerant of soggy garden soils, it has thrived on our well-drained loam with no supplemental watering even in drought years. It had already bloomed for two weeks when this late-July photograph was taken.

BOTTOM RIGHT Mountain clethra covers itself in flowers in late July in the North Carolina mountains. Unlike the flowers of sweet pepperbush, these are not noticeably fragrant.

pink forms occur, in tints from delicate to hot. Its suckering habit and broad tolerance of light conditions make it an ideal choice for massing at the woodland edge or in the understory.

As its name suggests, mountain clethra, *Clethra acuminata*, is truly a higher-elevation species, growing in rich mountain woods from Pennsylvania south to Tennessee and Georgia. Provided the cool, moist summer conditions it prefers, mountain clethra forms a large shrub or small multistemmed tree fifteen to twenty feet tall, and is most memorable for the cinnamon color of its bark. It is cold hardy into zone 5, but nowhere near as tolerant of heat and drought as sweet pepperbush.

ABOVE Cinnamon clethra is another, obvious name for mountain clethra, *Clethra acuminata*.

RIGHT This pond's-edge setting at Mount Cuba Center in Delaware closely emulates the familiar habitat of sweet pepperbush, *Clethra alnifolia*. Warmly reflected in the water, the gold autumn color is a reliable trait.

Clintonia

BEAD LILY, BLUEBEAD LILY
LILIACEAE, LILY FAMILY

Bead lilies are often encountered in huge patches, covering the floor of densely shaded acid woodlands. Their small lilylike flowers are subtle, but their glossy foliage makes a beautiful ground cover. Bluebead lily, *Clintonia borealis*, which ranges from Canada south through New Jersey and Pennsylvania and in the mountains to North Carolina and Tennessee, requires deep organic soil and moderate summer heat for best growth. Its deep blue berries are attractive from summer into fall. It is hardy into zone 2. Another bead lily of more southern distribution is *Clintonia umbellulata*, with blue-black berries. Cold hardy to zone 3, its greater resistance to heat and drought makes it adaptable to a wider range of conditions in the woodland garden.

Cornus

DOGWOOD
CORNACEAE, DOGWOOD FAMILY

Mention dogwood and, for most people, only one tree comes to mind: the flowering dogwood, *Cornus florida*. This is true whether you're posing the question in Quebec, Cape May, or Cape Town. It is truly the flowering emblem of the North American deciduous forest, yet the world renown of this magnificent tree sometimes seems to make other *Cornus* species invisible to the gardening eye. Other dogwoods, especially pagoda or alternate-leaved dogwood, *Cornus alternifolia*, and red osier dogwood, *Cornus sericea*, have much to offer the designed woodland landscape.

TOP RIGHT Bluebead lily, *Clintonia borealis*, covers the ground in a garden on Mount Desert Island, Maine, in late July.

CENTER RIGHT Viewed from below and behind, a flowering dogwood, *Cornus florida*, reaches toward the light over White Clay Creek in northern Delaware. The flowers are quite small and are surrounded by four leafy bracts, often mistaken for petals. Though typically white, pink dogwoods are sometimes encountered in the wild and many forms have been propagated in commerce.

BOTTOM RIGHT A late-January storm turns a flowering dogwood into an ice sculpture. Next year's flower buds decorate each branch tip, and the red tint of last year's growth is evident through the crystalline cover. The sympodial branching pattern common to both flowering dogwood and pagoda dogwood is easily observed in this photograph: the greatest extension in each year's growth comes from lateral buds, not terminal buds. This results in a lilting line when viewed up close and a strongly horizontal form when viewed from a distance.

Though dogwood anthracnose has wreaked havoc with native woodland populations in the northeastern United States, it does not appear this disease will eradicate the species from our landscapes. Caused by *Discula* fungi, the anthracnose is most troublesome under cool weather conditions, when moisture remains for long periods on the flowers and foliage. The problem is accentuated by the relatively low air circulation inside native forests, and trees in these habitats have fared much worse than those in open, sunny conditions. Though it is wise to provide the best air circulation and drying conditions possible, flowering dogwoods are still a viable choice for woodland gardens.

TOP LEFT I delight in observing the variation in autumn color found among seedling dogwoods. This pink-leaved tree, seen in early October in West Virginia, was growing near others that were deep red or purple-bronze. *Cornus florida* is truly a four-season tree, with spring blooms followed by fine summer form and foliage and then autumn color and berries followed by splendid winter architecture. The bright red fruits are favored by many birds and are usually taken quickly in early winter. The cold hardiness and heat resistance of flowering dogwood vary considerably with provenance, so it is important to select seedlings or cultivars suited to regional conditions. It naturally occurs in woods and clearings from Maine to Michigan and south to Florida and Mexico. The most cold-hardy trees are adapted to zone 5.

BOTTOM LEFT Red-osier dogwood, *Cornus sericea*, spreads naturally in colorful sweeps through an open swampy area in the northern New York State woodlands. Of the numerous shrubby dogwood species, this is probably most useful in the woodland garden, especially in northern regions. Native over much of North America, from Newfoundland to Alaska and south to Pennsylvania and northern Mexico, it is cold hardy to zone 2 but suffers in the summer heat and humidity of the Southeast.

BELOW LEFT The main appeal of red-osier dogwood is in its stem color, and this is most intense on new growth, from autumn into early spring. The color varies considerably from typical reds to bright yellow, and many clonal selections are available. Though this suckering shrub can grow nine feet tall, it is most colorful when cut back nearly to the ground each year in early spring, as we do with these plants of *Cornus sericea* 'Cardinal' positioned just outside a window. The stem color is enriched by the late-day sun in this photograph two days before Christmas.

Pagoda dogwood, *Cornus alternifolia*, can be one of the most architecturally stunning trees in the winter landscape, though it is typically overshadowed by its famous relative, flowering dogwood. Its horizontal branching habit is even more pronounced than that of flowering dogwood and adds powerfully to the tree's appeal whether covered with snow, flowers, or autumn foliage. Native to rich woods and thickets from Nova Scotia to Minnesota and south to Florida, Alabama, and Arkansas, pagoda dogwood is cold hardy to zone 3.

TOP LEFT The form and autumn coloration of this tree is typical of pagoda dogwood growing underneath a deciduous woodland canopy. The photograph was taken in early November in Pennsylvania.

TOP RIGHT Snow in late January highlights the branch structure of a pagoda dogwood seedling in our garden.

RIGHT The same tree is flower covered in early May.

Cotinus

AMERICAN SMOKETREE
ANACARDIACEAE, CASHEW FAMILY

Though it has a relatively narrow natural range in Alabama, Tennessee, and Texas, American smoketree, *Cotinus obovatus*, is cold hardy to zone 4, quite drought resistant, and adaptable to a wide range of soil types including the calcareous soils of limestone regions. I am always finding inspiration for design combinations directly from native habitats. In the late 1990s, legendary southern nurseryman Don Shadow showed me a native population near Winchester, Tennessee, and I was surprised to see that the ground-level companions of smoketrees, in relatively dry conditions, were fragrant sumac, *Rhus aromatica*, and pinkroot, *Spigelia marilandica*.

Crataegus

HAWTHORN
ROSACEAE, ROSE FAMILY

The hawthorns, *Crataegus*, constitute one of plant taxonomy's most magnificent black holes, swallowing up a number of intrepid taxonomists but not before they were able to name some several hundred North American species. Many of these

TOP LEFT I've never been able to find out who might have planted this venerable American smoketree, *Cotinus obovatus*, outside the men's pool in Warm Springs, Virginia, which dates from 1761. The tree is almost indescribably beautiful in mid October, when the foliage turns a smoky mix of orange, peach, salmon, and bronze.

BOTTOM LEFT Flowers are only incidental to the beauty of American smoketree, which is centered on its autumn color, but they can be effective in the spring light, as evidenced by this late-May image from the Henry Foundation in Gladwyne, Pennsylvania.

LEFT American smoketree is very late to leaf out, as seen in this early May photograph of a cultivated tree growing in the Virginia mountains. The mature bark is wonderfully scaly.

have proved dubious as we've come to understand that the hawthorn species are complicated by frequent hybridization, apomixis, polyploidy, and other genetic irregularities. That said, hawthorns can be uniquely beautiful trees, whatever their species, and include some of the wonderfully rounded, spreading forms that captivated Jens Jensen and other midwestern landscape artists in the twentieth century. Hawthorns are generally smaller trees, less than thirty feet in height, of open or disturbed habitats including thickets along streams, savannas, open second-growth forests, and woodland edges. Many are well adapted to alkaline soils.

Cyrilla

LEATHERWOOD, TI-TI

CYRILLACEAE, CYRILLA FAMILY

The only species in its family, leatherwood or ti-ti, *Cyrilla racemiflora*, is an unusually attractive shrub or small tree, typically ten to twenty feet tall, native to swamps and wet woods. It occurs mostly on the coastal plain from southeastern Virginia to Texas and into South America, and is reliably cold hardy into zone 6. It is fully evergreen toward the southern portion of its range, dropping most or all its leaves in northern winters. Leatherwood grows best on moist but well-drained

TOP RIGHT Cold hardy to zone 4, green hawthorn, *Crataegus viridis*, is native from Delaware to Florida and west to Texas and Oklahoma. Like many hawthorns, it produces red berries in autumn which last through much of winter. This species is often represented in commerce by the clonal cultivar 'Winter King', which may be a hybrid. Though birds eat hawthorn fruits, often the most important role of hawthorns for avian wildlife is to provide cover in otherwise open habitats.

RIGHT The form of this hawthorn, multistemmed with a rounded top and widespreading branches, is typical of those celebrated by Jens Jensen and used widely in his designs. Most likely red haw or downy hawthorn, *Crataegus mollis*, this tree is nearly silhouetted against the fading late-day light in January at Crab Tree Farm in Illinois. This species is common in limestone regions, from New England and southeastern Canada to Minnesota, and south to Alabama and eastern Texas. It is cold hardy to zone 4.

soil rich in organic matter. Its main appeal is its mid-summer flowering and its graceful, arching branch pattern.

LEFT Pendent flower clusters are plentiful on leatherwood, *Cyrilla racemiflora*, in late July in the Gentling garden in Asheville, North Carolina.

Delphinium
LARKSPUR
RANUNCULACEAE, BUTTERCUP FAMILY

The eastern forest flora includes two larkspurs worth growing in woodland gardens, both cold hardy to zone 4. Dwarf larkspur, *Delphinium tricorne*, is native to rich, moist woods from Pennsylvania to Minnesota and south to Oklahoma, Alabama, and Georgia. It is a spring bloomer, with typically purple-blue but sometimes white or pink flowers, growing one to two feet tall. My clear favorite is tall larkspur, *Delphinium exaltatum*, with six-foot stature and dark purple-blue flowers in July. It occurs naturally in rich woods from Pennsylvania south to North Carolina and west to Missouri, and it is easy to grow in a range of soil types and moisture conditions.

BOTTOM LEFT Tall larkspur, *Delphinium exaltatum*, blooms six feet tall in late July in the Virginia mountains. In woodland environment, blue and purple are common in spring but quite unusual in summer. This stately plant is an exceptional and superb choice for bringing rich color to edges and openings in the woodland garden.

Dentaria
TOOTHWORT
BRASSICACEAE, MUSTARD FAMILY

Dent means "tooth," and the genus name recognizes the cut-leaf margins common to toothworts. Sometimes lumped with the genus *Cardamine*, the *Dentaria* species are mostly spring ephemerals, subtly attractive in bloom but quickly going dormant. For garden purposes, the one truly worth mentioning is broad-leaved toothwort, *Dentaria diphylla*, which spreads strongly but not aggressively by rhizomes, often forming large patches of dark green leaves low to the forest floor. Most importantly, its basal foliage is evergreen in zones 6 and warmer. Cold hardy into zone 3, it occurs in rich woods from Canada south to North Carolina, Georgia, and Alabama. I've found it easy to grow and long persistent in the garden, even in dense shade and dry summer conditions.

Dicentra

SQUIRREL CORN, DUTCHMAN'S BREECHES, WILD BLEEDING HEART
FUMARIACEAE, FUMITORY FAMILY

One of my favorite spring treks is to the Susquehanna River in nearby Maryland where, each April, the steep, rocky, wooded banks are covered in a merry mix of native wildflowers including squirrel corn, *Dicentra canadensis*; Dutchman's breeches, *Dicentra cucullaria*; blue cohosh, *Caulophyllum thalictrioides*; bluebells, *Mertensia virginica*; trout lilies, *Erythronium americanum*; and *Trillium erectum*, along with myriad ferns. Despite the larger, more colorful flowers of some, the most curiously beautiful are the two ephemeral *Dicentra* species. Cold hardy into zone 3, both would be worth having in the garden if they did no more than produce their exquisitely cut foliage for a month or so in spring before going dormant. Add their flowering and you have two plants that deserve a place in any woodland landscape that offers deep, moist organic soil and sharp drainage.

The third eastern species, wild bleeding heart, *Dicentra eximia*, is much larger, growing up to eighteen inches tall, and persists through summer. I've seen it growing in densely shaded acid woodlands, but it is also fairly sun tolerant and heat resistant. The foliage is nowhere near as lacy and refined, and I've always found the pink color a bit muddy and far inferior to the pleasing whites of the other two. It is cold hardy to zone 4.

Broad-leaved toothwort, *Dentaria diphylla*, blooms in early May in the Virginia woods. The rich green lower leaves are evergreen in warmer parts of its range.

ABOVE Flowers of squirrel corn, *Dicentra canadense,* are cool white with a hint of lavender at the tips.

LEFT Flowers of Dutchman's breeches, *Dicentra cucullaria*, are warm white with golden-yellow tips. It takes little imagination to envision these as pantaloons hung out to dry.

TOP LEFT Wild bleeding heart, *Dicentra eximia*, grows naturally in shale along a sunny West Virginia mountain roadside, in full bloom in early May. Though smaller overall, this species is most similar in color and flower shape to Japanese bleeding heart, *Dicentra spectabilis*.

TOP RIGHT *Dicentra canadense* (left) is named squirrel corn for the tiny underground bulblets which form around the base of its underground stem. Similar in size and color to a grain of corn, the bulblets are easily separated to make more plants. *Dicentra cucullaria* (right) is also easily propagated by division.

Dioscorea

WILD YAM
DIOSCOREACEAE, YAM FAMILY

I was first intrigued by the common wild yam, *Dioscorea villosa*, when I discovered its dried seed capsules lingering in the winter landscape. Returning during the growing season, I found its stems twining gracefully up and over woodland companions, clothed in neatly elegant, glossy green leaves. Wild yams are easy to grow from seed, and for years I had *Dioscorea villosa* growing on a split-rail fence in our small city garden, where it was unfazed by poor soil and summer drought. This species is common to moist open woods, thickets, and roadsides from Connecticut to Minnesota south to Texas and Florida.

I've since become enamored of *Dioscorea quaternata*, which has leaves in whorls of four to seven. It's common in similar habitats throughout the Appalachian region and is likewise hardy through zone 4. *Dioscorea* species are dioecious, so if you want the seed capsules you need to grow female plants, but I believe both are worth considering for foliage alone, which can turn a stunning gold in fall.

Diospyros

PERSIMMON
EBENACEAE, EBONY FAMILY

Native in dry woods from Connecticut to Florida and west to Texas and Kansas, but generally neglected by gardeners, persimmon, *Diospyros virginiana*, is one of the unsung heroes of North America's accidental landscapes. The bright orange fruits seem so fitting in fall, hanging from trees in pastures, abandoned fields, hedgerows, and roadsides, planted by passing animals.

Nearly disease-free and cold hardy to zone 4, this tough tree has a habit of suckering, like sassafras, and has been similarly shunned by gardeners too enthusiastic about control. Indeed, it can be a nuisance if planted in the wrong location, but its colonial nature often results in a beautiful, enduring woodland composition. I always found the persimmon grove on the hill behind the fountains at Longwood Gardens to be a serene, restful place in summer and a delight in autumn. The grove now in our home garden is not entirely accidental.

Though the North American native persimmon's fruits are much smaller and much more astringent than the relatively tender Japanese species, *Diospyros kaki*, they are still edible. Absolutely mouth-puckering when firm, the fruits are palat-

TOP LEFT AND CENTER These two images from the Virginia mountains illustrate the texture and color appeal of wild yam, *Dioscorea quaternata*, first in late May contrasting with Christmas fern, *Polystichum acrostichoides*, and then in mid October, when its rich gold lights up the woodland landscape.

TOP RIGHT Ripening persimmons, *Diospyros virginiana*, enliven the autumn landscape in Virginia.

able once they become fully ripe and soft, and have traditionally been used in making pudding, preserves, bread, and brandy. They are favored by many wildlife and are picked from trees or eaten from the ground. Since fallen fruits can be messy, the tree is best planted away from paved surfaces and walkways. The species is dioecious, with fruits only on female trees. Though they spread by suckers, persimmons are deep rooted and companionable to shrub and ground layer plants.

Persimmons typically grow thirty to fifty feet tall in time, though they can reach nearly twice this height. If plants are trained as individual trees, suckering will eventually diminish or cease. Autumn color is a mix of yellow and bronze.

Diphylleia

UMBRELLA LEAF
BERBERIDACEAE, BARBERRY FAMILY

I've seen some fine patches of umbrella leaf, *Diphylleia cymosa*, growing in cool North Carolina mountain streams, but no population has ever matched the magnificence of the sweeping plantings I encountered at the Berlin-Dahlem Botanical Garden in 1989, before the Wall came down. At that time, the plant wasn't even on the radar screen of American horticulture, but the Germans had recog-

TOP Backlit by the late-May sun, foliage of umbrella leaf, *Diphylleia cymosa*, is dramatic against the shadow background of the deep North Carolina forest.

ABOVE Light blue berries of umbrella leaf are set off by crimson red stalks in this late-August image from Berlin, Germany.

RIGHT Cool New York nights support this healthy patch of umbrella leaf at Stonecrop, near Cold Spring, New York, not far from the Hudson River.

nized the beauty in its bold texture and could offer it the constant moisture and cool summer night temperatures it absolutely requires.

Native to wet places in the mountains from Virginia to Georgia and Tennessee, umbrella leaf is cold hardy to zone 4. It grows three feet tall, flowering in spring but most noteworthy for its paired leaves, each of which may be more than a foot across. Its dramatic presence easily exceeds that of its close American relative Mayapple, *Podophyllum peltatum*, as well as many of the oft-coveted Asian *Diphylleia* species. Many ferns appreciate similar growing conditions and superbly complement the texture of umbrella leaf.

Dirca

LEATHERWOOD, WICOPY, ROPEBARK
THYMELAEACEAE, MEZEREUM FAMILY

Leatherwood flowers are less than one-half inch long, but as they appear in late winter, their bright lime-yellow is a welcome harbinger of spring. Also known as wicopy and ropebark, *Dirca palustris* has laughably pliable branches, which can be literally tied into knots without splitting or cracking. Cold hardy to zone 5, it is frequent in rich woods from New Brunswick to Minnesota and south to Florida, and was once valued by American Indians for its elastic properties, as the common names suggest. Leatherwood is open branched in dense shade but forms a neat, rounded shrub if grown in more sunny spots. It is among the earliest to leaf out in spring, and the autumn color is typically a warm yellow.

Echinacea

CONEFLOWER
ASTERACEAE, ASTER FAMILY

These days, coneflowers are so popular you can buy them in pill form. The most commonly grown of them, purple coneflower, *Echinacea purpurea*, is traditionally a prairie and meadow species but is also native to openings in low woods from Illinois and Iowa to Oklahoma, Texas, and Louisiana. Cold hardy into zone 3, it is among the most shade tolerant coneflowers and is useful in edge situations and as a transition plant in newly planted woodland garden areas that are still mostly sunny.

Flowers of leatherwood, *Dirca palustris*, grace bare branches in late March at the Morton Arboretum in Illinois.

Purple coneflower, *Echinacea purpurea*, is well suited to edges and transitional spaces, and is drought tolerant enough to grow under shallow-rooted trees such as river birch, *Betula nigra*. In this mid-July image, the flowers complement pink hues in the birch bark.

LEFT Though it has a deserved reputation for being an erratic bloomer, trout lily, *Erythronium americanum*, can be quite floriferous, as seen in this population along the Susquehanna River in Maryland in early April. Trout lilies are often found on steeply sloping sites and usually grow on moist but well-drained soils.

RIGHT Trout lily leaves can be curiously beautiful even in the absence of flowers. All trout lilies grow from corms, and each fertile corm sends up two leaves and a flowering stalk. Both *Erythronium americanum* and *Erythronium albidum* are noted for producing numerous sterile corms, each producing a single leaf and several stolonlike offshoots. Dense clusters of single leaves from crowded, sterile corms appear much like schools of fish, as seen in this early April image of *Erythronium americanum*. Trout lilies are true spring ephemerals, going dormant by late spring or early summer when temperatures rise.

Erythronium

TROUT LILY, FAWN LILY, ADDER'S TONGUE, DOG-TOOTH VIOLET
LILIACEAE, LILY FAMILY

A name like dog-tooth violet is enough to raise the hackles on a well-bred taxonomist. It does not require a trained eye to see that *Erythronium* flowers are very much like miniature lilies, to which they are related, and not at all like violets, to which they are not. Each flower has six showy parts, called "tepals," the term for petals and sepals which look nearly alike. Each tepal is shaped much like a long canine tooth. *Erythronium*, comprising fifteen or more species, is exclusively North American except for the Eurasian native *Erythronium dens-canis*, the original dog-tooth violet. It has purple flowers held above low leaves and is violetlike if you don't look too closely.

The most common *Erythronium* species in the eastern deciduous forest are *Erythronium americanum* and *Erythronium albidum*. Though neither flowers as freely as the western species, they're quite pretty in bloom, and both are extensively colonial, often forming large patches. Tapered like the body of a fish, the leaves of *Erythronium americanum* are always mottled gray-green, often with a brown background, and their obvious resemblance to brook trout is the origin of the name trout lily. This species is native to moist woods and shaded bottomlands from Nova Scotia to Minnesota south to Florida and Alabama, and is hardy to zone 3. The flowers are typically solid yellow, but I've observed considerable variation among different populations and individuals, including some with white-speckled or maroon-suffused tepals. Native from Ontario to Minnesota and south to Oklahoma and Georgia, *Erythronium albidum* has white flowers and leaves that are less mottled or not mottled at all. It is cold hardy to zone 3. In the woodland garden, both do best in moist, richly organic soils, and they flower best when sunlit at least part of the day.

Euonymus
STRAWBERRY BUSH, HEARTS-A-BUSTIN'
CELASTRACEAE, STAFF-TREE FAMILY

The most-often encountered *Euonymus* species in North American woodlands, *Euonymus alatus* is escaped from gardens, originally introduced from Asia. Its burning red fall foliage has completely overshadowed the appeal of the North American strawberry bush, *Euonymus americanus*. Native to moist woods from New York to Ohio and south to Florida and Texas, this suckering green-stemmed shrub is loose and open-growing, to six feet tall in shade. It is unremarkable until fall, when the crimson-colored fruits burst open to reveal bright orange seeds. No wonder it's often called hearts-a-bustin'. Though susceptible to euonymus scale, it is easy to grow in sun or shade on a variety of soils, and is cold hardy into zone 5.

Taller and more treelike, wahoo, *Euonymus atropurpureus*, is rangy and open, but can still be a delight to discover in fruit in the autumn woodland. Hardy to zone 4, wahoo could be a worthwhile inclusion in larger woodland gardens and public landscapes. Its fruits are similar in color to those of strawberry bush but smooth and dramatically suspended from long stalks.

Eupatorium
THOROUGHWORT
ASTERACEAE, ASTER FAMILY

Broadly known as thoroughworts, *Eupatorium* species are mostly plants of sunny places, but a few are woods or woods-edge natives. Hollow-stemmed Joe-pye weed, *Eupatorium fistulosum*, the best-known garden species, is most frequent in moist meadows, but I often encounter it at the edges of woodland streams, busily attracting butterflies. It belongs in a taxonomically confused subgroup of species with whorled leaves, and partly due to the nomenclatural chaos, another one, woodland Joe-pye weed, *Eupatorium purpureum*, has been overlooked horticul-

Strawberry bush, *Euonymus americanus*, also known as hearts-a-bustin', is at its colorful peak in this late-October image from a Pennsylvania garden.

Hollow-stemmed Joe-pye weed, *Eupatorium fistulosum*, turns lime-yellow at the edge of a Virginia woodland in early October.

turally. It occurs in open, often dry woods and thickets, from New Hampshire to Virginia and in the mountains to Georgia and west to Oklahoma, and is cold hardy through zone 4. The leaf nodes are purple, but the flowers are typically white or very pale pink, appearing in late July and August. Often reaching six feet in height and capable of flowering in considerable shade, *Eupatorium purpureum* has a lot to offer woodland gardeners.

The familiar blue mistflower of gardens, *Eupatorium coelestinum* is native to woods and streambanks from New York to Florida and blooms fairly well in semi-shade. It self-sows readily, as does white snakeroot, *Eupatorium rugosum*, a true woodland species occurring from Nova Scotia south to Georgia and Texas, and flowering in September and October. White snakeroot is poisonous if ingested, and white-tailed deer leave it alone. This trait, combined with the horticultural introduction of the bronze-purple-leaved cultivar 'Chocolate', has significantly boosted the presence and popularity of a once-ignored plant.

Fagus
BEECH
FAGACEAE, BEECH FAMILY

I'm sometimes inclined to believe horticulturists are involved in an unwitting conspiracy against big trees. Though gardening books often extol their virtues, the final recommendation is often to plant them someplace other than in your own garden, or to leave their planting entirely to others. Surely trees like American beech, *Fagus grandifolia*, can be superb choices for large parks and public spaces, but with care and a little imagination, they can also contribute mightily to the more intimate landscapes in which so many of us make our homes.

If you live in an area where beech is native, and this includes a huge percentage of upland woods from Nova Scotia to northern Florida, west to Wisconsin, Illinois, Missouri, Oklahoma, and east Texas, then your experience might be like my own. We've planted a few beeches near one another in what is now still a sunny part of our garden. It's our intention they'll grow upright trunks with branches spreading from the periphery of the group to eventually provide this section of the property with high-quality shade. The trees are from seed of local provenance, which may account for why they've proved so vigorous and easy to transplant. In less than five years, they've grown five to ten feet tall, and, with no

TOP Woodland Joe-pye weed, *Eupatorium purpureum*, blooms six feet tall in mid August in a mature woodlands at Longwood Gardens.

BOTTOM White snakeroot, *Eupatorium rugosum*, flowers in late September under river birch, *Betula nigra*. By bloom time, the foliage of this species is nearly always marked by leaf miners, which are disfiguring but have little effect on plant health or vigor.

supplemental watering after the year they were transplanted, have survived a one-hundred-year summer drought unfazed.

Trees of northern provenance are cold hardy to zone 4, and those from southern extremes have considerable heat tolerance, often far superior to that of the ubiquitous and overplanted European beech, *Fagus sylvatica*. American beech

A nearly solid stand of American beech, *Fagus grandifolia*, is magnificent in late-February light at the Arnold Arboretum in Massachusetts. Beeches spread readily by seed, and they also increase by suckers arising from the extensive root systems of mature trees. Look closely in most large beech stands and you'll note that many of the smaller trees are not seedlings but root suckers.

typically grows fifty to seventy feet tall but can top one hundred feet in ideal conditions. If trees grow close together, as they often do, they become narrow and upright, with relatively few lower branches. Open-grown beeches are often as wide-spreading as they are tall.

Among the most beautiful aspects of beeches are their horizontal branching and their strong light-seeking (phototropic) tendency which is responsible for the graceful sweep of branches over the edges of innumerable rivers and streams. Beech nuts, produced each year in profusion, are among the most important food sources for woodland wildlife from birds to mammals.

American beech is extremely shallow rooted, and the roots are very sensitive to compaction by foot or vehicle traffic. The roots are highly moisture competitive, and few plants survive readily under ancient beeches, with the frequent exception of mosses, the more drought-tolerant ferns, and a number of flowering spring ephemerals.

LEFT, TOP TO BOTTOM The epithet *grandifolia* is perfectly descriptive of American beech, which is worth watching year-round just for the pageantry of its foliage. The honey-eyed green hues of new beech leaves are truly among spring's greatest color moments. The golden autumn foliage is alive with a sophisticated brilliance full of warmth and clarity. The light display continues through winter as dry leaves remain suspended from new growth, crisp, papery, and luminous against woodland shadows. On occasion, their low rattle paints an aural portrait of the winter wind.

Ferns

Woodland ferns are a wondrously diverse group, too numerous to afford thorough coverage in a book of this scope. They are grouped here under a single heading to provide an overview of their potential in the woodland garden, and to make it easy to compare the attributes of many I believe are among the most beautiful and widely adapted.

Ferns native to North American deciduous forests range in size from diminutive types that lie flat against the substrate to shrub-sized species three to six feet tall. Typically fine textured, they exquisitely complement the broad leaves of deciduous shrubs and flowering herbs. The look of all ferns, even evergreens, changes radically with the revolving seasons, and the unfurling of spring fronds is among the forest floor's most dramatic events. Deciduous ferns are responsible for some of the unique and appealing autumn and winter foliage colors in the woodland.

Including running forms and clumpers, deciduous types and evergreens, ferns are essential to the textural and seasonal beauty of the woodland garden, in designs both formal and informal. In early October, interrupted fern, *Osmunda claytoniana*, holds the foreground while Christmas fern, *Polystichum acrostichoides*, covers a creek bend in the Ward garden in northern Delaware.

The majority of ferns spread by rhizomes, sometimes forming vast colonies. Others are distinct clump formers. As a group, they are a cold-hardy lot, with a great many reliable into zone 3, though some southern species are more tender. Ferns transplant readily in spring or fall and are generally easy to grow if provided well-drained, moist organic soil and a shaded situation. Typically native on slightly acid soils, most ferns are tolerant of pH ranging from acid to near neutral, though some species from specialized habitats are more specific in their needs. For example, the cliff brakes, *Pellaea* species, typically found on limestone outcrops, require somewhat alkaline soils for healthy growth. At the other extreme, the chain ferns, *Woodwardia* species, native to wet acid swamps and bogs, are demanding of a wet, highly acid site. Though it may be possible to alter growing conditions in a garden to accommodate such specialized types, it is usually easier and more satisfying to devote your efforts to the many beautiful, broadly adapted ferns, which are certain to become favorite, enduring elements in your landscape.

If you're new to woodland ferns, cinnamon fern, *Osmunda cinnamonea*, is a fine one to begin with, since it offers so much over the seasons and is undemanding and adaptable. At home we chose cinnamon ferns to provide important focal points in one of our most appreciated views: from the bathroom window. Native to moist shaded habitats from Labrador to Minnesota and south to Florida, Texas, and New Mexico, this clump-former is fully deciduous. Though all ferns reproduce by spores, some have separate sterile and fertile fronds, and cinnamon fern is in this group. It is among the first ferns to begin new growth in spring, and first to arise are the fertile fronds, felty-white with fine hairs (ABOVE LEFT). Over the next three weeks, these will unfurl and become the bright cinnamon-colored stalks for which the plant is named. The changes in a short period of time can be startling, as these images from May 10 (FAR LEFT) and May 13 illustrate (LEFT). The cinnamon fertile fronds are extraordinarily translucent, glowing when side-lit in May and complementing the textures and colors of sweetshrub, *Calycanthus floridus* 'Edith Wilder' (page 253 TOP

LEFT). By mid October, the fertile fronds have folded and the sterile fronds have begun turning deep gold (TOP RIGHT). Their hue will darken to amber by autumn's end. *Osmunda* belongs in the royal fern family, Osmundaceae.

Interrupted fern, *Osmunda claytoniana*, ranges from Ontario to Minnesota and south to Georgia, and though frequently found in moist conditions, is slightly more comfortable in dry situations than cinnamon fern. It is much like cinnamon fern except its fronds are all leafy, interrupted in the middle by a fertile, frond-bearing section (ABOVE). It often occurs in large groups, growing three to four feet tall, as here in Maine in late July (RIGHT).

Of the three *Osmunda* species, royal fern, *Osmunda regalis*, is most often associated with moist to wet environments, occurring naturally from Newfoundland to Saskatchewan, south to Florida and Texas. It prefers somewhat acid soil and will grow well in moderately moist soil if provided sufficient shade. It is at its best at water's edge, as seen in late July in a private New England garden (ABOVE) and growing in the wild among river rocks in Virginia in mid October (ABOVE RIGHT), when its fall color is nearing peak.

Christmas fern, *Polystichum acrostichoides*, in the wood fern family, Dryopteridaceae, offers no autumn color, but it is one of the sturdiest and most widely adapted evergreen ferns, and is a year-round delight. Native from Nova Scotia to Wisconsin and south to Florida and Texas, it is a distinct clump former. Fiddleheads unfurl in spring (TOP LEFT), expanding into new fronds that are first quite upright above foliage from the previous season (LEFT), gradually relaxing as summer goes by. Christmas fern is exceptionally shade tolerant and will grow underneath shrubs or in the summer shade of other herbs. As the architecture of the woodland canopy becomes apparent again with the autumn thinning of leaves, and most herbaceous plants begin to wither with winter's approach, the evergreen presence of Christmas fern is accentuated in the ground layer. Often occurring naturally on slopes, as seen in this view of a shaded roadbank in northern Delaware (OPPOSITE BOTTOM RIGHT), Christmas fern can be very useful in woodland soil stabilization.

ABOVE Evergreen but strongly rhizomatous, common polypody fern, *Polypodium virginianum*, is most often found growing in thin layers of decaying organic matter atop rocks and between tree roots, as here in mid October in western Pennsylvania. It is one of the most cold-hardy ferns, occurring from the Yukon south to Alabama and Arkansas. Its close relative, *Polypodium polypodioides*, is more southern in distribution, growing naturally from Maryland to Illinois and south to Texas. It is called resurrection fern for its ability to coil and uncoil in response to alternating periods of drought and moisture. *Polypodium* belongs in the polypody family, Polypodiaceae.

The delicacy of two native maidenhair ferns, *Adiantum* species, belies their durability. Members of the maidenhair family, Adiantaceae, both are tough, long-lived plants if provided proper conditions. Northern maidenhair fern, *Adiantum pedatum*, prefers soils near neutral or only slightly alkaline, and occurs natively from Alaska to Newfoundland, south to California and Georgia. It is often seen on sloping ground, as in this photograph from a Virginia woodlands where the graceful fronds overtop the broad straplike foliage of plantain-leaved sedge, *Carex plantaginea* (LEFT). Though much less cold hardy, reliable only into zone 7, southern maidenhair fern, *Adiantum capillus-veneris*, grows lush and full if provided moist neutral to slightly alkaline conditions, as here growing over limestone at the Birmingham Botanical Gardens in Alabama (RIGHT). It is native to moist calcareous rocks and banks from Virginia south into the tropics.

Known as wood ferns or shield ferns, the *Dryopteris* species, also in the family Dryopteridaceae, include some of the finest ferns for woodland gardens. They are a diverse group, including deciduous and evergreen types, and their identification is often complicated by frequent hybridization. The majority are distinct clump formers. Among the evergreens, *Dryopteris intermedia* is called fancy wood fern for the fine-cut lacy quality of its rich green fronds (TOP). It is native to moist woods and swamps from Newfoundland to Georgia and west to Arkansas and Minnesota. One of the most distinctive species is the marginal wood fern, *Dryopteris marginalis*, which has blue-green fronds. Native from Ontario to Newfoundland and south to Oklahoma and Georgia, its color varies with provenance, and is sometimes intensely blue as seen in this Alabama plant (BOTTOM). This genus includes a giant among deciduous forest species, *Dryopteris goldiana*, Goldie's wood fern, which easily grows six feet tall in rich, moist soil.

The spreading rate of different running ferns varies from polite to overly rambunctious. Some such as sensitive fern, *Onoclea sensibilis*, in the wood fern family, Dryopteridaceae, and bracken fern, *Pteridium aquilinum*, in the bracken family, Dennstaedtiaceae, are almost impossible to keep within defined boundaries, but with careful siting, even the most enthusiastic types can play an important role in the woodland garden.

Wide-ranging in moist woods, meadows, and streambanks, lady fern, *Athyrium filix-femina*, in the cliff fern family, Woodsiaceae, is a slow, creeping deciduous species growing two to three feet tall (TOP). The stems (called "stipes") of its new fronds are often attractively red or wine-tinted. Lady fern is easily managed in the garden and can serve as a durable ground cover, as here at Ashland Hollow in northern Delaware in early June (BOTTOM).

Ostrich fern, *Matteuccia struthiopteris*, another member of the cliff fern family, is circumboreal in distribution. In North America it is found in swamps and moist woods, typically in near-neutral soils, from Canada south to Virginia. It is an aggressive runner, with long-creeping thick black rhizomes, and can be an ideal choice for covering a large area, especially one with poorly drained soil. Dry conditions will check its spread. It is deciduous, growing three to six feet tall, and its fronds are beautiful from the time they open (ABOVE) and through summer (TOP LEFT) as their delicate patterns catch the light. The foliage often becomes tired-looking by autumn, and it has no significant fall color.

New York fern, *Thelypteris noveboracensis*, another creeping deciduous species, is less aggressive and is well adapted to the dry shade common underneath deciduous trees including maple, beech, and birch. It is fairly fine textured (OPPOSITE TOP RIGHT) and can be used effectively as a ground cover and stabilizer in densely shaded sloping (ABOVE). Its close relative, the broad beech fern, *Phe-gopteris hexagonoptera* [synonym *Thelypteris hexagonoptera*], is quite different in appearance, with fronds that are nearly triangular (OPPOSITE BOTTOM RIGHT). Though appearing more delicate, it spreads modestly by underground rhizomes and can form large patches even in dense shade. Both genera belong to the marsh fern family, Thelypteridaceae.

Hay-scented fern, *Dennstaedtia punctilobula*, in the bracken family, Dennstaedtiaceae, is a strongly running species most often found in open woods and clearings, and on difficult, rocky slopes from Canada south to Georgia, Alabama, and Arkansas. Though it can be difficult to manage in rich, moist organic soils, it is a superb choice for tough wood-land sites that tend toward summer drought. It is worth considering for its autumn color alone, which varies from light cream (RIGHT) to bright yellow or deep amber (ABOVE), depending upon light conditions and moisture.

Fothergilla

WITCH ALDER

HAMAMELIDACEAE, WITCH HAZEL FAMILY

Fothergillas are close relatives of witch hazel, *Hamamelis*, and their foliage is very similar in appearance until fall, when fothergillas often turn intense shades of red, scarlet, and orange that are truly unsurpassed. Though they've become readily available through nursery propagation, the two North American fothergilla species are rare in the wild. The larger of the two, *Fothergilla major*, is a mountain species, found only in dry woods and openings in North Carolina, Tennessee, Georgia, and Alabama. Cold hardy to zone 4, it can grow ten feet tall as a rounded, multistemmed shrub. Dwarf fothergilla, *Fothergilla gardenii*, also called dwarf witch alder, is uncommon but occurs with greater frequency, typically in savannas and low boggy areas called "pocosins," from North Carolina into northern Florida and west to Mississippi. It is more of a coastal plain species, which explains its lesser cold hardiness (zone 5), and it rarely grows more than three feet tall.

Though the majority of plants in cultivation and in horticultural literature have been labeled *Fothergilla gardenii*, this identification is frequently suspect. Clonal selections including 'Blue Mist' and 'Jane Platt' are good representatives of this diminutive species, but many garden plants are more typical of *Fothergilla major*. Some are likely hybrids between the two species. Unfortunately, though chromosome numbers differ between the two species, there are no significant visual characteristics which can be relied upon for positive identification and differentiation.

TOP LEFT *Fothergilla gardenii* becomes a kaleidoscope of colors by early November in our Pennsylvania garden. The autumn color typically begins gold and yellow and gradually deepens to red and bronze hues. We can count on nearly two months of color in October and November each year.

CENTER LEFT Growing only three feet tall without any pruning, plants in the foreground at the Morris Arboretum in Pennsylvania are true representatives of the diminutive stature of *Fothergilla gardenii*. This particular form has been named and propagated as the clonal cultivar 'Blue Mist'. Plants in the background represent *Fothergilla major*.

BOTTOM LEFT Foliage of *Fothergilla gardenii* 'Blue Mist' is glaucous-blue, here in mid May. Fall color on this cultivar and other blue-leaved forms in general is never as vibrant as that of green-leaved types. Though 'Blue Mist' is valuable for its compact size, it is somewhat tender and not at all drought tolerant.

ABOVE Occurring in April or early May, usually before the leaves, the puffy white flowers of fothergillas lack petals: they are mostly comprised of clusters of stamens with long white filaments. The shrubs shown here represent forms that are commonly sold as *Fothergilla gardenii*, and though they may belong to this species, they are capable of growing nearly ten feet tall—I know from experience—which is more characteristic of *Fothergilla major*. Whatever they are, their branching habit makes it easy to keep them pruned gracefully to a height of four to five feet, which is often the proper scale for plantings along walks and in other intimate spaces. Pruning should be done just after flowering, or bloom buds for the following year will be lost.

Fraxinus

ASH

OLEACEAE, OLIVE FAMILY

Though green ash, *Fraxinus pennsylvanica*, is more cold hardy, to zone 3, and very widely adaptable, it is particularly prone to storm damage, and its form and fall color are inferior to the form and fall color of white ash, *Fraxinus americana*, which is only hardy to zone 4. White ash easily grows sixty to seventy feet tall and can exceed one hundred feet. Native from Nova Scotia west to Minnesota and south to Texas and Florida, it is easy to transplant and reasonably adapted to a wide range of soil and moisture conditions.

TOP In late October, furrows of white ash, *Fraxinus americana*, are green with lichens. The bark patterns of big trees can contribute boldly to the texture of the woodland garden.

BOTTOM White ash may turn gold in fall, but it characteristically becomes a rich mix of pink-red and bronze-purple tones. Ash leafs out late in spring and drops its leaves early in autumn.

TOP Flowering in mid June this patch of *Galax urceolata* has survived without care for nearly half a century in Elizabeth White's garden on New Jersey's coastal plain, proving that acid, sharply drained soil is more critical than cool summer nights. Galax has an amazing capacity to flower in dense shade as well as sunny spots.

BOTTOM The glossy round leaves of *Galax urceolata* are a rich wine color, especially where they're exposed to sunlight, in the North Carolina mountains in mid February.

Galax

DIAPENSIACEAE, DIAPENSIA FAMILY

Given sharp drainage and acid conditions, *Galax urceolata* can form a dense, enduring carpet of extraordinarily glossy round leaves. It is native to both moist and dry woods, mostly in the mountains from Maryland south to Alabama but also on the coastal plain in North Carolina and Virginia. Anyone who has walked Appalachian trails knows galax as a constant companion, appealing in all seasons. It is cold hardy to zone 4.

Gentiana

GENTIAN
GENTIANACEAE, GENTIAN FAMILY

The rich blue and blue-purple hues of gentians are always a delight to come upon in the autumn landscape. The common American woodland species are "bottle" types, meaning they have flowers with petals closed at the top. Container production of native wildflowers has resulted in ready availability of gentians, which transplant easily from a pot but resent disturbance once established in the ground. Among the best are the meadow gentian, *Gentiana clausa*, hardy to zone 3 and native to woods, meadows, and thickets from Maine to Ohio and south in the mountains, and the very similar prairie gentian, *Gentiana andrewsii*, which has a slightly more western distribution and is cold hardy to zone 5.

Geranium

WILD GERANIUM, CRANESBILL
GERANIACEAE, GERANIUM FAMILY

The best of the perennial wild geraniums, *Geranium maculatum*, is often criticized for its capacity to self-sow, but this characteristic can be of good use in the woodland garden, especially in relaxed designs. Cold hardy into zone 3, wild geranium grows from a stout, almost woody rhizome and is common in woods from Maine to Georgia and west to Oklahoma. Attractive even when not in bloom, *Geranium maculatum* is easily grown in a wide range of soil, moisture, and light conditions.

Prairie gentian, *Gentiana andrewsii*, flowers at a woodland edge at Mount Cuba Center, Delaware, in mid October.

Blooming in early May, this dark-flowered form of wild geranium, *Geranium maculatum*, comes from a population in the Virginia mountains. Flowers range from such dark purple-pinks to light lavender or snow white.

Gillenia

BOWMAN'S ROOT, INDIAN PHYSIC
ROSACEAE, BUTTERCUP FAMILY

Depending upon your nomenclatural bias, the two American *Gillenia* species may belong in the genus *Porteranthus*. By whichever name, they are garden-worthy plants, particularly the larger of the two, bowman's root, *Gillenia trifoliata*. Both are cold hardy to zone 4.

Also known as Indian physic for its emetic properties, *Gillenia trifoliata* is native to both moist and dry woods from Ontario south through Delaware, North Carolina, and Georgia and west to Missouri. I've admired it innumerable summers driving and hiking through the Virginia and West Virginia mountains, where it frequently occurs in large drifts along roadsides and sunny edges, blooming brightly in June. It has proved very easy to grow in the woodland garden, flowering well in shady spots and magnificently at sunnier edges, and is quite drought tolerant once established.

Western Indian physic, *Gillenia stipulata*, is smaller and finer textured, with deeply cut leaves. It is nowhere near as splendid in flower.

TOP Flowering in mid June in the Virginia mountains, this drift of bowman's root, *Gillenia trifoliata*, is growing in dry, rocky soil.

BOTTOM Pink suffused when first opening, the starlike flowers of bowman's root are held above the leaves on fine dark stems. In most years, the foliage turns dark purple-bronze mixed with orange and red by late October.

Grasses, Sedges, and Wood-rushes

Grasses and grasslike plants make up another vast group that is usually present though not often prominent in deciduous woodlands. They are grouped here for easier comparison.

True grasses, members of the Poaceae or grass family, are mostly plants of sunny environments. Though uncommon in shaded woodland interiors, there are a few showy, shade-tolerant species specially worthy of mention.

Wild oats, *Chasmanthium latifolium*, is so tough it is often grown in full sun in traditional borders, but it is a native of wooded slopes, moist thickets, and river bottoms, and tolerant of considerable shade. Occurring from New Jersey and Pennsylvania south to Texas, it is cold hardy through zone 5.

Crinkled hair grass, *Deschampsia flexuosa*, occurs in dry woods and clearings from Canada south to Oklahoma and Georgia, and is delightful in mass, when its delicate flower and seed heads create a soft, billowy effect. It is cold hardy to zone 4.

Bottlebrush grass, *Hystrix patula*, is native to moist or rocky woods from Nova Scotia to North Dakota and south to Georgia and Arkansas. Cold hardy to zone 4, it grows three feet tall in moist shade and typically one to two feet tall if conditions are dry, and I've admired it in both situations. I've seen it in late July along partly sunny, moist edges of the Blue Ridge Parkway, flowering with tall bellflower, *Campanula americana*, and various *Monarda* species. I've also observed it in seed in mid October on an extremely dry slope in West Virginia, growing be-

TOP LEFT Wild oats, *Chasmanthium latifolium*, can grow in dry shade under shallow-rooted trees. Exquisite in detail, it leans affectionately against the bark of river birch, *Betula nigra* 'Heritage', in late August.

CENTER LEFT In late October, the dried seed heads of wild oats stand out against the deep autumn colors of *Fothergilla gardenii*.

BOTTOM LEFT Bottlebrush grass, *Hystrix patula*, mixes with tall bellflower, *Campanula americana*, along the Blue Ridge Parkway in late July.

OPPOSITE LEFT Prairie dropseed, *Sporobolus heterolepis*, catches the early November light in a transitional area in our garden, off the north side of small beeches, *Fagus grandifolia*, and pawpaws, *Asimina triloba*.

OPPOSITE TOP RIGHT Pennsylvania sedge, *Carex pensylvanica*, gracefully clothes the bank lining a woodland path in the Smoky Mountains of North Carolina in July.

OPPOSITE BOTTOM RIGHT Plantain-leaved sedge, *Carex plantaginea*, sweeps around a boulder in late July in the Gentling garden, in Asheville, North Carolina.

neath hickories, *Carya glabra*, and alongside fragrant sumac, *Rhus aromatica*, both of which were in glorious fall color. Bottlebrush grass is especially easy to grow from seed.

Cold hardy to zone 4, prairie dropseed, *Sporobolus heterolepis*, is primarily a plant of open prairies but also grows in partly shaded savanna habitats. It will tolerate partial shade in the woodland garden and can be useful at edges and in transition areas. Others similarly useful are the plume grasses, *Saccharum* species, and to lesser extent, switch grass, *Panicum virgatum*.

The sedge family, Cyperaceae, includes a much greater number of shade species, mostly belonging to the genus *Carex*, the sedges. Pennsylvania sedge, *Carex pensylvanica*, is easy to overlook when it occurs as a few scattered plants, but it is capable of growing as a dense, woodland lawn and can be quite impressive when it does. It is native to woods and thickets across North America, and is cold hardy to zone 4.

Many sedges such as *Carex stricta*, the tussock sedge, are plants of moist to wet woodland habitats. Its beauty is primarily in its grassy foliage, which is a perfect foil for broad-leaved companions such as skunk cabbage, *Symplocarpus foetidus*. A few other moist-habitat sedges have interesting seed heads, including Gray's sedge, *Carex grayi*; hop sedge, *Carex lupulina*; and fringed sedge, *Carex crinita*. Among the most ornamental woodland sedges are species with broad,

ABOVE New foliage of tussock sedge, *Carex stricta*, rises above skirts of last year's leaves in early May in a wet Delaware woodlands.

TOP LEFT One of a number of attractive, broad-leaved woodland sedges, *Carex flaccosperma*, adds its blue-green hues to a bed of fallen pawpaw leaves, *Asimina triloba*, in early November.

CENTER LEFT The glaucous-blue leaves of

silver sedge, *Carex platyphylla*, are typically one inch wide.

BOTTOM LEFT Fraser's sedge, *Cymophyllus fraseri*, flowers in late April along a trail in North Carolina's Smoky Mountains. Restricted to rich mountain woods from southern Pennsylvania, Virginia, and West Virginia into the Carolinas and Tennessee, this beautiful sedge is demanding of sharp drainage, cool nights, and steady moisture.

straplike leaves, including plantain-leaved sedge, *Carex plantaginea*; silver sedge, *Carex platyphylla*; and *Carex flaccosperma*.

Fraser's sedge, which is unique enough to be placed in its own genus as *Cymophyllus fraseri*, is perhaps the showiest woodland sedge, with conspicuous white flowers and glossy evergreen leaves.

Wood-rushes, *Luzula* species, in the rush family, Juncaceae, are subtle but interesting shade denizens worthy of further consideration in the woodland garden. They are often found on woodland slopes and sometimes turn attractive bronze-purple tones during fall and winter. Hairy wood-rush, *Luzula acuminata*, and *Luzula multiflora*, are two that are wide-ranging and easy to grow.

RIGHT I admired many autumn and winter sunsets fading against the silhouette of this female Kentucky coffee tree, *Gymnocladus dioica*, planted near my former Longwood Gardens office, seen here in mid January.

FAR RIGHT The huge, compound leaves of Kentucky coffee tree catch the early June light and shade the porch of the Peirce–du Pont House at Longwood Gardens. This tough, tall-growing tree is long lived and trouble-free.

BOTTOM RIGHT Tough enough for wooded city gardens, Kentucky coffee tree turns bright gold at the Delaware Center for Horticulture in urban Wilmington in October. Photo by Dan Benarcik.

Gymnocladus
KENTUCKY COFFEE TREE
CAESALPINIACEAE, CAESALPINIA FAMILY

Kentucky coffee, *Gymnocladus dioica*, is a large, fast-growing, graceful tree that casts a fine shade and is virtually free from pests or diseases. Its main drawback is that female trees produce large woody pods filled with incredibly sticky pulp, and these can be messy if crushed against pavement. It is often possible to purchase male trees, but fruiting trees have their own appeal in the right situations. Native to rich, moist woods from New York to Minnesota and south to Tennessee and Oklahoma, Kentucky coffee tree is cold hardy into zone 3 and adaptable to a wide range of soil and moisture conditions. The common name refers to its use in the Colonial period as a coffee substitute.

Halesia
SILVERBELL
STYRACACEAE, SNOWBELL FAMILY

I've known silverbells since I was a child. Mountain silverbells, *Halesia tetraptera* var. *monticola*, were part of the original plantings designed by the Olmsted brothers for Grover Cleveland Park in northern New Jersey. They'd thrived for nearly forty years by the time my brother and I were playing beneath them in the late fifties and early sixties. Many had become forest-sized trees, and seedlings from these had filled countless niches in the park, lining a few paths and forming small groves. While I vaguely recall the ground being carpeted each April and May with delicate white bells, I remember being most intrigued by the four-winged seeds (fruits, in truth), which felt so comfortable in the hand, fingers fitting between the wings. They turned from green to amber brown with the passing of summer, and we picked them at various stages or collected them, fallen from the ground, hoarding them and bartering with them. They were literally the currency of our youth. Years later, living within the limits of the deciduous forest, how could I not have this tree in my garden?

I eventually met mountain silverbells in the Smoky Mountains of Tennessee and North Carolina, where the plentiful rainfall allows them to attain a height of more than eighty feet and girth exceeding four feet. The species epithet *tetraptera* literally means "four (*tetra*) wing (*ptera*)," and silverbells with four-winged fruits are native from Virginia to Illinois and south to Texas and Florida, but they're not all the same. The mountain giants found in the heart of the Appalachians were named *Halesia monticola*, and middle-sized trees that occur at lower elevations from Virginia to Florida were called Carolina silverbell, *Halesia carolina*. As botanists have concluded there are no clear lines distinguishing these types, the name *Halesia tetraptera* has been adopted as the single name describing a broad-ranging, variable species, with the mountain silverbell recognized only as a botanical variety, *Halesia tetraptera* var. *monticola*. By a confusing quirk of nomenclatural fate, the scientific name *Halesia carolina* has now been accepted as the correct name for the rare, small-flowered silverbell of riverbanks and alluvial woods in South Carolina, Georgia, Florida, and Alabama. This species is rarely cultivated.

From a garden perspective, variations in silverbells can be significant. The largest mountain types are spectacular when flowering and naturally tend toward single-stemmed growth. Mid-sized types are still quite dramatic in bloom, especially when grown as multistemmed trees, which is frequently their natural form. They will often sprout from the base even when aged, and this tendency can be used to renew and maintain trees in modest scale. I long marveled at two multistemmed silverbells planted off the east side of Longwood Gardens Outdoor Theater. Though they'd been there seventy years or more, they had grown barely twenty feet tall, with equal spread. Looking at them closely, each was comprised of a ring of trunks that had expanded over the decades as individual stems died back or were removed. At the center, where the original trunk grew, only a patch of earth remained. A deliberate garden strategy that allows such a succession of stems will result in a modest-sized tree that is virtually immortal.

Silverbells are among the most disease- and pest-free flowering trees of the deciduous forest. They're quite tolerant of dry shade once established and are at home on a wide range of soil types except those with high pH, which may cause the leaves to be somewhat chlorotic. All silverbells begin flowering when they are very young—as early as third-year seedlings—and their habit of flowering before the leaves provides uncommon drama in the spring garden. Pink-flowered forms occur, and some are offered as named cultivars, but they're often muddy colored and have never pleased my eye as much as the typical snow white. Although they hold their own against any spring-flowering tree, silverbells have something to offer every season. Their summer foliage is clean and bright green, and the trunks are distinctively striped silver gray. The autumn foliage reliably turns golden yellow, and the bare branches hung with winged fruits make striking silhouettes against the winter sky.

The two-winged silverbells, *Halesia diptera* (from *di* meaning "two" and *ptera* meaning "wing"), are quite distinct and equally garden-worthy. This species grows from Ohio south to Florida but is much more common in the southern part

TOP Seen here in mid November, the four-winged fruits of silverbell, *Halesia tetraptera*, often remain suspended from branches well into winter.

ABOVE Although pink-flowered forms sometimes are found among silverbells, most are not a pleasing color. The form shown here, however, is an exception.

LEFT The blooming of silverbell, *Halesia tetraptera*, overlaps with pinkshell azalea, *Rhododendron vaseyi*, in early May in our Pennsylvania garden.

of its range. It is not as shade tolerant as *Halesia tetraptera* and will have a neater habit if provided more sunlight. Though *Halesia diptera* is cold hardy into zone 4, its likely mature height increases from twenty-five to nearly fifty feet in the southern states. The fruits are flat affairs with only two wings, and though the flowers are pendent and still bell-like, the petals are mostly separate, unlike the fused petals of four-winged silverbells. I'm fond of the flowers when they're in bud stage, before the petals separate; the branches look like they're hung with tiny white eggs. Most spectacular is the large-flowered two-winged silverbell, *Halesia diptera* var. *magniflora*, which produces a profusion of blossoms, each more than one inch across. In full bloom, this tree is unquestionably the world's showiest member of its family, which includes the Asian snowdrop trees, *Styrax* species. I've enjoyed *Halesia diptera* var. *magniflora* interplanted with *Halesia tetraptera* in our home garden. It blooms a week or two later, and between the two species, we have silverbells blooming for most of a month in April to May.

TOP LEFT A magnificent large-flowered, two-winged silverbell, *Halesia diptera* var. *magniflora*, blooms in mid May at the Henry Foundation in Gladwyne, Pennsylvania.

BOTTOM LEFT Petals of *Halesia diptera* var. *magniflora* are separate, easily distinguishing the flowers of this species from the fused bell-like flowers of *Halesia tetraptera* and *Halesia carolina*.

BELOW *Halesia diptera* var. *magniflora* typically turns gold in autumn, shown here in late October in our Pennsylvania garden.

Hamamelis

WITCH HAZEL

HAMAMELIDACEAE, WITCH HAZEL FAMILY

The most memorable individual witch hazel I've seen was growing beside a mountain stream near Seneca Rocks in the West Virginia mountains. Growing up and over a ring of huge boulders that naturally formed a space as big as an average dining room, the witch hazel's branches stretched horizontally more than fifteen feet, literally putting a roof on the room. Whenever I think of witch hazel, I'm reminded of its capacity to grow treelike in time and of its sometimes impressive spread.

My West Virginia plant was autumn witch hazel, *Hamamelis virginiana*, the more common of the two North American species, which is native to moist and dry, often rocky woods from Quebec to Minnesota and south to Texas and Florida. It is often classed as a shrub since it grows multistemmed, but has the capacity to exceed thirty feet in height, which is treelike by my book. Its spreading vase shape is distinctive and attractive when growing singly or in a group. I've seen a number of abandoned quarry sites colonized by witch hazels to beautiful effect. I've not yet had the opportunity to create a garden room reminiscent of the naturally occurring one at Seneca Rocks, but I've used multiple autumn witch

TOP Nearly twenty feet tall along the banks of White Clay Creek in northern Delaware, an autumn witch hazel, *Hamamelis virginiana*, is bright clear gold in mid October.

ABOVE Nearly one inch across, the flowers of autumn witch hazel brighten bare stems in mid October in West Virginia.

LEFT Autumn witch hazel is a superb small tree for spaces close to the house, as here in the Lennihan garden in northern Delaware in early November.

hazels over a steep rocky grotto on a client's property, where the branches have ample room to drape and spread.

Of course, the unique and appealing attribute of autumn witch hazel is its timing—what other woody plant is in full bloom in October and November? Though individual plants vary, with some dropping their leaves before flowering and others blooming with the leaves, the display is always a delight. *Hamamelis virginiana* is easy to transplant when young, but difficult once it has attained size. It is cold hardy to zone 3 and adapted to a wide range of soil, moisture, and light conditions. When produced naturally, witch hazel extract is distilled from the bark of this plant.

The second species, Ozark witch hazel, *Hamamelis vernalis*, is native to Missouri, Arkansas, Oklahoma, and Texas. Hardy to zone 4, it is also known as vernal witch hazel due to its late winter to early spring flowering. Its flowers are considerably smaller than those of autumn witch hazel, rarely more than three-quarters inch across, with color varying from amber red to yellow.

Heuchera

ALUMROOT
SAXIFRAGACEAE, SAXIFRAGE FAMILY

It is a recent phenomenon that common alumroot, *Heuchera americana*, has found favor in American gardens. Its changing fortune can be traced to nursery growers paying closer attention to the natural diversity within the species.

The common form of this durable, easy-to-grow native has unremarkable solid green leaves and green flowers that are so slight they are barely noticeable. The species is wide-ranging, occurring on loamy, often calcium-rich wooded slopes from Connecticut to Georgia and west to Michigan and Oklahoma. In some parts of its range, particularly in the Smoky Mountains of North Carolina and Tennessee, the leaves are richly and dramatically marked with silver, gray-green, and bronze-purple.

In the late 1980s Dale Hendricks of North Creek Nurseries, a wholesale plug supplier, became aware of this variation and began producing plants from seed of these populations. Instead of choosing a single variant and propagating it asexually to produce identical plants, Dale deliberately offered seedlings in the belief they were all attractive and that the variation from one seedling to the next was part of the intrigue and interest of natural genetic diversity. 'Dale's Strain', as it came to be known, introduced countless gardeners to a previously ignored species and has resulted indirectly in a raft of named, asexual cultivated varieties offered by other nurseries, each representing variations on the original theme. 'Garnet', selected at Mount Cuba Center in Delaware, was one of the first cultivars marked with deep garnet-bronze tones.

Heucheras hybridize readily, often by accident. Richly purple-toned 'Montrose Ruby' resulted from an inadvertent cross of 'Dale's Strain' and 'Palace Purple' at the now-defunct Montrose Nursery.

In the garden, the clonal cultivars can be used to dramatic effect when planted in large groupings, sweeps, and masses; however, these plantings require some vigilance, since the hybridizing heucheras are likely to blur the edges of such formality with naturally occurring seedlings. In our Pennsylvania garden, we've grown a number of seedlings and cultivars, and have come to delight in the chance seedlings that add to our landscape's dynamic diversity. On more than one occasion, a garden visitor has asked "What is the cultivar name?" of one of these seedlings. I'm always tempted to say it is simply "Serendipity."

Botanists recognize many species of *Heuchera* growing within the limits of the deciduous forest, but they've not been clear about distinguishing one I believe is among the very finest for gardening purposes. I first visited the Birmingham Botanical Gardens in Alabama a number of years ago and was introduced to plants labeled *Heuchera macrorhiza*, growing in the woodland wildflower garden.

TOP RIGHT Leaves of alumroot, *Heuchera americana*, are typically solid green, as seen in a plant from a wild population in northern Delaware. This wide-ranging species is cold hardy into zone 3 and is easy to grow in light to dense shade on a variety of soils. It grows well on sloping ground and is tolerant of dry shade but looks best when the soil remains moist.

CENTER RIGHT Strongly marked with silver and gray, a seedling of *Heuchera americana* 'Dale's Strain' stands out dramatically from the yellow-green new foliage of white wood aster, *Aster divaricatus*, in our garden in early May. This seed cultivar represents some of

the beautiful diversity in alumroot's leaf patterning. In zones 6 and warmer, the lower leaves remain in good condition through winter, typically darkening and acquiring purple-bronze tones which provide a contrasting background for newly emerging spring foliage.

BOTTOM RIGHT This *Heuchera* seedling in our garden is typical of the accidental progeny of other alumroots growing nearby, including *Heuchera americana* from Smoky Mountains provenance, 'Garnet', and 'Montrose Ruby'. Unabashed botanists typically refer to such readily hybridizing plants as promiscuous, with no slight intended.

Growing on flat ground and perched in thin soil atop rock outcrops, these plants had large, hairy leaves and a mature spread of nearly three feet. Most distinctively, they formed large almost-woody rhizomes that spread at surface level, and I later learned they bloom, dramatically, in autumn. Though pioneering southern botanist John Kunkel Small recognized this particular heuchera as a distinct species, modern thinking has lumped these plants with *Heuchera villosa*, which, while similar in its hairiness, lacks the large surface rhizomes, the huge size and

TOP LEFT Autumn alumroot, *Heuchera macrorhiza* [synonym *Heuchera villosa* var. *macrorhiza*], grows from a distinctive rootstock with creeping one-inch diameter rhizomes that spread just below the soil surface. It has exceptionally hairy leaves which are typically light yellow-green in spring, turning darker over summer and fall.

CENTER LEFT Though autumn alumroot grows easily from seed, it also is easy to propagate by removing and transplanting rhizome sections in spring. It is the latest eastern alumroot to bloom, and one of the few with showy flowers, as seen in this early November image from our Pennsylvania garden.

BOTTOM LEFT The purple-leaved form of *Heuchera villosa*, sometimes called 'Atropurpurea', is imaginatively mixed with autumn alumroot and *Fothergilla gardenii* 'Blue Mist' in this container in the entry plaza of Peirce's Woods at Longwood Gardens in early June.

BELOW Maple-leafed alumroot, *Heuchera villosa*, grows naturally from a rock face in North Carolina, flowering in this late-July photograph. This very variable species is typically hairy leaved and occurs on moist, shaded cliffs and ledges, mostly in the mountains from Virginia and West Virginia south to South Carolina and Tennessee and west into the Ozarks.

bold texture, and the fall blooming habit. The beauty and utility of the form I saw in Birmingham have since been recognized, and the plants are variously offered as *Heuchera villosa* or sometimes with the cultivar name 'Autumn Bride' attached. I'd rather stick with Small and say autumn alumroot, *Heuchera macrorhiza*, is a distinct species of immense value to woodland gardeners. Having grown it now for many years, it has proved the longest-lived, dry-shade or nearly full-sun-tolerant heuchera I know.

Hexastylis

EVERGREEN WILD GINGER, MOTTLED WILD GINGER
ARISTOLOCHIACEAE, BIRTHWORT FAMILY

Closely related to the deciduous wild ginger, *Asarum canadense*, the *Hexastylis* species are all evergreen, with glossy, thick, leathery leaves that are sometimes strikingly mottled. Nearly all are clumping, never spreading to form a continuous carpet like *Asarum canadense* often does. Though especially susceptible to slug damage, the evergreen wild gingers are reasonably easy to grow if provided a shady location with moisture-retentive but well-drained, acid soil high in organic matter. Their flowers are typically at ground level, hidden by the foliage or by forest duff, and sometimes exquisite in extreme detail but never showy. Their dark maroon to brown coloration is responsible for the alternate common name, little brown jugs.

Depending upon your taxonomic leanings, there are four to ten species native to North America, centered in the Appalachian Mountains region. They can be confusing since plants of the same species may have heavily patterned leaves or no pattern at all. All are cold hardy to zone 5, some into zone 4.

TOP RIGHT New leaves of little heartleaf or cyclamen-leaved wild ginger, *Hexastylis minor*, mix with Christmas fern, *Polystichum acrostichoides*, in Virginia in early May. This species is common in low mountain areas and the piedmont of Virginia and the Carolinas, and may be solid green, as here, or mottled.

CENTER RIGHT A heavily patterned plant of mottled wild ginger, *Hexastylis shuttleworthii*, growing at the Birmingham Botanical Gardens in early May. Native to rich woods from Virginia and West Virginia to Georgia and Alabama, this species is often vividly marked. It is cold hardy into zone 4.

BOTTOM RIGHT Arrow-leaved ginger, *Hexastylis arifolia*, has leaves more triangular in outline, as illustrated by this distinctly patterned plant growing at Springwood in Pennsylvania in mid June. This species is native to moist and dry woods from Virginia and Kentucky south to Florida and Alabama, and is cold hardy to zone 5.

ABOVE Mountain bluet or thymeleaf bluet, *Houstonia serpyllifolia* [synonym *Houstonia michauxii*], has larger, deeper blue flowers, as seen on this plant growing on a mossy rock in the middle of a Smoky Mountains stream in late April. This species is native from Pennsylvania to Georgia.

ABOVE RIGHT In a moss bed at Mount Cuba Center in Delaware in early April, *Houstonia caerulea*, also called Quaker ladies, is the best-known bluet. Native from Nova Scotia to Wisconsin south to Georgia and Arkansas, it is most common on moist soil in open woods and meadows though I've often seen it flowering on relatively dry banks at woodland edges. Bluets are easy to establish from seed. Started this way, they persisted for many years in moss, growing between the shaded patio stones in my former Newark city garden in northern Delaware.

Houstonia

BLUETS, QUAKER LADIES
RUBIACEAE, MADDER FAMILY

The ten native bluet species include some of the most delicate perennials and are wonderful additions to the woodland garden, particularly when conditions allow them to naturalize. All prefer dappled light on a fairly open surface and cannot survive much competition, though they grow well in a moss bed. Most are hardy into zone 3.

Hydrangea

HYDRANGEACEAE, HYDRANGEA FAMILY

Oakleaf hydrangea, *Hydrangea quercifolia*, is easily the more alluring of two native eastern species, interesting in virtually every season. In winter, the light cinnamon-colored bark adds real color to the landscape, and I've always been especially fond of the period in spring when the new leaves unfold in the lightest shades of green. Few temperate wood plants rival the coarse summer texture of oakleaf hydrangea, which is augmented by huge panicles of white flowers that frequently turn pink toward fall. Autumn foliage is bronzed on plants in deep shade, but may be brilliant red and wine colored where it is hit by direct sunlight.

ABOVE The flower panicles of one seedling plant of oakleaf hydrangea, *Hydrangea quercifolia,* in our garden routinely turn deep pink by late August and are matched by rich foliage colors in late October.

TOP LEFT The exfoliating, light cinnamon-colored bark of oakleaf hydrangea enlivens the winter landscape of the Connecticut College Arboretum in New London.

BOTTOM LEFT A bold mass of oakleaf hydrangea flowers in mid-June shade at Springwood in Pennsylvania.

Wild hydrangea, *Hydrangea arborescens*, blooms in late June along a rocky bank in West Virginia. The flower clusters of this plant are all fertile, lacking the larger sterile florets sometimes occurring around the circumference of each cluster. The commonly grown garden forms 'Grandiflora' and 'Annabelle' bear very little resemblance to the common wild plant, having snowball-like flower clusters made up almost entirely of sterile florets.

Though cold hardy into zone 5, oakleaf hydrangea is a native of the Deep South, occurring naturally in shaded woodlands in Georgia, Florida, Alabama, Louisiana, and Mississippi, often on banks and slopes. It needs shade in southernmost zones but will grow satisfactorily in full sun in the northern portion of its hardiness range and can be very useful in establishing a shrub layer in mixed woodland plantings lacking the shading of a mature canopy. It adapts to a wide range of soil conditions and is surprisingly drought tolerant once established.

I've seen plants twelve feet tall in Alabama, though in our Pennsylvania area nine feet is the more realistic maximum height in flower. Oakleaf hydrangea can be easily contained by pruning and by removing older, taller stems and allowing new suckers to replace them.

Wild or woodland hydrangea, *Hydrangea arborescens*, suffers in comparison but is a pleasant shrub for relaxed woodland gardens. Native to moist or dry, often rocky woods and hillsides from New York south to Florida and west into Oklahoma, it is cold hardy into zone 3.

Hydrastis

GOLDENSEAL, YELLOWROOT
RANUNCULACEAE, BUTTERCUP FAMILY

Valued as an antiseptic and an immune system stimulant, goldenseal, *Hydrastis canadensis*, is probably better known for its herbal properties than as a woodland garden plant. Lately it seems to be becoming more widely available through native plant nurseries, which may help to offset its increasing rarity in native woods. Goldenseal naturally occurs only in deep, rich woodlands from Vermont to Minnesota south to Arkansas and North Carolina. It is easily started from seed but slow growing. The plants require moist well-drained organic soil and filtered light for best growth, but are very long lived if properly sited.

Ilex

HOLLY
AQUIFOLIACEAE, HOLLY FAMILY

Both evergreen and deciduous hollies occur within the North American deciduous forest, and both groups can play important roles in woodland gardens.

Best known of the deciduous species is winterberry, *Ilex verticillata*, a very variable shrub native to wet woods and swamps from Newfoundland to Michigan south to Indiana, West Virginia, and Maryland, and cold hardy to zone 3. Though typically six to eight feet tall, it can reach fifteen feet under ideal circumstances. It is broadly adaptable and will tolerate soggy, poorly drained soils as well as fairly dry conditions. Though the summer foliage is often a rich dark green, the fall and winter berries are uniquely capable of coloring the woodland landscape. I enjoy seeing this shrub at a distance in the designed landscape and in the woods, its bright berries acting as both a focal point and a beckoning presence in the winter garden. Since hollies are mostly dioecious, it is important to include male plants to ensure good berry crops on the females. Other deciduous hollies include smooth winterberry, *Ilex laevigata*; mountain holly, *Ilex montana*; serviceberry holly, *Ilex amelanchier*; and possum haw, *Ilex decidua*; however, none of these is capable of a winter show equivalent to common winterberry.

American holly, *Ilex opaca*, is the most wide-ranging and broadly adaptable of the evergreen tree species, occurring along the coast from Maine to Maryland and inland from Virginia to Kentucky and south to Florida and Texas. As with many plants, hardiness varies considerably with provenance, but with informed

The maplelike leaves of goldenseal, *Hydrastis canadensis*, are still expanding beneath the late-April flowers in our Pennsylvania garden. By July, the flowers have become clusters of bright red berries, which remain attractive into late summer.

TOP RIGHT For twenty years I've visited this winterberry, *Ilex verticillata*, growing naturally in a woodland swamp within the nearby White Clay Creek Preserve in northern Delaware. It's stunning whether snow covered or bare branched and berried. Winterberry can be an enduring element in the woodland garden on a range of soils from wet to dry.

ABOVE Though red is the typical color, berries of *Ilex verticillata* may also be orange or salmon, as seen in this naturally occurring form.

regional selection American holly is adaptable from zone 5 to 9. American holly is remarkably shade tolerant and is often observed growing fully under a deciduous canopy.

Of southern distribution and hardy only to zone 7, yaupon, *Ilex vomitoria*, is another evergreen tree species that will tolerate some shade. Native from Nova Scotia to Florida, the shrubby inkberry holly, *Ilex glabra*, is a third useful native evergreen that will grow in light shade among deciduous trees and shrubs. It is cold hardy into zone 4.

Iris
IRIDACEAE, IRIS FAMILY

The two most common eastern North American woodland irises are valuable in the garden for both flowers and foliage. Despite its diminutive stature and apparent delicacy, dwarf crested iris, *Iris cristata*, which usually flowers less than six inches tall, is tough enough to serve as a ground cover. Found on rich woods floors, banks, and cliffs, typically in slightly acid soils, it is cold hardy to zone 4.

American holly, *Ilex opaca*, is remarkably shade tolerant, growing well even under a deciduous tree canopy (TOP LEFT). In autumn, its evergreen foliage and bright berries add to the foliage hues of deciduous species, while in winter its green becomes the most obvious color (BOTTOM LEFT). A male pollinator is needed to ensure good berry set on female American holly (TOP RIGHT).

ABOVE Inkberry holly, *Ilex glabra*, has small evergreen leaves and ink-black berries.

TOP LEFT Dwarf crested iris, *Iris cristata*, blooms in mid-May shade in Pennsylvania, with typical light blue flowers. Some forms are dark blue.

TOP RIGHT *Iris cristata* 'Alba' creates a flowering ground cover under a large deciduous tree at Mount Cuba Center in Delaware in late April. Though dwarf crested iris is typically blue flowered, white forms occur and are readily available commercially. Photo by Melinda Zoehrer.

ABOVE The taller of the two dwarf irises, *Iris verna* blooms in open, sandy soil beneath a deciduous woodlands in Virginia in early May.

Though it prefers steady moisture, it will persist for many years in relatively dry conditions once established. Its close relative, *Iris verna*, is slightly taller, and its leaves extend considerably above the flowers. More common in open, often sandy woods from Pennsylvania to Georgia, it is cold hardy to zone 5. It is less inclined to form a continuous sweep, growing most readily as single plants or small groups.

Isopyrum
FALSE RUE ANEMONE
RANUNCULACEAE, BUTTERCUP FAMILY

It is not easy to stroll through the woodland gardens of Mount Cuba Center in Delaware in early April and not be smitten by eastern false rue anemone, *Isopyrum biternatum* [synonym *Enemion biternatum*], which grows in large flowering patches along the paths. Although it is not widely grown or even mentioned in garden literature, perhaps because it is among the true spring ephemerals that disappear by summer, it is obviously an easy thing to grow, from seed or by division of the tuberous roots. Native to moist woods from New York to Minnesota and south through the Carolinas to Florida, it is cold hardy through zone 4.

Itea

VIRGINIA SWEETSPIRE, VIRGINIA WILLOW
GROSSULARIACEAE, GOOSEBERRY FAMILY

Every time I've encountered Virginia sweetspire, *Itea virginica*, growing in its native habitat, I've been either standing in water or riding in a canoe. It's amazing how adaptable this running shrub is to garden soils of average moisture. Native to swamps, wet woods, and streambanks from southern New Jersey and eastern Pennsylvania south to Florida and north along the Mississippi River valley into southern Illinois, Virginia sweetspire is cold hardy through zone 5 if proper attention is paid to provenance. Toward the northern end of its range, it rarely exceeds four feet, but in the South it approaches ten feet and runs much more vigorously.

The story of *Itea virginica*, like that of several other species, is one in which a selected cultivar, 'Henry's Garnet', has drawn attention to an underused native plant and brought it widespread popularity. All plants of Virginia sweetspire offer June flowers and autumn color which is typically orange-red, but the longer-flowering racemes and deep red hues of 'Henry's Garnet' represent perhaps the best this species has to offer. Like many suckering shrubs, it can be renewed almost indefinitely by periodic cutting back to the ground.

TOP LEFT Eastern false rue anemone, *Isopyrum biternatum*, nestles between root flares anchoring the deciduous canopy at Mount Cuba Center in Delaware in early April.

TOP RIGHT AND ABOVE The long pendent racemes of *Itea virginica* 'Henry's Garnet' are dramatic in mid June, and then in fall, the arching branches and foliage turn rich maroon and red.

As is true for many shrubs native to wet habitats, Virginia sweetspire will tolerate poorly drained or soggy soils. I've often seen it growing natively alongside sweet pepperbush, *Clethra alnifolia*, and since *Itea* turns red and *Clethra* turns gold, they make a vibrant combination in autumn.

Jeffersonia
TWINLEAF
BERBERIDACEAE, BARBERRY FAMILY

The flowers of twinleaf, *Jeffersonia diphylla*, are so fleeting they are easy to miss, often gone in a day or two. They are pretty enough, appearing at the very beginning of spring, but it is the foliage of twinleaf that makes the most significant impact in the woodland landscape. Held in horizontal pairs at the top of each wiry petiole, the leaves are chalky blue-green and last late into autumn, contributing a uniquely bold texture to the herbaceous layer.

This plant named for Thomas Jefferson is fittingly common in Virginia but also occurs from New York to Minnesota south to Maryland and Alabama, in rich woods and typically in calcareous soils associated with limestone. In the garden it is quite adaptable and will thrive within the normal range of soil acidity. Twinleaf grows twelve to eighteen inches tall from a very dense crown which is difficult to divide. It is best propagated by seed.

Juniperus
JUNIPER
CUPRESSACEAE, CYPRESS FAMILY

Although eastern red cedar, *Juniperus virginiana*, rarely persists as an integral part of the mature forest, it is often an important bit player in the early evolution

TOP LEFT Twinleaf, *Jeffersonia diphylla*, flowers on leafless stalks in early April at Mount Cuba Center in Delaware. The flowers mature into a curious seed capsule which in fall flips open at the top like a kitchen trash can.

CENTER LEFT Held up to eighteen inches high on sturdy stalks, the twin leaves of *Jeffersonia diphylla* are a bold presence in the woodland landscape from spring into late fall. Twinleaf will live for many years if pro-

vided a situation that is moist and partly sunny in spring, and shaded through summer. Once established, it is very tolerant of summer dryness.

BOTTOM LEFT Red cedar, *Juniperus virginiana*, can be quite ornamental in fall and winter when covered with the light blue "juniper berries" (actually fleshy cones) that are used to flavor gin.

of deciduous woodland landscapes, and as such may have a place in the developing woodland garden, or in one that tells the story of woodland succession.

Eastern red cedar is native from Maine to North Dakota and south to Florida and Texas, especially on dry, calcareous soils. Cold hardy into zone 3, it is an extremely variable species, including a wide range of foliage colors from dark green to blue-green. Some plants remain green in winter, others turn olive or brown. When choosing plants for northern climates it is important to select ones with single leaders to reduce the likelihood of splitting from snow loads. Though eastern red cedar cannot survive deep woodland shade, it has the capacity to live more than a century if it receives sufficient sunlight.

Kalmia

MOUNTAIN LAUREL
ERICACEAE, HEATH FAMILY

When conditions are to its liking, mountain laurel, *Kalmia latifolia*, grows with great enthusiasm, forming huge thickets to nearly thirty feet tall, but it is very particular and sometimes unaccountably difficult to establish in cultivation. In its native habitat this much-loved evergreen shrub is restricted to acid, sharply drained soils, and these are absolute requisites for garden culture. It ranges naturally from Maine to Florida and west to Ohio and Mississippi, typically in shady deciduous woods, though I also know it from full sun environments on the sandy, acid New Jersey coastal plain, where it withstands hot summer temperatures and re-sprouts from occasional fires. It is cold hardy to zone 4.

Closely related sheep laurel, *Kalmia angustifolia*, has deep red-pink flowers and grows only two to three feet tall, but is more a plant of acid bogs and open areas in the Northeast. It is exceptionally cold hardy, adaptable even to zone 1.

TOP RIGHT Winter is one of mountain laurel's best seasons, when the often-picturesque trunks of older plants are silhouetted against snowy ground. This mid-March view from northern Delaware shows older shrubs growing in typical habitat: sloping, well-drained, acid soil under a deciduous canopy with occasional openings. In dense shade, mountain laurel may flower sparsely or not at all.

BOTTOM RIGHT Mountain laurel, *Kalmia latifolia*, blooms in early June in a sunny opening in the New Jersey woodlands. The flowers naturally range in color from nearly white to light pink. Clonal cultivars are available with dark pink to purple-red blooms.

RIGHT At home we've used a cultivar of coastal leucothoe, *Leucothoe axillaris* 'Red Sprite', to provide a low evergreen presence along a paved walk. It has proved tough enough to grow within the competing roots of river birches, *Betula nigra*, and once established has survived hot droughty summers without supplemental watering.

ABOVE Flowers of coastal leucothoe are attractive in early May but have a strong musky odor for about two weeks, not an ideal presence in an outdoor dining area.

Leucothoe

DOG-HOBBLE
ERICACEAE, HEATH FAMILY

Like *Kalmia*, *Leucothoe* is also a member of the typically acid-loving heath family, but it is nowhere near as particular about its conditions and is much easier to grow. Though the literature is filled with confusing and superfluous names, there are reasonably two native evergreen *Leucothoe* species, and both are worth consideration in woodland gardens. The traditional common name is dog-hobble, referring to the hobbling capacity of these dense shrubs when they occur in large masses in native habitats. The name leucothoe is gaining favor with gardeners and nursery marketing departments, understandably.

The more malleable of the two species is coastal leucothoe, *Leucothoe axillaris*, which is native to wet woods from southeastern Virginia to Florida and Louisiana, almost exclusively on the coastal plain. Reliably cold hardy to zone 5, it typically grows three to five feet tall and is a superb choice when a relatively low, compact evergreen shrub is needed for winter color or to create a year-round sense of enclosure. Unlike inkberry holly, *Ilex glabra*, it is not subject to snow damage. Coastal leucothoe appreciates markedly acid, well-drained conditions but adapts to average garden soils and drainage, with winter drainage most important. This species also better tolerates heat and sun, and is capable of growing in the strong sun of new woodland plantings as well as under the dense shade of an established canopy.

Mountain leucothoe, *Leucothoe fontanesiana* [synonym *Leucothoe walteri*], has been much more commonly cultivated but really requires cool, moist, acid conditions for good health, and is best suited for northern or mountain regions. Native mostly near mountain streams and wet hillsides from Virginia to North Carolina, Tennessee, Georgia, and Alabama, it is cold hardy into zone 4. It is larger growing, typically closer to six feet tall, with long, arching branches.

Lilium

LILY

LILIACEAE, LILY FAMILY

The flowers of the larger American woodland lilies, Turk's cap, *Lilium superbum*, and Canada lily, *Lilium canadense*, are so winning it's easy to forget that these plants are also dramatic before they bloom. Their leaves, in whorls of four to a dozen, rise in multiple tiers up stems to eight feet tall. While neither blooms well in dense shade, both are frequently found flowering magnificently at the edges of wet woods and in clearings. Both require moist to wet conditions in the garden.

Canada lily has a slightly more northern distribution, occurring from Quebec to Maryland and south in the mountains to Alabama. It grows to five feet tall, with flowers mostly light yellow or orange in northern regions and often deep red in the South. It is hardy to zone 3.

Hardy to zone 4, Turk's cap lily ranges from Massachusetts and New Hampshire south to Georgia and Alabama, and often reaches eight feet in height.

Smaller and less common are wood lily, *Lilium philadelphicum*, which is found in drier, open woodlands from New Hampshire to Kentucky, and Gray's lily, *Lilium grayi*, a southern mountain species.

TOP RIGHT Normally yellow or yellow-orange, Canada lily, *Lilium canadense*, is sometimes deep red, as this West Virginia plant shows.

CENTER RIGHT Turk's cap lily, *Lilium superbum*, blooms in late July along a wet, sunny edge in the North Carolina mountains. It may often be found flowering with black snakeroot, *Cimicifuga racemosa*.

BOTTOM RIGHT Named for famed American botanist Asa Gray, *Lilium grayi* is typically less than three feet tall and is found only in rich, moist habitats high in the mountains of Virginia, North Carolina, and Tennessee.

Lindera

SPICEBUSH

LAURACEAE, LAUREL FAMILY

This widespread woodland native is one of North America's most undervalued shrubs, with great potential for designed landscapes. One of the big things it has going for it these days is its virtual invulnerability to browsing by deer, which find it extremely unpalatable. It truly has multiple seasons of interest. Spice-bush, *Lindera benzoin*, like its relative *Sassafras albidum*, blooms early in spring, covering branches with bright green-yellow flower clusters. Also like sassafras, it is dioecious, but female plants are often stunningly bedecked with scarlet berries by late summer, and these last into winter. The fall foliage color of spicebush is

Among the earliest spring flowers, spice-bush, *Lindera benzoin*, is appealing whether backlit against woodland shadows, as here in early April at Mount Cuba Center in Delaware (TOP LEFT) or flat-lighted against a stucco wall, as here in our Pennsylvania garden in mid April (CENTER LEFT).

BOTTOM LEFT Bright scarlet berries deco-

rate the branches of a female spicebush in late September in eastern Pennsylvania.

BELOW Tolerant of dense shade or nearly full sun, spicebush can be counted upon for bright golden color in autumn, as here in late October. Its size can be easily managed by pruning or by periodic cutting back to the ground.

always a vibrant golden yellow, whether growing in deep shade or nearly full sun, and the delicate tracery of its branches adds to the beauty of the winter woods, especially when dusted in snow.

Spicebush is common and abundant in moist woods from Maine to Minnesota and south to Texas and Florida, and is cold hardy to zone 4. It typically grows as a multistemmed shrub six to ten feet tall, though it is capable of reaching twice that height. It adapts to a wide range of soils and will even thrive in somewhat soggy, poorly drained conditions.

Liquidambar

SWEETGUM
HAMAMELIDACEAE, WITCH HAZEL FAMILY

No other tree matches the autumn colors often produced by the uniquely five-lobed leaves of sweetgum, *Liquidambar styraciflua*, which can be clear yellow, brilliant scarlet, bright orange, or dark purple, sometimes all at once on the same tree. Native to moist or even wet woods from Connecticut to southern Illinois and south to Florida, sweetgum is cold hardy through zone 5 and adaptable to an extremely wide range of soil, moisture, and drainage conditions, though it does best when pH is slightly acid. It is best transplanted as a small tree, but long

ABOVE The woody fruits of sweetgum, *Liquidambar styraciflua*, enliven the winter landscape as they move with the wind, suspended from fine stalks against a clear-blue January sky. Though they're tough on bare feet and can be a nuisance when they accumulate on paved surfaces or lawns, the fruits are relatively innocuous in a wooded garden setting. The younger branches of sweetgum are gray barked and sometimes dramatically lined with corky ridges which add to winter interest.

LEFT Sweetgum is backlit by the late-October sun.

lived and usually disease-free. Sweetgum often occurs in dense stands, with trees growing narrow and next to one another, and it can be particularly beautiful when planted this way in larger woodland gardens.

Liriodendron
TULIPTREE, YELLOW POPLAR
MAGNOLIACEAE, MAGNOLIA FAMILY

Now that the American chestnut, *Castanea dentata*, is mostly a memory, tuliptree, *Liriodendron tulipifera*, is increasingly significant as one of the longest-lived, tallest trees in the deciduous forest, capable of growing two hundred feet tall and surviving for centuries. It is among the largest trees in my local Pennsylvania woods, its trunks forming massive columns free of any branches for sixty feet or more, but these giants are dwarfed by those still standing in Joyce Kilmer Forest in western North Carolina, any of which can barely be encircled by two grown men with arms stretched. Native to rich woods from Vermont to Michigan and south to Florida and Louisiana, tuliptree is cold hardy to zone 4. Its size suits it best to larger landscapes, and its tendency to shed branches in storms suggests care when planting it near drives or walkways.

Lonicera
HONEYSUCKLE
CAPRIFOLIACEAE, HONEYSUCKLE FAMILY

Unlike the introduced Japanese honeysuckle, *Lonicera japonica*, which is truly a curse on the North American woodlands, the native honeysuckles are well-behaved woody vines that offer easy ways to bring flowers and foliage up in the woodland garden.

Most common and easy to acquire as seed-grown plants or in many cultivated varieties, trumpet honeysuckle, *Lonicera sempervirens*, is native to woods and thickets from Connecticut to Florida and west to Oklahoma. It is hardy through zone 4. Capable of climbing twenty feet or more, it blooms for many weeks in spring and sporadically through summer. Flowers are typically orange-red, but many variations occur from dark scarlet to light yellow. The leaves are perfoliate, meaning the stem runs through the joined pairs of leaves. Unfortunately, the plant is commonly disfigured by aphids, though this rarely discourages flowering.

TOP Large green-and-orange flowers are distinctive on a low-hanging branch in late May at Ashland Hollow. Though responsible for the name tuliptree, the flowers of *Liriodendron tulipifera* are structured more like those of magnolias, to which this tree is closely related.

BOTTOM In autumn, the high deciduous canopy is bright with the golden foliage of tuliptrees.

Trumpet honeysuckle blooms well in shade or in sun, though aphids are usually more pronounced on sun-stressed plants.

Less common in cultivation but worth seeking, the aptly named yellow honeysuckle, *Lonicera flava*, occurs in rocky woods and thickets from Missouri and Arkansas to North Carolina and Georgia. It is cold hardy to zone 5. The flowers are a deep sulfur yellow.

TOP RIGHT In full bloom in mid May, this trumpet honeysuckle, *Lonicera sempervirens* 'Cedar Lane', has brightened our shaded north porch for more than a decade with no care except occasional minor pruning.

CENTER RIGHT Gracing a trellis off the south side of our house but in filtered light

from a nearby tree, the yellow trumpet honeysuckle, *Lonicera sempervirens* 'Sulphurea', has proved every bit as attractive to hummingbirds as the red-flowered form.

BOTTOM RIGHT The deep yellow flowers of *Lonicera flava* make this uncommon species worth seeking for the woodland garden.

Magnolia

MAGNOLIACEAE, MAGNOLIA FAMILY

Though none of the many North American magnolias can match the floral display of Asian species that bloom before the leaves, as a group they include some very fine large and small trees which can serve a multitude of purposes in the woodland garden and enrich the passing seasons with flower, foliage, and fruiting interest. Magnolias in general are surface rooted, and since their fleshy roots generally don't like to be disturbed, they are best transplanted in smaller sizes.

The tallest of the deciduous species, *Magnolia acuminata*, is called cucumber tree for its flowers, which are typically blue-green and covered with a waxy bloom like a cucumber. This magnolia can grow seventy-five feet tall, with a massive columnar trunk resembling a tuliptree. Native to rich woods from New York and Ontario south to Florida and Louisiana, it is cold hardy to zone 5. This species was among those that captured the imagination of early botanists exploring the grand diversity of the North American deciduous forest. Sometime in the early eighteen hundreds two brothers, Joshua and Samuel Peirce, planted it in their arboretum near Kennett Square, Pennsylvania, on ground that is now at the heart of Longwood Gardens. Some of those plantings have survived to the present, and when I was at Longwood I always enjoyed visiting one particularly magnificent tree that still stands east of the original house. The Peirces also planted the rarer yellow cucumber tree, which is usually distinguished as *Magnolia*

acuminata var. *subcordata*, and today that tree is the national champion. The flowers are nearly banana yellow.

Bigleaf magnolia, *Magnolia macrophylla*, is so coarse textured it truly evokes the tropics. The individual leaves can be nearly three feet long and are clustered in whorls. Cold hardy to zone 5, it occurs over a wide range from Ohio and Kentucky south to Arkansas, Louisiana, and Georgia, but is rare and only found in small, scattered populations, often growing in shady ravines and gorges. It can reach fifty feet in height, while a southern variety, sometimes distinguished as Ashe's magnolia, *Magnolia ashei*, is typically shorter and cold hardy only to zone 6. Both have huge, fragrant cream-white flowers, often with purple blotches.

Two small large-leafed magnolias are easier to integrate in woodland garden designs. Fraser's magnolia, *Magnolia fraseri*, looks like a smaller version of bigleaf magnolia and has similar lobes at the base of its leaves, which are usually up to eighteen inches in length. I've often seen this tree venturing out into the sunlight in forest clearings and on steep slopes in the Smokies, blooming in late April. Native from the Virginia mountains south to Georgia and Alabama, it is cold hardy to zone 5.

Smaller still is umbrella magnolia, *Magnolia tripetala*, which has long been a personal favorite. Though it can grow fifty feet tall under unusual circumstances, it more frequently forms a multistemmed tree or even a large shrub under twenty feet in height. Its leaves taper at the base and can be nearly two feet long, arranged in distinctive umbrella-like whorls. Though the unpleasant scent of the flowers is often noted in literature, it is not much of an issue in the landscape since it doesn't carry far. Umbrella magnolia is widely adaptable and hardy to zone 5.

By far the best for smaller garden spaces, sweet bay, *Magnolia virginiana*, occurs naturally in wet woods and around the margins of swamps, mostly on the

TOP LEFT I am always amazed when I hear people say magnolias have no appreciable fall color. Who could discount the brilliant gold of this cucumber tree, *Magnolia acuminata*, in mid October at Mount Cuba Center in Delaware?

CENTER LEFT Cucumber magnolia flowering at Longwood Gardens in late May.

BOTTOM LEFT The yellow cucumber magnolia, *Magnolia acuminata* var. *subcordata*, is relatively rare in the wild, but many forms are available in cultivation. One distinct advantage native magnolias have over the precocious-blooming Asian species is that their flowering is never blighted by late frosts.

TOP LEFT Almost tropically bold textured, bigleaf magnolia, *Magnolia macrophylla*, dwarfs ferns in the ground layer at the Birmingham Botanical Gardens.

CENTER LEFT Bigleaf magnolia produces fragrant flowers nearly one foot in diameter in late May at Longwood Gardens.

BOTTOM LEFT Fraser's magnolia, *Magnolia fraseri*, flowers in late April on a sunny hillside clearing in the Smoky Mountains of North Carolina.

RIGHT, TOP TO BOTTOM Umbrella magnolia, *Magnolia tripetala*, has multiple seasons of interest, as seen here at Longwood Gardens. May flowers develop into brilliant scarlet fruits by September, and gold autumn foliage is backlit by the late-October sun.

coastal plain from Massachusetts south to Florida and Texas. It usually grows as a multistemmed tree up to twenty feet tall. Also known as swamp magnolia, it will tolerate poorly drained soils but prefers somewhat acid conditions. I've often seen it growing with sweet pepperbush, *Clethra acuminata*, and highbush blueberry, *Vaccinium corymbosum*, and the three make a colorful combination in fall when the sweet bay is still green and its companions are yellow and red. It is cold hardy to zone 5. Much taller-growing plants toward the southern part of the range are often segregated by botanists as *Magnolia virginiana* var. *australis*. These are typically evergreen in the South and semi-evergreen when grown in northern zones. I've never seen them appear truly comfortable with winters even in my zone 6 and personally prefer sweet bays that cleanly drop their leaves for winter rather than keeping them to dangle somewhat discolored and forlorn.

A quintessentially Southern tree, *Magnolia grandiflora*, the bull bay or southern magnolia, is the only completely evergreen species in eastern North America, ranging in low woods and swamp forests, often near the coast, from Virginia to Mississippi, Alabama, Georgia, and Florida, frequently mixed with *Magnolia virginiana* in the South. It is potentially a huge tree, capable of growing nearly one hundred feet tall with half that in spread. Though many forms of southern magnolia have been selected for cultivation, the most cold hardy of these are reliable only into zone 6.

TOP LEFT The sweetly lemon-scented flowers of sweet bay, *Magnolia virginiana*, begin in late May and continue into summer. In two gardens and for nearly a quarter century, I've enjoyed this tree planted within sniffing distance of regularly used walkways. An older, now obsolete botanical name for this species is *Magnolia glauca*, referring to the glaucous (white wax-covered) underside of the leaves.

BOTTOM LEFT With dark glossy leaves that are orange brown below, the clonal cultivar 'D. D. Blanchard' is a fine representative of southern magnolia, *Magnolia grandiflora*. The deliciously sweet-fragrant flowers are produced most heavily in May and June and then sporadically through the remainder of the growing season.

Maianthemum

CANADA MAYFLOWER
LILIACEAE, LILY FAMILY

Looking something like a miniature lily-of-the-valley, *Convallaria majalis* (a European native), Canada Mayflower, *Maianthemum canadense*, frequently carpets the woodland floor with myriad glossy-green teardrop-shaped leaves and delicate white blossoms. Common in both moist and dry shady woodlands from

Canada south into the North Carolina mountains, it is cold hardy to zone 3 and easy to grow on acid soils in dense shade or in part sun in northern zones. It spreads rapidly by rhizomes and can be an extremely useful and durable ground cover in the woodland garden.

Mertensia
BLUEBELLS
BORAGINACEAE, BORAGE FAMILY

Often occurring in hundreds of thousands along shaded floodplains, *Mertensia virginica* is one of spring's coolest blues and a truly electrifying sight when it forms a virtual river of its own blooms. Its beauty has motivated different regions to claim it for their own. Known simply as bluebells in the larger scheme of things, it is called Virginia bluebells throughout the Shenandoah and Roanoke valleys, and Brandywine bluebells where it carpets the banks of the Brandywine River in Pennsylvania and northern Delaware. Occurring naturally in rich, moist woods and clearings from New York and Minnesota south to South Carolina, Arkansas, and Alabama, bluebells will grow in zones 3 to 9, though the flowers last longer in regions with cool, lingering springs.

Typically sky blue at their peak, the flowers undergo a number of color shifts

ABOVE LEFT Glowing in the late-April sunlight, the new leaves of Canada Mayflower, *Maianthemum canadense,* cover the ground below small trees and shrubs in a northern Delaware woodlands.

ABOVE Canada Mayflower blooms in a solid carpet in late May in a densely shaded Virginia woodlands, a clue to its potential as a ground cover for low-light areas in the woodland garden.

as they emerge and mature. Appearing with the first unfurling shoots, the flower buds are deep blue-purple and are attractive in their own right. As the stems elevate and the buds open into bells, their hue shifts through pink on the way to blue. Occasional plants with pink or smoky white flowers are found in large populations. The young leaves and stems are quite glaucous and appear gray-green. Mature foliage is a light, bright green, and the broad-bladed lower leaves contribute to the plant's overall bold texture.

This sturdy, long-lived perennial is a classic spring ephemeral: an herbaceous species that leafs out and flowers in early spring, sets seed and dies back to the ground by early summer, and is nowhere in evidence for the duration of the growing season. Blending such a plant into a woodland garden requires a different strategy than that normally employed, and observing the plant's pattern in its native habitat provides easy clues to garden opportunities. Bluebells typically grow around and under deciduous shrubs such as spicebush, *Lindera benzoin*, small trees such as ironwood, *Carpinus caroliniana*, and pawpaw, *Asimina triloba*, and canopy trees including beech, *Fagus grandifolia*, sycamore, *Platanus occidentalis*, and swamp hickory, *Carya cordiformis*. All such companions are leafless when bluebells bloom, and by the time the tree and shrub foliage darkens the

TOP Bluebells, *Mertensia virginica*, locally called Brandywine bluebells, add their vibrant blue hues to the landscape of the Delaware Center for Horticulture in urban Wilmington, in late April.

BOTTOM At home, we enjoy bold bluebell foliage as it contrasts with Christmas ferns, *Polystichum acrostichoides*, along our entry walk in early May. By the time the bluebells are going deciduous, they'll be hidden by the expanding fern fronds.

Bluebells bloom with abandon among the still-bare stems of bottlebrush buckeye, *Aesculus parviflora*, at Ashland Hollow in north-ern Delaware. This ingenious combination makes the best of the bluebell spring ephemeral nature.

woodland floor, the bluebells have retreated to dormant, thick tuberous roots unaffected by the dearth of sunlight. In the garden, they're an ideal choice for planting immediately underneath shrubs and low-spreading trees. Their flowers and fresh foliage will brighten the ground level, and their dormant period will be hidden by the foliage of the woody plants. Herbaceous companions, especially in slightly sunnier edge conditions, include asters, *Aster* species; foamflower, *Tiarella cordifolia*; Mayapples, *Podophyllum peltatum*; and a multitude of ferns, both deciduous and evergreen.

Bluebells may be grown from seed but dividing the roots is an easier method of propagation. Root division is most easily accomplished just as the leaves are going yellow, in late spring, since plants can be difficult to locate later in the season. Early spring division, when new growth just begins to show above ground, will also succeed.

Mitchella

PARTRIDGEBERRY
RUBIACEAE, MADDER FAMILY

Much slower to spread than the deciduous *Maianthemum* species but capable of covering large patches in time, partridgeberry, *Mitchella repens*, is a delightfully diminutive evergreen suited to moist, shady spots in the woodland garden. It is not particular about pH but does require good drainage and will not tolerate a heavy leaf cover over winter. For this reason, it is often observed growing naturally on slopes, where leaves are less inclined to accumulate. Cold hardy to zone 3, it is native to woodlands from Nova Scotia and Ontario to Minnesota and south to Texas and Florida.

Mitella

BISHOP'S CAP, MITREWORT
SAXIFRAGACEAE, SAXIFRAGE FAMILY

This delicate beauty really rewards those who pay it close attention. Bishop's cap or mitrewort, *Mitella diphylla*, has lobed basal leaves that are similar but smaller than those of its relatives *Tiarella* and *Heuchera*. From these, in April and May, a fine flowering stalk ascends twelve to sixteen inches. A pair of leaves (*di* means "two" and *phylla* means "leaves") is positioned part way up the stalk, and above it are quarter-inch flowers that are fringed like snowflakes. The flowers mature

The evergreen leaves and bright scarlet fruits of this patch of partridgeberry, *Mitchella repens*, have come through winter in fine condition, as seen here in a Pennsylvania woodland bank on March 31.

Bishop's cap, *Mitella diphylla*, blooms in early May on sloping ground in a slightly acid Delaware woodlands. Though subtle from a distance, the flowering stalks are often noticed when sunlit against a dark background.

into green capsules shaped like tiny bishop's caps (or mitres), each holding a number of shiny jet-black seeds. This plant is on my "A" list for gardens aimed at children of all ages.

The only eastern representative of a largely western North American genus, bishop's cap, *Mitella diphylla*, is native to woodlands from Quebec to Minnesota and south to Virginia, Georgia, and Missouri, and is cold hardy to zone 3. In native habitats it usually grows on banks and steep slopes, which provide sharp drainage and freedom from accumulating leaves. In the Smokies, I've seen it growing in moss running up the sides of a nurse log, and it is frequently found with *Trillium* species.

TOP AND CENTER LEFT Up close, the fringed flowers of bishop's cap look like snowflakes. They mature to form green cuplike fruits with exposed, jet-black seeds.

Monarda

OSWEGO TEA, BEE BALM, WILD BERGAMOT
LAMIACEAE, MINT FAMILY

Though *Monarda* species are often associated with meadow habitats, a few are truly at home in the woods and woods edge. Generally cold hardy to zone 3, they are rhizomatous perennials capable of developing into substantial masses when growing conditions are suitable, and all are favorites of butterflies.

Easily the most spectacular, the red-flowered Oswego tea, *Monarda didyma*, occurs in moist woods and thickets from Maine to Michigan south to New Jersey and Ohio, and in the mountains to Georgia. It is relatively easy to grow in shade or sun if provided rich organic soil and plenty of moisture. Purple bergamot, *Monarda media*, is more eastern in distribution and similar except slightly shorter, with red-purple flowers. The white woodland bergamot or basil bee balm, *Monarda clinopodia*, has smaller flowers which fade to brown.

BOTTOM LEFT Oswego tea, *Monarda didyma*, blooms in mid July at a sunny edge along the Blue Ridge Parkway in Virginia. Though most often red, the flowers of Oswego tea are sometimes white.

Neviusia

ALABAMA SNOW WREATH
ROSACEAE, ROSE FAMILY

Alabama snow wreath, *Neviusia alabamensis*, is a good example of a plant that may be rare or even endangered in native habitats yet proves easily amenable to cultivation and conservation in the garden. It grows, divides, and transplants so readily in our Pennsylvania garden that we've taken to using it as a flowering hedge and low deciduous screen in shade and part sun.

Over the years, I've collected regional floras (botanical accounts of the plants growing in various regions) and have found these invaluable to my education about North America's native plants. On page 133 of A. W. Chapman's *Flora of the Southern United States* published in 1883, *Neviusia alabamensis* is listed as growing only on shady cliffs near Tuscaloosa, Alabama, and having "flowers very numerous and showy." Since Chapman's time, small, scattered populations have been found in Arkansas, Tennessee, Missouri, Mississippi, and Georgia, but the bit about the flowers is still quite true.

Alabama snow wreath spreads strongly but not aggressively, producing a rounded mass of arching branches up to five feet high. It blooms heavily for more than two weeks in late April and early May, in either shade or sun. I've found it one of the most shade-tolerant flowering shrubs in the garden, thriving even in the dim spaces on the north side of white pines. The flowering stems have also proved excellent cut material for indoors.

Cold hardy to zone 4, *Neviusia alabamensis* adapts to various soil and drainage conditions, and though it is most vigorous when provided moist, well-drained soil, it is extremely tolerant of dry shade once established. Fall color is an unremarkable gold, but the densely woody growth has a pleasing presence over winter. Much more than a botanical curiosity, Alabama snow wreath is a broadly useful shrub for modern woodland gardens.

Nyssa

TUPELO
NYSSACEAE, TUPELO FAMILY

Nyssa sylvatica has many common names, and I've run into all of them at one time or another as I've traveled. In different regions, it is called black gum, sour gum, black tupelo, upland tupelo, and pepperidge. This last name has long been asso-

TOP Arching stems of Alabama snow wreath, *Neviusia alabamensis*, are covered with flowers in early May.

BOTTOM Delicate but long lasting as cut material, *Neviusia* flowers have no petals: the showy parts are the thin filaments holding the pollen-producing anthers.

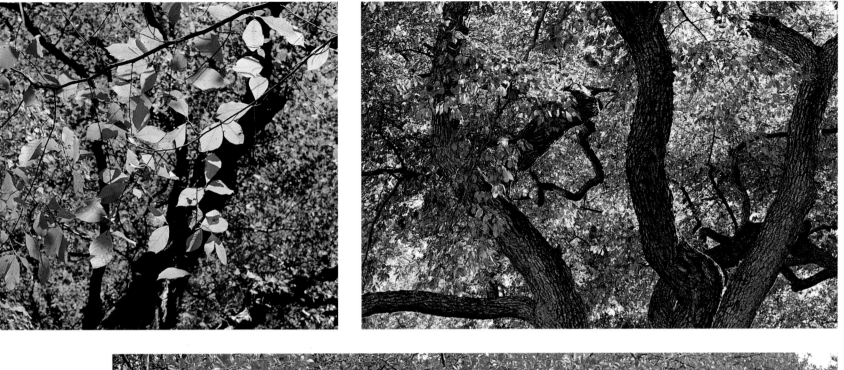

ciated with a well-known brand of cookies, and though diminished in size in recent years, a pepperidge tree is still visible in the logo, behind the farm barn.

Black gum, as I know it best, is common over a broad range in upland and lowland woods from Maine to Florida, west to Wisconsin and south to Texas. Cold hardy to zone 4, it adapts to various soil and moisture conditions, though as usual, provenance plays an important role in regional performance. This deep-rooted tree would surely be planted more widely if not for its relative difficulty in transplanting. It is almost imperative to plant trees when small and particularly important to avoid girdling roots if purchasing container-grown trees. Once established, black gums are typically disease-free and drought tolerant, and make superb overstory trees in the woodland garden, since their deep roots are easy on underplantings of shrubs and herbs. *Nyssa sylvatica* is mostly dioecious, and female trees produce dark purple-blue fruits in fall. The fruits are only subtly attractive but are very important food for birds. Though mature trees may grow over one hundred feet tall with half that in spread, black gum is very late to leaf out, allowing light to reach the herbaceous layer into late April or early May. Its autumn color is early, and is among the richest and most brilliant of any deciduous tree.

Van Morrison fans should know that black gum's close relative, the water tupelo, *Nyssa aquatica*, is the bee tree from which tupelo honey is produced. Native to swamps from Virginia to Florida and Texas, it often grows to towering heights with large buttressed trunks. It is unforgettable when rising from drifts of Louisiana iris in early spring. It will grow in soils of average moisture, but more slowly than black gum, and is cold hardy only to zone 6.

OPPOSITE The autumn color of black gum, *Nyssa sylvatica*, is variable but always extraordinary, as illustrated by these mid-October images of tall salmon-pink trees in my local White Clay Creek Preserve (TOP LEFT), a magnificent orange-bronze specimen on the campus of Swarthmore College (TOP RIGHT), and a group of intensely scarlet-red trees growing wild on Cape Cod (BOTTOM).

Ostrya

HOP HORNBEAM, IRONWOOD
BETULACEAE, BIRCH FAMILY

Closely related to hornbeam, *Carpinus caroliniana*, hop hornbeam, *Ostrya virginiana*, is a small to medium-sized tree with almost equally hard wood, which is why both are sometimes called ironwood. Its range, from Nova Scotia to Manitoba and south to Florida and Texas, is also nearly identical; however, whereas

TOP The common name of *Ostrya virginiana*, hop hornbeam, refers to the hoplike fruits which are evident from late summer through autumn. Fall foliage color is insignificant.

BOTTOM This venerable tree at the Rutgers Gardens on the Cook College campus in New Jersey is testimony to the size and bark character which hop hornbeam may develop.

Carpinus grows in moist woods and alluvial soils, *Ostrya* is a distinctly upland tree, usually found in dry woods and on rocky banks and slopes.

Cold hardy into zone 3, hop hornbeam is a tough, long-lived tree capable of enduring difficult soils and droughty conditions in the woodland garden, but it is more often found growing naturally than in nursery offerings due to the difficulty its deep roots pose to commercial production and transplanting. Hop hornbeam can grow over fifty feet tall but is typically less than half that height. The mature bark is a rich mixture of silver gray and red brown, exfoliating lightly in vertical strips.

Oxydendrum

SOURWOOD

ERICACEAE, HEATH FAMILY

Widely acknowledged as one of the most beautiful North American trees in all seasons, sourwood is both monotypic and endemic, meaning the genus is comprised of only one species and that species is native only to North America. It grows naturally from Pennsylvania to Indiana, south to Florida. I've never seen it more spectacular than in the Smoky Mountains, where its summer blooms and autumn hues grace seemingly every roadside and forest edge, and where, in the deepest coves, it grows nearly one hundred feet tall.

Sourwood is very late to leaf out and among the earliest trees to turn color, in autumn or often in late summer. Individually resembling the flowers of blueberries, sourwood's tiny white urns are suspended in June and July along the stems of slender, nearly horizontal racemes. The fruits turn upward as they mature while the racemes become gently pendent, all colored bright cream-white and set against the deepening bronze and crimson tones of the foliage.

Like its relatives, the blueberries, azaleas, and rhododendrons, sourwood prefers well-drained, somewhat acid soil. It is notoriously unpredictable about transplanting, and gardeners' varying experiences may be related to genetic dif -

TOP LEFT When grown in the open, sourwood, *Oxydendrum arboreum*, makes a neatly pyramidal specimen, but I am always intrigued by the exquisitely irregular shapes of trees forming at the edge of the forest in native habitats, as typified by this tree in the Smoky Mountains, in late July. Sourwood honey is a rare delicacy, sometimes available regionally.

BOTTOM LEFT In late October, sourwood's combination of pendent white racemes against crimson foliage is uniquely memorable.

ferences in seedlings as well as cultural conditions of the site. Even in the best of circumstances it is slow to re-establish but worth the wait. When eventually settled and growing well, sourwood is quite drought tolerant. Though showy enough to serve as a garden focal point, sourwood is gorgeous planted in groupings when space permits.

Pachysandra

ALLEGHENY SPURGE, ALLEGHENY PACHYSANDRA
BUXACEAE, BOXWOOD FAMILY

The rich green and bronze foliage of Allegheny pachysandra, *Pachysandra procumbens*, reminds me of matte finishes on some of the best Arts and Crafts pottery. Weaving a thick carpet six to twelve inches high, this plant can cover ground in the woodland garden with uncommon grace and sophistication.

Native to rich woods from West Virginia, Kentucky, and North Carolina to Florida and Louisiana, it is actually quite a tough character, evergreen through zone 5 and root hardy to zone 4. It is mostly immune to the plethora of pests and diseases that affects the ubiquitous and tiresome Japanese species, *Pachysandra terminalis*.

Allegheny pachysandra can be rooted from cuttings and is easily divided in spring or fall. It is most vigorous on moist, well-drained organic soils but will

TOP Matte-textured and richly patterned, the evergreen foliage of Allegheny pachysandra, *Pachysandra procumbens*, is still quite handsome in late March after enduring winter in our Pennsylvania garden.

BOTTOM Though a fleeting presence in late April, the fragrant white flowers of Allegheny pachysandra are an added attraction, appearing before new leaves.

LEFT Allegheny pachysandra has seasonal personalities, here in early May at Springwood in Pennsylvania when the bright green new foliage overtops the old.

Be sure to add dwarf ginseng, *Panax trifolius*, to your short list of plants that will thrive between the root flares of beeches and other surface-rooted trees, as observed here in late April in the Ward garden in northern Delaware.

grow well enough on lesser soils, and is tolerant of summer-dry shade once established. Its growth is never aggressive and choking like that of its Asian relative, and I've found it well suited for planting around and under shrubs.

Panax
AMERICAN GINSENG, DWARF GINSENG
ARALIACEAE, GINSENG FAMILY

American ginseng, *Panax quinquefolius*, is now grown in large quantities as a substitute for the original Asian ginseng species, which were earlier collected to near-extinction for their medicinal properties. Once common in rich woodlands from Canada to the Gulf coast, it is now rare in native habitats, never having recovered from overcollecting.

As a landscape plant, ginseng is more curious than attractive, but its smaller relative, dwarf ginseng, *Panax trifolius*, can be a delightful presence in the woodland landscape, both native and designed. Ranging widely in rich woods and bottomlands from Quebec to Minnesota and south along the mountains to Georgia, dwarf ginseng is often found in large colonies that dot the ground with small dark green leaves and small spheres of snow-white flowers in early spring. A true ephemeral, it disappears into dormancy by early summer. Cold hardy to zone 3, dwarf ginseng can be grown from seed or by division.

Parthenocissus
VIRGINIA CREEPER
VITACEAE, GRAPE FAMILY

Yes, it can creep, but Virginia creeper, *Parthenocissus quinquefolia*, is more often like Mercury, flying over the ground surface and up into the high canopy of deciduous trees. I've even observed (and admired) red cedars, *Juniperus virginiana*, garlanded with scarlet-hued Virginia creeper in October and ready to give any store-bought Christmas tree some serious competition. For all its exuberance, Virginia creeper has won a reputation as something to be approached cautiously, if at all, but I believe it has real utility in the designed landscape if imaginatively employed. Certainly no other North American vine, and few native trees, can rival its autumn color.

Found in the wild on moist and dry soils of all sorts, from Maine and Ontario to Nebraska and south to Texas and Florida, this vigorous woody vine is cold hardy through zone 4. It will grow in clay, sand, or loam, whether wet or dry, and is quite salt tolerant. It colors best when the foliage receives some direct sunlight but will grow and color subtly even in dense shade. Climbing fifty feet or more by adhesive-tipped tendrils, Virginia creeper is capable of scaling stone or other masonry walls.

TOP RIGHT Virginia creeper, *Parthenocissus quinquefolia*, is brilliant in mid-October sunlight in West Virginia.

CENTER RIGHT In late September, the rich red hues of Virginia creeper grace a stone pillar at Grey Towers, the former home of forester Gifford Pinchot, in Pennsylvania.

Phacelia

HYDROPHYLLACEAE, WATERLEAF FAMILY

The phacelias are mostly annual species. Their blooming is often a breathtaking event in the Smoky Mountains springtime, as myriad flowers float above the forest floor like a low cloud.

Mention annuals to most gardeners and the image conjured is one of tender tropicals, with color as constant and unyielding as a coat of epoxy paint, grown in geometrically ordered confines. Including native annual flowers in designed landscapes, even naturalistic ones, is relatively uncommon. Nowhere near as obedient as perennials, annuals can be coaxed but never coerced, and the most effective way to do this is by working with the essential order of habitats within your garden. With a little luck, annuals may flock to niches predisposed to their needs, as they do in native habitats.

The phacelias are mentioned here because they present that possibility. Seeds and plants are sometimes offered by nurseries, and they deserve to be more often. Among the showiest are Appalachian phacelia, *Phacelia dubia*, with blue or white flowers; forest phacelia, *Phacelia bipinnatifida*, a blue-flowered biennial; and Blue Ridge phacelia, *Phacelia fimbriata*, with fringed white flowers. All are native to moist deciduous woodlands.

BOTTOM RIGHT The annual Blue Ridge phacelia, *Phacelia fimbriata*, flowers on the woods floor in North Carolina in late April.

ABOVE LEFT Growing wild, woodland phlox, *Phlox divaricata*, blooms in drifts in dappled shade at the edge of a Virginia woodlands in early April. Though sometimes called blue phlox for the most common flower color, it has forms with pink or white flowers.

ABOVE RIGHT Creeping phlox, *Phlox stolonifera*, wends its way through clouds of foamflower, *Tiarella cordifolia*, in early May at Longwood Gardens. These two are relatively well balanced in vigor and, though the patterns will evolve over seasons, can be maintained in combination with minimal intervention. Many cultivated varieties are available including white- and pink-flowered types.

Phlox

POLEMONIACEAE, PHLOX FAMILY

Most North American phlox species are sun plants, but two true woodland phlox are among the most beautiful and useful perennials for woodland gardens. In addition to their spring floral displays, both are spreading species valuable as ground covers.

Flowering twelve to fifteen inches high, woodland phlox, *Phlox divaricata*, is the taller and earlier blooming of the two. Native to rich, moist woods from Quebec to Minnesota south to Texas and Georgia, it is cold hardy to zone 3. Woodland phlox produces two types of growth: short sterile stems that form a low year-round cover of basal foliage, and leafy upright stems that support flowers in April. Woodland phlox spreads underground by rhizomes but not aggressively. Easily grown in well-drained organic soil, it blooms best with some direct sun but will flower within a deciduous canopy. Woodland phlox is easily divided, and it readily self-sows if conditions are moist and lightly shaded, making it an ideal choice for naturalizing.

More of a mountain species, growing naturally from Ohio and Pennsylvania south to Georgia, creeping phlox, *Phlox stolonifera*, is even more shade tolerant and will bloom in surprisingly low light. Like woodland phlox, it has separate flowering stems and sterile stems, but it spreads by stolons to form a dense foliage mat less than two inches high which remains over winter. The slender flowering stems are leafless. Creeping phlox is less inclined to self-sowing and naturalizing.

Pieris

MOUNTAIN PIERIS, MOUNTAIN FETTERBUSH
ERICACEAE, HEATH FAMILY

Native to mountain woods from Virginia and West Virginia south to Georgia, mountain pieris, *Pieris floribunda*, is a handsome evergreen shrub growing four to six feet tall. Its white flower clusters appear in April and early May, and stand out sharply against the dark green foliage. Cold hardy to zone 4, it requires moist, well-drained organic soil and does best in regions with cool to moderate summer night temperatures. Though more particular about siting than the ubiquitous Japanese pieris, *Pieris japonica*, it is nearly immune to the lacebug that so often disfigures those shrubs. Mountain pieris is little known and little grown, but it clearly deserves further consideration in woodland gardens.

Platanus

SYCAMORE, BUTTONWOOD
PLATANACEAE, PLANE TREE FAMILY

Long before I ever dreamed of studying botany and horticulture, I frequented a nearby hilltop overlooking the White Clay Creek valley. The view was most captivating in winter, when the course of the creek was revealed by a double line of sycamores, standing brilliant white among the grays, blacks, and browns of other trees. Native to moist or wet alluvial soil from Maine to Minnesota south to Texas and Florida, sycamore, *Platanus occidentalis*, is unique in the drama of its winter presence.

Cold hardy to zone 4, sycamores are fast growing and broadly tolerant, colonizing bottomlands in the wake of disturbance by floods and storms, as well as seeding into nooks and crannies in semi-urban environments. They can grow over 150 feet tall, surpassed in height by few if any deciduous North American species except tuliptree, *Liriodendron tulipifera*. Though too large for many residential landscapes and somewhat messy as a street tree due to dropping leaves and seeds, sycamores are something to be appreciated and conserved in regional

Mountain pieris, *Pieris floribunda*, blooms in early May in the mountains of eastern West Virginia. Though it is sometimes seen in apparently sunny exposures in the mountains, it is effectively shaded by the frequent cloud cover of such places. The filtered light of deciduous woodlands is ideal for plants grown at lower altitudes.

Brilliant and chalk-white, sycamores, *Platanus occidentalis*, stand out against autumn foliage in West Virginia in early October.

woodlands and parks. In part of the twentieth century they suffered increasingly from anthracnose disease, but while they are often temporarily defoliated, trees usually recover from bouts. The sycamore-like trees most frequently used in street plantings are London plane trees, which are hybrids between *Platanus occidentalis* and the oriental plane tree, *Platanus orientalis*. Their bark is never as white as sycamore bark.

Podophyllum
MAYAPPLE
BERBERIDACEAE, BARBERRY FAMILY

It is a curious phenomenon that when Americans visit eastern Asian landscapes they are enthralled by the native *Podophyllum* species there, yet when I've had

Asian visitors in my Pennsylvania garden and local woodlands, they've marveled at the local Mayapple, *Podophyllum peltatum*.

Though Mayapples do flower, it is their foliage that is enthralling. Rising in early spring like tiny parasols, the leaves open twelve to sixteen inches across. The largest leaves arise singly on stout stalks, directly from the underground rhizome. Smaller leaves are produced in pairs arising from short vertical stem segments, attached at a node and accompanied by a single flower. Porcelain-white and fragrant, the flowers are more than two inches in diameter and mature into one-and-one-half-inch-long fruits that are applelike only in their smooth yellow-green skin. They are toxic until ripe and are then edible but not particularly palatable.

Native to deep, rich woods from Vermont to Minnesota and south to Arkansas, Tennessee, and North Carolina, Mayapple typically spreads by its thick rhizomes to form huge colonies covering the woodland floor. Though they share space with other sturdy herbaceous plants in their native habitat, they can easily overpower delicate companions in the garden and are best reserved for less precise plantings. Many ferns will co-exist with Mayapples, and evergreen ferns in particular make a good combination since they persist after the Mayapple foliage goes dormant in late summer or fall. Cold hardy to zone 3, Mayapples are easily propagated by root divisions.

Polemonium
JACOB'S LADDER
POLEMONIACEAE, PHLOX FAMILY

The most common eastern Jacob's ladder, *Polemonium reptans*, is long lived and easy to grow on moist, well-drained soil. Despite its species epithet (*reptans* means "creeping"), Jacob's ladder is a clump-forming perennial which frequently spreads by seed to form large patches in low woods and floodplains and is covered in late April and early May with sky-blue blossoms. It grows naturally in rich woods and shaded bottomlands from New York to Minnesota and south to Virginia, Alabama, and Oklahoma, and is cold hardy to zone 3 but suffers in regions with high summer night temperatures. Less common but also worth considering for the woodland garden, Appalachian Jacob's ladder, *Polemonium van-bruntiae*, is a blue-purple-flowered eastern species often found at higher altitude in acid environments.

Mayapple, *Podophyllum peltatum*, decorates the forest floor with foot-wide foliage in mid April. Some leaves are solid green; others are strongly bronze patterned.

The common eastern Jacob's ladder, *Polemonium reptans*, flowers in large drifts on a Pennsylvania floodplain in early May.

Polygonatum

SOLOMON'S SEAL
LILIACEAE, LILY FAMILY

Solomon's seals grow from a thick, horizontal rhizome which typically sends up one new stalk each year. The common name refers to the round scars on the rhizome marking the attachment points of stalks from former years. Two eastern woodland plants share these characteristics, the true Solomon's seals, *Polygonatum*, which have flowers suspended in clusters along the arching stem, and the false Solomon's seals, *Smilacina*, which have flowers in clusters at the end of the stem.

The most common and widespread true Solomon's seal is *Polygonatum biflorum*, which grows from New Hampshire to Minnesota, Manitoba, and North Dakota and south to Mexico and Florida, often on sloping ground associated with stream and river valleys. Cold hardy to zone 3, it is easy to grow in moist well-drained soils under deciduous shade. The species is extremely variable, and plants may be barely one foot tall or over five feet tall. At one time, Solomon's seal

ABOVE Although its species name means "two-flowered," *Polygonatum biflorum* has pendent blossoms grouped in twos, threes, or fours. If pollinated, the flowers mature into attractive dark-blue berries.

RIGHT Giant Solomon's seals, *Polygonatum biflorum*, stretch architecturally to five feet in height from a moist woodland bank in Virginia in late May.

was split into two separate species, with *Polygonatum commutatum* describing the tallest plants, which are frequently tetraploid. From a horticultural perspective, the giant Solomon's seals are quite different plants from their diminutive relatives; however, all manner of intermediates can be found between the largest and the smallest, which is why botanists lump them together.

Downy Solomon's seal, *Polygonatum pubescens*, is a very similar-looking plant of more northern distribution, ranging south only in the mountains to northern Georgia. It is slightly hairy, whereas *Polygonatum biflorum* is smooth.

Quercus
OAK
FAGACEAE, BEECH FAMILY

The oaks are a large and complex group whose diversity far exceeds the scope of this book (over 100 species are native to North America); however, they are key elements in the forest canopy and in the seasonal beauty of deciduous woodlands, and their acorns are among the most important food sources for woodland wildlife. Often relegated to parks and forests, oaks have significant potential for residential landscapes, too.

The deep-rooted nature of most oaks, which is desirable in the garden, makes them generally difficult to transplant in any size, and this has unfortunately limited the selection of oaks commonly offered by nurseries. Growing quality oak trees for transplanting requires significant root pruning and training during nursery production. The most commonly planted species, pin oak, *Quercus palustris*, is readily available not because it is a superior oak—it is not—but because it is one of the most shallow-rooted and easy to produce and transplant. If you can't find the oak species you're looking for, consider starting trees from acorns, which is easy and surprisingly fast. It's also the best way to obtain trees of local provenance.

Oaks are generally segregated into two groups: the white oaks, which typically have round-lobed leaves, and the red oaks, whose leaves are usually sharp pointed. Of the first group, the white oak, *Quercus alba*, is the preeminent eastern species. Capable of living for centuries, it is native to upland woods from Maine to Minnesota and south to Florida and Texas. It is cold hardy to zone 3 and requires well-drained soil that is at least slightly acid. Autumn color is often rich

The round-lobed leaves of white oak, *Quercus alba,* are fresh bright green in mid May and typically amber to red brown in autumn.

Growing in the open in southern New Jersey, a majestic white oak, *Quercus alba*, spreads nearly one hundred feet wide, silhouetted against the December sky near twilight.

amber or red brown. In time, white oak can reach more than one hundred feet tall, and if growing in the open, its spread can equal or exceed its height. White oak is not very shade tolerant and is among the most difficult to transplant in any size, though extremely easy from acorns. A white oak seedling in our garden has grown more than twenty feet in less than a decade.

Swamp white oak, *Quercus bicolor*, is a better choice in poorly drained sites. Native on floodplains and other wet soils from Quebec to Minnesota and south to Arkansas, Tennessee, and North Carolina, it is cold hardy to zone 4. Overcup oak, *Quercus lyrata*, is especially flood tolerant. Native to wet woods and swamps, from New Jersey to Illinois and south to Texas and Florida, it is cold hardy to zone 5.

Also in the white oak group, burr oak, *Quercus macrocarpa*, is the classic midwestern oak. Native to moist woods and floodplains from New Brunswick to Ontario and south to Virginia, Louisiana, and Texas, it is cold hardy to zone 2 and tolerant of limestone soils. It can also grow over one hundred feet tall with equal or greater spread. Its fall color is subtle, usually brown or tan.

Leaves of chestnut oak, *Quercus prinus*, another in the white oak group, look very much like those of American chestnut, *Castanea dentata*, except they are smaller and the lobes are rounded. It is an extremely tough oak, native mostly to dry, upland rocky woods in the Appalachian region from Maine to Georgia, cold hardy to zone 4, and able to grow in extremely dry, poor soils. The mature bark is typically deeply furrowed. Among the easier oaks to transplant, it is often available commercially. Trees from rocky mountain habitats are sometimes referred to as rock chestnut oak, *Quercus montana*.

The red oak group includes some of the best species for red fall color, but pin oak, *Quercus palustris*, is not one of these. Its fall color is unremarkable, usually brown, or amber at best. Native from Massachusetts to Delaware and west to Wisconsin and Arkansas, it is cold hardy to zone 4. Though pin oak is widely adaptable, its lower branches droop strongly downward and it typically requires considerable pruning to produce a form that is practical in the designed garden.

Red oak, *Quercus rubra* [synonym *Quercus borealis*], is very common. A fast-growing tree that can easily exceed one hundred feet in height, it is cold hardy to zone 3 and relatively easy to transplant. It is also among the more shade-tolerant oaks and can be introduced under an existing canopy. New leaves typically emerge bright velvet-red. Autumn color may be orange, red, or russet but is sometimes unremarkable, varying with individual seedlings. One of the most distinctive characteristics of red oak is its vertically striped bark, which has dark furrows alternating with flat gray areas. The species ranges widely from Minnesota to Quebec and south to Oklahoma and into the North Carolina mountains. Its close relative black oak, *Quercus velutina*, is more common on poor soils but is difficult to transplant and not readily available.

Scarlet oak, *Quercus coccinea*, is among the oaks with consistent, dark red to maroon autumn color. Native to upland habitats from Maine to Georgia and west to Michigan, Missouri, and Mississippi, it grows up to seventy-five feet tall and is cold hardy to zone 4. It transplants reasonably well and is becoming increasingly available. Cold hardy to zone 5, its southern relative, Shumard oak, *Quercus shumardii*, is native to bottomlands and usually has good red fall color.

Among the many other oaks are those known as scrub oaks, typically small to

TOP Burr oak, *Quercus macrocarpa*, is the quintessential midwestern oak, capable of growing over one hundred feet tall with massive trunk and wide-spreading branches.

BOTTOM New leaves of red oak, *Quercus rubra*, emerge felty and pink-red in late April in eastern Pennsylvania.

ABOVE LEFT Though autumn color varies considerably among seedlings, red oak, *Quercus rubra,* can be spectacular, as illustrated by this early October image of a West Virginia mountain tree.

ABOVE RIGHT Young scarlet oaks, *Quercus coccinea,* add their distinctive deep red color to the late-October landscape of the Hendricks garden in eastern Pennsylvania.

ABOVE Glowing dark amber in late October in coastal New Jersey, the lyre-shaped leaves of blackjack oak, *Quercus marilandica,* will remain on the branches through winter.

medium-sized trees found on dry, somewhat sterile soils. Best known among these is blackjack oak, *Quercus marilandica,* which ranges widely from New York to Iowa and south to Florida and Texas. Though it can reach ninety feet if provided rich growing conditions, it is more commonly fifteen to twenty-five feet tall. It is very difficult to transplant, except when young, but an interesting tree to consider starting from an acorn.

Rhododendron

AZALEA, RHODODENDRON
ERICACEAE, HEATH FAMILY

The genus *Rhododendron* includes both evergreen rhododendrons and azaleas, and the deciduous azaleas of eastern North America, comprising fifteen or more species, are among the most versatile and satisfying shrubs for woodland gardens, offering fine form, foliage, flowers, and often fragrance.

Though there are species native from Quebec to Maine and south to Texas and Florida, deciduous azaleas are most common in the Southeast. Flower color ranges from the rose-purple blooms of rhodora, *Rhododendron canadense,* through pink, red, orange, yellow, white, and all shades in between. Many species

I've long been fond of my local native pinxter azalea, *Rhododendron periclymenoides*, which enlivens the April and May woods with delicate pink blossoms, but I became truly enamored of the deciduous azaleas as a group while researching their potential for the Peirce's Woods garden at Longwood Gardens.

ABOVE Pinxter azalea flowers in late May in a shaded northern Delaware woodlands. Native to moist and dry woods from New England to Illinois and south to the Carolinas and Tennessee, this species is cold hardy into zone 4. Flowers vary in color from deep pink to white with pink suffusion, and are

unscented or only lightly fragrant. A close relative, the piedmont azalea, *Rhododendron canescens*, is very similar except the flowers are always sweetly fragrant.

TOP RIGHT Pinxter azalea blooms heavily at the sunny edge of a Delaware woods in early May. The long-exerted stamens are part of the characteristic charm of native deciduous azaleas.

BOTTOM RIGHT The foliage of pinxter azalea is richly colored in late October in our Pennsylvania garden.

readily hybridize in cultivation and in their native habitats. I've climbed the North Carolina mountains in mid to late June to find populations of naturally occurring hybrid azaleas in an almost dizzying mix of color and fragrance. Such experiences are unforgettably inspiring to a woodland gardener.

Deciduous azaleas are an easy group to grow, preferring moist, well-drained organic soil for best performance. They are shallow rooted and transplant readily even in surprisingly large sizes, though small plants will more quickly establish. Some of the more northern species, including *Rhododendron prinophyllum*

Alabama azalea, *Rhododendron alabamense*, blooms in late May at Winterthur Museum and Gardens in northern Delaware. Native to Alabama and Georgia, this extremely fragrant species typically has white flowers with a prominent yellow blotch, and is cold hardy to zone 6.

ABOVE Roseshell azalea, *Rhododendron prinophyllum*, blooms heavily in dappled light near the edge of a West Virginia woods in late May. Native to moist or dry woods from Quebec and Maine south to Oklahoma, Arkansas, and Kentucky, mostly in the moun-tains, this species is cold hardy to zone 4.

TOP LEFT The characteristically deep-pink flowers of roseshell azalea are among the most fragrant of all deciduous azaleas, with a sweet-spicy clovelike scent.

and *Rhododendron canadense*, do best in regions with cooler summers, but others from the Southeast such as *Rhododendron austrinum* and *Rhododendron serrulatum* are quite heat resistant. The most common limitation is cold hardiness. *Rhododendron canadense* is hardy to zone 2, and *Rhododendron prinophyllum* to zone 4; however, many of the most floriferous are plants best suited to zones 5 and warmer.

The flowering period of native azaleas as a group is surprisingly long. After selecting and amassing over 100 different species and varieties at the Longwood Gardens research nursery, we had plants that bloomed from April into September. Flowering is best when shrubs are sited at edges and in openings; however, even heavily shaded plants are likely to produce some blooms. Many deciduous azaleas also have fine fall color when touched by the sun.

TOP LEFT Pinkshell azalea, *Rhododendron vaseyi*, blooms in early May in the Peirce's Woods garden at Longwood Gardens, under a high deciduous canopy. Among the largest deciduous azaleas, this species can grow to fifteen feet tall. Cold hardy to zone 5, it is native only to the mountains of western North Carolina.

BOTTOM LEFT Growing along a western Pennsylvania riverbank, sweet azalea, *Rhododendron arborescens*, and witch hazel, *Hamamelis virginiana*, present a fine balance of form and texture. The glossy dark green leaves make this azalea a particularly handsome shrub even when not in bloom. Also called smooth azalea, it is native to upland woods from Pennsylvania to Kentucky and

south to Alabama and Georgia, especially in mountains toward the southern part of its range. It is cold hardy to zone 4.

BOTTOM CENTER Sweet azalea is covered in fragrant white flowers with characteristic red styles in late June at Longwood Gardens. This species typically flowers in early to mid summer, later than many deciduous azaleas.

TOP RIGHT Blooming heavily in sun on May 3 at Longwood Gardens, seedlings of pinkshell azalea vary in color from deep clear pink as shown, to light pink or rarely, white. Though large, the flowers of this species are not fragrant.

BOTTOM RIGHT Fall foliage of pinkshell azalea is bright scarlet in a sunny location at Longwood Gardens in late October.

ABOVE Flowering in early June in coastal New Jersey, swamp azalea, *Rhododendron viscosum*, is fragrant and characteristically white flowered. Even within New Jersey populations, swamp azaleas bloom anytime from early June to late July. Sometimes called swamp honeysuckle, this species is native to wet woods and swamps from Maine to Ohio and south to Florida, and is cold hardy to zone 4. Its close relative, the Florida hammocksweet azalea, *Rhododendron serrulatum*, is very similar in appearance and fragrance, though the flowers are smaller. Native to wet habitats in Florida, Georgia, and Louisiana, it is cold hardy through zone 7.

TOP CENTER Coast azalea, *Rhododendron atlanticum*, flowers quite fragrantly in our Pennsylvania garden in mid May. Shorter in stature than many of the deciduous azaleas, this species is usually less than four feet in height, with white or light pink flowers. Native to sandy soil mostly on the coastal plain from New Jersey to Texas, it is cold hardy to zone 5.

TOP RIGHT Flame azalea, *Rhododendron calendulaceum*, blooms in early June in a sunny location at Longwood Gardens. Bright orange is the most characteristic color of this tall-growing species, but yellow forms are often found. Native to mountain woods and clearings from Pennsylvania and Ohio to Georgia and Alabama, flame azalea is cold hardy to zone 5. Though among the most vividly colored, the flowers of this species are unscented.

BOTTOM RIGHT Many years ago, I saw this magnificent clear yellow flame azalea blooming in late May beside a house in Parsons, West Virginia. Hiking the hillsides and mountain slopes nearby, I found many other plants varying from typical orange to gold and yellow. The local populace obviously valued these native mountain shrubs, commonly conserving and transplanting them on farm and residential properties through the valley.

TOP LEFT Cumberland azalea, *Rhododendron bakeri*, blooms in partial shade at Winterthur Museum and Gardens in mid June. Closely related to flame azalea, the flowers are typically orange to deep red, and are unscented. Native to the Cumberland Plateau in Kentucky, across Tennessee to the mountains in Georgia, Alabama, and North Carolina, this azalea is cold hardy to zone 5.

TOP CENTER An exceptionally deep red-flowered form of Oconee azalea, *Rhododendron flammeum*, blooms in partial shade at Winterthur Museum and Gardens in late May. Native to the lower piedmont region of Georgia and South Carolina, this species is more heat tolerant than most and is cold hardy to zone 6. Flowers are typically in ball-like trusses, varying in color from red or pink to yellow. Though the species is not fragrant, hybrids with fragrant species are common in cultivation.

TOP RIGHT Florida flame azalea, *Rhododendron austrinum*, flowers in early May in a sunny location at Longwood Gardens. Flower color of this extraordinarily fragrant species varies from typical red-orange to yellow. Native to woods and streambanks in Florida, Georgia, Alabama, and Mississippi, this heat-tolerant species is cold hardy to zone 6.

BOTTOM LEFT Plumleaf azalea, *Rhododendron prunifolium*, blooms in early August in relatively dense shade at Longwood Gardens. The unscented flowers are typically orange to red. Native to moist shaded woodlands and streambanks in Georgia and Alabama, this late flowering azalea is hardy into zone 5.

BOTTOM RIGHT In late June on Gregory bald, a sunny opening in the North Carolina mountain forest, naturally occurring hybrids of native deciduous azaleas produce kaleidoscopic colors. This population and others on similar heath balds in the Smoky Mountains have served as seed sources for many nursery breeding and evaluation programs.

The clonal cultivar *Rhododendron* 'Yellow Delight', having fragrant, light yellow flowers, originated as an open-pollinated seedling of *Rhododendron atlanticum*, possibly involving *Rhododendron austrinum*. Introduced by Transplant Nurseries of Georgia, it represents one of the finer selections built entirely upon the natural genetic diversity of North American deciduous azaleas.

Though limited in color and rarely as splendid in bloom as the deciduous species, native evergreen rhododendrons also have much to offer woodland gardeners.

Rosebay rhododendron, *Rhododendron maximum*, is the hardiest of the lot and will withstand zone 3. Native from Nova Scotia and Ontario south to Georgia, Alabama, and Ohio, it truly requires cool, moist, richly organic soils and suffers if exposed to summer sun and heat. Flowers are typically white to purple-pink in early summer.

A close relative, the Catawba rhododendron, *Rhododendron catawbiense*, is much more adaptable and heat tolerant. Cold hardy to zone 4, it ranges naturally in mountain woods and openings from Virginia to Kentucky and south to Georgia and Alabama. Flowers are typically an intense lilac-purple but may also be white. This species has been used extensively in the production of garden hybrids.

Native from Kentucky through the Carolinas to Tennessee, Alabama, and Georgia, the piedmont rhododendron, *Rhododendron minus*, is smaller in all aspects, with lighter lavender-pink flowers. The widely cultivated Carolina rhododendron, *Rhododendron carolinianum*, has smaller, glossy dark green leaves and flowers varying from lilac and pink to white. Cold hardy through zone 5, it is native mostly to the mountains of North and South Carolina and Tennessee.

LEFT Rosebay rhododendron, *Rhododendron maximum*, blooms in mid June in typical habitat along a cool stream in North Carolina.

BELOW Piedmont rhododendron, *Rhododendron minus*, blooms light pink in late May at

the Henry Foundation in Gladwyne, Pennsylvania.

BELOW RIGHT Catawba rhododendron, *Rhododendron catawbiense*, blooms deep rose-purple in the Virginia mountains in mid June.

Rhus

SUMAC

ANACARDIACEAE, CASHEW FAMILY

The infamy of the toxic *Rhus* relatives often overshadows the multiseason interest other members of this group contribute to the regional landscape. Though motivated by nomenclatural rule, not marketing, in recent years taxonomic botanists have done sumacs, *Rhus* species, a small public-relations favor by segregating those that cause blistering and itching in the genus *Toxicodendron*. As opposed to the red-fruited friendly sorts, this group is white berried and includes the familiar poison ivy, *Toxicodendron radicans* [synonym *Rhus radicans*] and the true poison sumac, *Toxicodendron vernix* [synonym *Rhus vernix*], which is a relatively uncommon shrub that occurs only in woodland swamps from Maine to Minnesota and south to Texas and Florida. For the adventurous or the immune, poison sumac does have splendid autumn color, as does poison ivy.

Most red-fruited sumacs are strongly running plants of open spaces, often venturing up to sunny woodland edges but never continuing under the full shade of the canopy. The one exception is fragrant sumac, *Rhus aromatica*, a low-running shrub typically two to five feet tall, occurring in both open woods and sunny habitats from Quebec south to Florida and west to the Pacific coast. I've seen it scrambling over rock outcrops and steep wooded slopes in the Appalachian region, producing small yellow flowers in late March or early April and turning bright red in fall. Tolerant of shade or full sun on a wide range of soil types, it is extremely drought tolerant and cold hardy to zone 3. Though it runs, it is much less aggressive than the larger sumacs and is a useful tall groundcover or soil-stabilizing shrub for difficult areas.

Autumn colors of the larger sumacs are among the season's most vibrant, and winter fruit and stem characters are often uniquely appealing. They are useful in sunny edge situations in the larger woodland garden, where their strongly spreading growth can be accommodated. The most spectacular in autumn, staghorn sumac, *Rhus typhina*, is also best in winter, with fuzzy stems that glow when backlit, and bright red fruit clusters on female plants. Native to dry open places from Nova Scotia to Minnesota and south to Alabama and Georgia, it is cold hardy to zone 4. An elegant cut-leafed form is common in commerce. Also cold hardy to zone 4, winged sumac, *Rhus copallinum*, is typically solid red or

TOP Fragrant sumac, *Rhus aromatica*, blooms on the first day of April on a rocky outcrop in the Virginia mountain woodlands. Despite the common name, the flowers are better described as mildly malodorous.

BOTTOM Fragrant sumac colors vividly even within an open oak-hickory woods in West Virginia in mid October.

TOP LEFT We've found staghorn sumac, *Rhus typhina*, useful and manageable at the sunny edge of our Pennsylvania garden, where its fuzzy stems may catch the winter sunlight, as in this early December photograph.

TOP RIGHT Staghorn sumac is rainbow-hued in mid October as it ventures near the edge of a West Virginia mountain forest.

ABOVE AND OPPOSITE TOP LEFT Flowering raspberry, *Rubus odoratus*, blooms in late July along the Blue Ridge Parkway in Virginia. It is often in flower from June through August.

burgundy in autumn, and smooth sumac, *Rhus glabra*, cold hardy to zone 3, is often a brilliant mix of orange and crimson-red. Cut-leafed forms of smooth sumac exist, along with a superb hybrid between *Rhus glabra* and *Rhus typhina* which has been called 'Red Autumn Lace'.

Rubus
BRAMBLE, BLACKBERRY, RASPBERRY
ROSACEAE, ROSE FAMILY

Of the myriad native brambles, only flowering raspberry, *Rubus odoratus*, stands out as a superb possibility for woodland gardens. It lacks the thorns that make most *Rubus* species painful to work with and its broad, maplelike leaves are so attractive this running shrub is worth growing for foliage alone. For many weeks in summer, it produces large, fragrant rose-purple flowers in clusters at the stem tips. Native to moist shady places and woods margins from Nova Scotia to Michigan south to North Carolina and Tennessee, it is cold hardy to zone 5 and of easy culture on a wide range of soil types.

Sambucus

ELDER, ELDERBERRY
CAPRIFOLIACEAE, HONEYSUCKLE FAMILY

Native to moist woods and meadows across much of North America, common el-derberry, *Sambucus canadensis*, has long been valued for its purple-black fruits, which are used in making wine, juice, jam, and pies, and are important to birds. Its generally rangy growth and floppy form, however, make it difficult to inte-grate in all but the most naturalistic woodland garden designs.

   A more intriguing alternative is American red elder, *Sambucus pubens* [syn-onym *Sambucus racemosa*], a brilliantly red-berried shrub native to rich, moist woods from Newfoundland to British Columbia, south through Illinois and Pennsylvania into the North Carolina mountains. Growing upright-spreading to nine feet tall, it is cold hardy to zone 4. Quite shade tolerant, red elder grows best with even moisture, in regions with cool to moderate summer night tempera-tures. The berries are also favored by birds.

TOP RIGHT Fading flower panicles of Amer-ican red elder, *Sambucus pubens*, catch a bit of the late-May light along a stream in the Smoky Mountains.

BOTTOM RIGHT Berries of red elder are brilliant in woodland shade as seen in this late-June image from North Carolina.

Sanguinaria

BLOODROOT
PAPAVERACEAE, POPPY FAMILY

Bloodroot, *Sanguinaria canadensis*, is such a commonplace harbinger of spring, it's hard for me to imagine a woodland garden without it. Native to moist woodlands and floodplains from Nova Scotia to Manitoba, south to Oklahoma and Florida, this delicately beautiful but rugged plant often spreads by seed to form patches in the woods or extensive sweeps along shaded roadbanks. Though the flowers quickly drop their snow-white petals, the leaves expand to become a significant, bold-textured presence in the woodland ground layer, remaining attractive long into autumn. Easy to grow from divisions of the rhizome and often easy to naturalize by seed, bloodroot adapts to a wide range of soil and moisture conditions and is cold hardy to zone 3.

TOP LEFT Flowering in late April in our Pennsylvania garden, bloodroot, *Sanguinaria canadensis*, has proved one of the longest-lived, carefree-flowering perennials.

TOP RIGHT The leaves of bloodroot have expanded by early May and will remain an attractive ground cover through summer and into autumn.

CENTER LEFT Many poppy family members have colored sap, but the sap of bloodroot is among the most brilliant red. Bloodroot is easily propagated by divisions of the thick-ened rhizomes, which normally lie horizontally one to three inches below the soil surface.

BOTTOM LEFT I'm typically ambivalent or uninterested in most double-flowered forms; however, it is difficult to discount the elegance and appeal of *Sanguinaria canadensis* 'Multiplex'. This clonal cultivar is sterile and must be vegetatively propagated. I wouldn't grow it in lieu of the innumerable fertile seedlings that are native and naturalized in our garden, but our patch of 'Multiplex' is an innocuous and stunning presence in their midst.

Sassafras

LAURACEAE, LAUREL FAMILY

Sassafras albidum has many personalities. It can be a pioneer, reclaiming land laid open by agriculture, transportation systems, or various types of natural disturbance. Though often viewed as a transient, it can also live for more than a century and reach over one hundred feet in height. Native from Maine to Michigan and Missouri, south to Texas and Florida, sassafras adapts to a variety of soil and moisture conditions, and is cold hardy to zone 4. Truly a tree with four seasons of interest, sassafras deserves wider appreciation in North American gardens.

Appearing at the beginning of spring, the bright yellow flowers of sassafras are splendidly displayed against clearing blue skies. The species is dioecious, and the flowers of female trees produce dark blue fruits. These are favorites of birds and are often quickly plucked from their scarlet pedicels, which remain colorful and attractive into autumn. Summertime foliage is a bright green, with leaves in various shapes including some that look remarkably like mittens. Fall color is variable but always superb, and in the best trees, it is a riot of gold, apricot, peach, and red.

Like dogwoods, sassafras has a sympodial branching pattern, meaning the new growth extends from lateral buds instead of from terminal buds as is typical with most woody plants. Sassafras branches are markedly horizontal and often tiered, resulting in a graceful winter architecture.

TOP LEFT A grove of sassafras, *Sassafras albidum*, is covered in light yellow flowers in late April in northern Delaware.

TOP RIGHT Produced only on female trees, the dark blue sassafras berries are quickly taken by birds, leaving only the scarlet pedicels. The bark on young growth is green throughout the year.

BOTTOM RIGHT Sassafras autumn color is among the most dazzling of any deciduous tree, as typified by these trees along a Delaware roadside in late October.

LEFT In many regions, sassafras groupings like this one in southern New Jersey are taken for granted in hedgerows and other often-temporary niches in the accidental landscape. The trees' suckering habit leads to such close spacing. In winter, the tiered effect of the branches will be even more apparent than in this late-October photograph.

BELOW Growing on sloping ground in a former farmyard not far from our Pennsylvania garden, this magnificent old sassafras is testimony to the potential of the species. Sassafras can be easily trained as a single-stemmed or multistemmed tree by removing extra shoots while young and then preventing root disturbance, which promotes suckering.

The commercial availability of sassafras has increased along with growing interest in North American native flora; however, it is limited by the relative difficulty of transplanting large trees. I've experienced nearly complete success transplanting trees up to one-inch caliper in late winter, which is the ideal time. Sassafras is easy to grow from seed, and young seedlings transplant readily. The species is prone to suckering, especially in disturbed situations, and root suckers are nearly impossible to transplant. Due in part to its suckering habit, sassafras is often found growing in groves, and this is an attractive way to use it in the woodland garden. Free of any significant pests or diseases, sassafras grows fastest in full sun and will decline if eventually shaded by a continuous overstory.

The root bark of this highly aromatic tree has been traditionally used for numerous medicinal purposes and in the making of sassafras tea; however, it contains safrole, which is a suspected human carcinogen, and commercial production of foods containing safrole is now prohibited by the U.S. Food and Drug Administration. Other research has confirmed safrole's antibacterial and antiviral properties. Much less controversial, sassafras leaves are safrole-free, and are dried and ground to make the famous *filé* powder used in gumbos and in other Creole and Cajun cuisine. Sassafras is common along the Gulf coast and reportedly was used by Choctaw Indians for its flavoring and thickening properties long before the Acadians (Cajuns) drifted south to Louisiana.

Sedum
STONECROP
CRASSULACEAE, STONECROP FAMILY

Few woodland ground covers are as willing or versatile as wild stonecrop, *Sedum ternatum*, which will grow in the deepest deciduous shade, its creeping stems spreading and rooting to create a low, light-green mat of evergreen foliage. It is a fine choice for a ground cover directly under shrubs or trees, or will thrive in considerable sun if provided moist soil. In late April and early May, wild stonecrop can literally cover itself in bright white flowers, especially in partly sunny locations. Found naturally on forest floors, rocks, and cliffs, wild stonecrop is native from New Jersey to Georgia, west to Iowa and Arkansas, and is cold hardy to zone 4. It is easy to divide and almost equally easy to propagate by rooting stem cuttings directly in the ground in early spring.

Two other useful low sedums are cliff stonecrop, *Sedum glaucophyllum*, and

TOP Wild stonecrop, *Sedum ternatum*, grows below pagoda dogwood, *Cornus alternifolia*, and serves as evergreen ground cover around the base of a pot that is the focal point of our heavily shaded front walk. Few woodland ground covers could produce such a precise yet low-maintenance effect in this narrow space. The wild stonecrop was rooted in place from vegetative stem cuttings planted in very early spring.

BELOW LEFT AND RIGHT Growing in part sun, this ground cover of *Sedum ternatum* is appealing both in and out of flower. Plantings in heavy shade may be less dense and will not flower nearly as fully.

TOP RIGHT Allegheny stonecrop, *Sedum telephioides*, grows in pockets of soil atop a rock outcrop in the Virginia mountains in late May.

TOP LEFT Heart-leaved golden ragwort, *Senecio aureus*, flowers between dogwoods, *Cornus florida*, at Mount Cuba Center in Delaware in early May.

Sedum nevii. Both are southeastern mountain natives, typically growing on top of rocks and rocky cliffs, and they do best in regions with cool or moderate summer night temperatures. Their growth is much more delicate and not as widespreading as *Sedum ternatum*. Both are cold hardy to zone 5.

Allegheny stonecrop or wild live-forever, *Sedum telephioides*, looks surprisingly like the common garden plants *Sedum telephium* and *Sedum spectabile*, natives of Europe and Asia. It produces stout stems and grows upright to two feet tall, blooming light pink in late summer. Native to dry, rocky places, mostly in the mountains from Pennsylvania to North Carolina and occasionally west to Illinois and Indiana, it is cold hardy to zone 4.

Senecio
GOLDEN RAGWORT
ASTERACEAE, ASTER FAMILY

Two perennial *Senecio* species are worth considering for the ease with which they can create drifts of golden flowers under the developing shade of the early May woodland garden. Most commonly available is heart-leaved golden ragwort, *Senecio aureus*, a native of moist woods and shaded swamps from Labrador to Minnesota south to Florida. Cold hardy to zone 3, it is easy to grow on moist organic soil in shade or part sun and often self-sows and naturalizes. It is an excellent choice for partly sunny streamsides and the edges of woodland ponds. Running golden ragwort, *Senecio obovatus*, is similar but spreads slowly by stolons. It grows naturally in rich woods and on rock outcrops, often in calcareous soil, from Vermont to Florida and west to Texas and Kansas, and is cold hardy to zone 4.

Silene

WILD PINK, FIRE PINK, STARRY CAMPION
CARYOPHYLLACEAE, PINK FAMILY

The most spectacular of the wild pinks is unfortunately among the most fleeting. Fire pink, *Silene virginica*, one of the most intensely red native wildflowers, sometimes behaves more like an annual than the perennial it technically is. In its native haunts, it often seeds into open ground cleared by fire or disturbance, flowers madly in late spring or early summer, and may be gone the next year. Native to woods and rocky, often sloping ground from Michigan to Ontario and south at higher elevations to Oklahoma and Georgia, fire pink is cold hardy to zone 4 but does best in regions with cool to moderate summer night temperatures. If your climate is suitable, it is worth trying from seed, which is readily available. Individual plants may also persist longer if cut back after flowering to preserve energy reserves.

Completely different in appearance and much easier to grow, starry campion, *Silene stellata*, has white flowers with exquisitely fringed petals. Growing two to three feet tall and blooming in mid to late summer, it occurs naturally in woods and woodland edges from Connecticut to Nebraska, south to Georgia and Texas. Cold hardy to zone 4, it is easy to grow in a variety of soil and moisture conditions in part shade, and often self-sows pleasantly.

Smilacina

FALSE SOLOMON'S SEAL
LILIACEAE, LILY FAMILY

The false Solomon's seals, *Smilacina*, are more inclined to form large sweeps and masses than the true Solomon's seals, *Polygonatum*, and since their leafy stems are so ordered and architectural, they would be worth growing for this reason alone. The two larger eastern species are dramatic plants for woodland

TOP Fire pink, *Silene virginica*, blooms heavily in late May in West Virginia, where it has seeded into newly opened ground along a mountain roadcut.

BOTTOM Starry campion, *Silene stellata*, blooms profusely in late July along the Blue Ridge Parkway in Virginia.

TOP LEFT AND CENTER A late-May rainstorm wets false Solomon's seal, *Smilacina racemosa*, as it blooms above the foliage of wild ginger, *Asarum canadense*, and bloodroot, *Sanguinaria canadensis*, on a shaded streambank in southeastern Pennsylvania. The berries of false Solomon's seal are nearly ripe by September.

TOP RIGHT Starry false Solomon's seal, *Smilacina stellata*, forms a dense mass growing wild in the Ohio woodlands in mid June.

gardens, offering spring flowers and autumn berries in addition to their foliage appeal. Both are easy to grow in moist, well-drained soil, in shade or part sun, and propagate readily by division.

The most common false Solomon's seal, *Smilacina racemosa*, occurs naturally in rich woods from Nova Scotia to British Columbia and south to Arizona and Georgia, and is cold hardy to zone 3. In May it produces a large cluster of small cream-white flowers at the end of each stem. Over summer, these become clusters of glossy berries that are at first green, then milk-glass white with red speckles, and finally translucent red by the beginning of autumn. The foliage generally remains in good condition as the berries ripen, and plants make attractive companions to woodland wreath goldenrod, *Solidago caesia*, which blooms about this time. Wild ginger, *Asarum canadense*, is frequently found with false Solomon's seal in native habitats and makes a good combination in the woodland garden, balanced both culturally and aesthetically.

Naturally wide-ranging in woods and prairies on moist, often sandy soils from Newfoundland to British Columbia, south to California and New Jersey and further in the mountains to Georgia, starry false Solomon's seal, *Smilacina stellata*, is cold hardy to zone 3 but prefers slightly cooler climates than *Smilacina racemosa*. Its individual flowers are larger but the clusters are smaller and less conspicuous. The berries are similarly ornamental.

Solidago
GOLDENROD
ASTERACEAE, ASTER FAMILY

Though most goldenrods grow only in full sun, there are three shade species truly worth considering for the woodland garden. They are undemanding plants, easy to grow in a wide range of soil and moisture conditions, and are capable of bringing their yellow and gold hues beyond the edges and into the shaded interior in late summer and early autumn.

My favorite, wreath goldenrod or blue-stemmed goldenrod, *Solidago caesia*, begins upright but by early autumn is transformed into long, arching wands lined with light golden flowers. Native to moist and dry woods, from Nova Scotia to Wisconsin and south to Texas and Florida, it is cold hardy to zone 3.

Less showy but still attractive, zigzag goldenrod, *Solidago flexicaulis*, is so-named because its stem angles back and forth at each successive leafy node. Growing mostly upright to two feet tall, it is native to moist and dry woods from Nova Scotia to North Dakota and south in the mountains to Georgia, and is cold hardy to zone 3.

Native to open, sometimes rocky woods, often on calcareous soils, from Virginia to Georgia, west to Illinois and Kentucky, autumn goldenrod, *Solidago sphacelata*, has been popularized in recent years by 'Golden Fleece', a selection from Mount Cuba Center in Delaware. This species produces a wide clump of basal foliage that is useful in keeping the ground covered over the summer growing season. Lax, widely branched flowering stems extend from the clump in September and early October, often lying nearly on the ground, and creating the effect of a golden carpet. Cold hardy to zone 4, it is easy to grow a wide range of soil types and is tolerant of dry shade once established.

TOP Wreath goldenrod, *Solidago caesia*, blooms from a steep woodland bank in the West Virginia mountains in early October.

BOTTOM Flowering in late September in our Pennsylvania garden, autumn goldenrod, *Solidago sphacelata*, has proved to be a durable ground cover under river birches, *Betula nigra*, and a reliable source of late-summer color.

Blooming in our Pennsylvania garden in mid June, this bright yellow-throated seedling of *Spigelia marilandica* is a descendent of a form originally grown at Longwood Gardens.

Spigelia

PINKROOT, INDIAN PINK
LOGANIACEAE, LOGANIA FAMILY

Pinkroot, *Spigelia marilandica*, was growing at Longwood Gardens when I first arrived there in the late 1970s. It had been established from seed brought in by the Gardens' taxonomist, Donald G. Huttleston, and always elicited questions from visitors when its bright scarlet flowers appeared anytime from June through September. Certainly few native wildflowers have such intense red color.

Though the Longwood plants were all seedlings, their flowers were consistently bright yellow in their throats and on the spreading upper sides of the corolla lobes. The plants were also relatively short, rarely exceeding twelve inches in height. Longwood frequently received requests for plants, and though seeds germinated readily, they were quite frustrating to collect. *Spigelia* has what is technically termed *explosive dehiscence*, meaning the seed capsules burst open suddenly when ripe and expel the seeds with surprising force. The tiny seeds of this plant are impossible to find once scattered, so you have to watch the capsules carefully and try to pick them just as they are becoming ripe, allowing them to open in the confines of a jar or other container.

As I came to know pinkroot from its native habitat and other gardens, I learned that the red outer color of the flowers varies from orange-red to deep scarlet, the throats may be bright yellow or lime green, and plants may grow as tall as two feet. These characteristics are often consistent in any particular local population and usually come true from seed. Cutting propagation and tissue culture have made pinkroot more economically viable for commercial production, but though it is much more widely available, its not often easy to know what forms are being offered.

Spigelia is native from North Carolina west to Indiana and Oklahoma and south to Texas and Florida. I've encountered it in moist thickets, but I've also seen it growing on a dry, rocky, sloping site under American smoketree, *Cotinus obovatus*, and fragrant sumac, *Rhus aromatica*. Cold hardy to zone 4, it is easily grown in a variety of soils and moisture conditions, and persists even in dry partly shaded locations. It has readily naturalized in our Pennsylvania garden in both sunny and shaded spots, and we enjoy a wide range of variation in our plants, which all originated from seed. In a typical year, *Spigelia* blooms for a few weeks in June, then sporadically into September. If plants are cut back after their initial flowering, they will re-bloom heavily in autumn. Individual plants are long lived.

Staphylea

BLADDERNUT
STAPHYLEACEAE, BLADDERNUT FAMILY

The delight of American bladdernut, *Staphylea trifolia*, is as much aural as it is visual. This running shrub is common in moist woods and thickets from Quebec to Minnesota and south to Oklahoma and Florida. It has interesting striped bark, especially on young growth, and pendent greenish-white bell-shaped flowers in April and May, but its fruits, curious inflated bladderlike affairs, are where the fun is. Beginning soft and green in summer, they turn brown and crisply papery by late autumn, enclosing several hard seeds in each of their three chambers. The seeds become loose inside, and they rattle in autumn and winter winds. I often hear bladdernuts long before I see them.

American bladdernut can form a mass or thicket up to fifteen feet tall, though it is frequently half that height. It has no appreciable fall foliage color but is easy to grow and cold hardy to zone 4. It's an interesting choice for enlivening the winter landscape and is useful as a stabilizer of alluvial soils on floodplains, at the edge of woodland ponds, and along shaded streams and riverbanks.

Stewartia

SILKY CAMELLIA
THEACEAE, TEA FAMILY

The tea family includes many beautiful and useful plants, the majority native to eastern Asia. Among them are tea, *Camellia sinensis*, as well as trees and shrubs valued for their flowers, such as *Camellia japonica*, *Camellia sasanqua*, *Stewartia pseudocamellia*, and *Stewartia monadelpha*. Of the North American representatives of this family, *Franklinia alatamaha*, now extinct in the wild but conserved in gardens, is perhaps best known; however, none of these surpasses the uniquely elegant beauty of the two southeastern natives *Stewartia malacodendron* and *Stewartia ovata*.

Mountain stewartia, *Stewartia ovata*, is the more cold hardy of the two, na-

Papery fruits of American bladdernut, *Staphylea trifolia*, remain suspended from bare branches in mid February along a Pennsylvania stream. Enclosing loose, hard seeds, they rattle distinctively in winter winds.

ABOVE Flowers of silky stewartia, *Stewartia malacodendron*, typically have stamens with red-purple filaments tipped by blue-purple anthers.

RIGHT Silky stewartia blooms in mid May in the Birmingham, Alabama, garden of Louise Smith. Grown from seed, some plants in this garden are fifteen feet tall with a nearly thirty-foot spread.

tive to mountain woods from Kentucky to Virginia and Alabama, and adaptable to cultivation into zone 5. It is a large shrub or small tree, typically up to fifteen feet tall with similar spread, blooming from June into August depending upon the region. The flowers are three to four inches wide, usually white with yellow stamens, but in some naturally occurring forms, they are rich purple. Fall color is often deep orange or scarlet-bronze.

Silky stewartia or silky camellia, *Stewartia malacodendron*, is rarely found inland, occurring mostly on the coastal plain from Virginia to Florida and Louisiana. Cold hardy to zone 7, it can grow fifteen feet tall with nearly twice that in spread. Appearing in May and June, its three- to four-inch diameter flowers typically have deep purple stamens and are among the most beautiful in the tea family. Fall color can be a rich mix of orange and dark red, especially when the foliage is touched by direct sunlight.

Both native stewartias require rich, moist, well-drained soil and partial shade; however, mountain stewartia is the less demanding of the two.

Celandine poppy, *Stylophorum diphyllum*, blooms in mid April at Ashland Hollow in northern Delaware, intermingled with Mayapples, *Podophyllum peltatum*.

Stylophorum

CELANDINE POPPY, WOOD POPPY
PAPAVERACEAE, POPPY FAMILY

Stylophorum diphyllum, called celandine poppy or wood poppy, is among the easiest flowering perennials to naturalize in woodland garden interiors. Cold hardy to zone 4 and easily grown in moist, well-drained organic soil, it is native to rich woods from Pennsylvania to Wisconsin and south to Arkansas and Tennessee. Though sometimes confused with its weedy Eurasian relative, lesser celandine, *Chelidonium majus*, *Stylophorum* is a much larger plant, with deep yellow flowers up to two inches across. Celandine poppy blooms in April and May, and then the foliage usually dies back by mid summer, so it is best to interplant with lingering companions including ferns. Under some conditions it can be a bit over-enthusiastic in its self-sowing, in which case it may be advisable to remove some seed capsules before they ripen.

American snowbell, *Styrax americanus*, flowers profusely in late May at Jim Plyler's Natural Landscapes nursery in Pennsylvania.

Styrax

SNOWBELL

STYRACACEAE, SNOWBELL FAMILY

American snowbell, *Styrax americanus*, is closely related to silverbells, *Halesia* species, but is shrubbier, rarely growing above ten feet tall, and typically multi-stemmed. Though not often seen in gardens, it is easily grown in moist organic soil in shade or part sun, and is cold hardy to zone 6. Native to wet woods and shaded swamps, mostly on the coastal plain, it ranges from Virginia to Florida and Louisiana and north and west in scattered locations to Pennsylvania, Indiana, and Kentucky.

Even less common is bigleaf snowbell, *Styrax grandifolius*, which has leaves up to eight inches across. Native to drier woodland habitats from Virginia to Illinois and south to Arkansas and Florida, it is cold hardy into zone 6. Plants of both these species have grown for decades at the Henry Foundation in Gladwyne, Pennsylvania, located in zone 6.

Symplocarpus

SKUNK CABBAGE

ARACEAE, ARUM FAMILY

There's nothing skunky about skunk cabbage, *Symplocarpus foetidus*, unless it is deliberately tormented: its parts are only noticeably malodorous when bruised or broken. Native to wet or moist woods, shaded swamps, and floodplains from Quebec to Minnesota south to North Carolina, skunk cabbage has some of the most magnificent foliage of any woodland perennial, with leaves more than two feet long and up to fourteen inches wide. It is also among the earliest to flower, often beginning in the "dead" of winter. The plant draws on energy reserves in its huge underground rhizome to push curiously shaped inflorescences up through snow and ice, respiring at such a rate that temperatures inside the purple-mottled spathe are significantly above freezing, allowing pollination by small flies just emerging from hibernation.

Cold hardy to zone 3, skunk cabbage really does require constantly moist or

CENTER AND BOTTOM LEFT Appearing before the leaves in mid to late winter and remaining attractive into early April, hooded green-purple spathes enclose the flowers of skunk cabbage. The leaves eventually expand to nearly tropical proportions and seem particularly Amazonian when backlit by the spring sun.

wet soil for good growth but is a natural and attractive companion to many other denizens of wet woods including marsh marigold, *Caltha palustris*, and innumerable ferns. The foliage lasts into mid summer, going dormant by the time temperatures reach their highest.

Tiarella

FOAMFLOWER
SAXIFRAGACEAE, SAXIFRAGE FAMILY

Filled with low clouds of foamflowers in late April and early May, the woodland garden is a truly memorable experience. Though the individual blossoms of *Tiarella cordifolia* are quite small, they are often spectacularly profuse. There are two varieties of foamflower, each with different utility in the garden. The most common variety spreads fairly quickly by stolons and is most effective as a flowering ground cover. I've seen it growing wild in the dense shade of an Ohio woodlands where it literally created a continuous carpet of neat green foliage. The second variety is called Wherry's foamflower, *Tiarella cordifolia* var. *collina*, in honor of the celebrated Pennsylvania botanist Edgar T. Wherry. It is deeper

ABOVE LEFT Skunk cabbage, *Symplocarpus foetidus*, and marsh marigold, *Caltha palustris*, are complementary companions in a low, wet Maryland woods in late April.

ABOVE The typical variety of foamflower, *Tiarella cordifolia* var. *cordifolia*, runs by stolons to form a flowering sweep at Springwood in Pennsylvania in early May.

Wherry's foamflower, *Tiarella cordifolia* var. *collina*, makes a floriferous but distinct clump in my former Newark, Delaware, garden in late April.

rooted and not stoloniferous. Its energy is directed more to flowering, and it is by far the showier of the two in any comparison of individual plants.

The typical foamflower is native to rich woods from Nova Scotia to Wisconsin and south to Alabama and Georgia, and is cold hardy to zone 3. Wherry's foamflower has a more southern distribution, occurring north only as far as West Virginia, but is nearly as cold hardy. Both are easy to grow in rich, well-drained organic soil and are very shade tolerant but flower best with some sun. Forms with pink-suffused flowers and purple-marked leaves in many shapes are common in any large seedling population. We grow a diversity of seedling plants in our Pennsylvania garden, often mixing the running and clumping varieties. Many clonal cultivars are offered commercially.

Trillium

WAKE ROBIN, TOADSHADE
TRILLIACEAE, TRILLIUM Family

Trilliums come with a caveat. Though tissue culture may eventually remedy the situation, at present the majority of eastern North American trilliums offered for sale originated as plants dug from the wild. True, they may have been "nursery grown," but only for a while. This is not to say there aren't nurseries offering ethically produced trilliums: there are, but they are a minority. Responsible gardeners should make inquiries before purchasing plants and use common sense. The problem is that, though trilliums can easily be grown from seed, they are uneconomically slow. Many studies have proved it takes five to seven years from germination to flowering-sized plant. Unless your nursery supplier is a not-for-profit enterprise, seed-grown trilliums must reflect the cost of many years of care. A ten-dollar flowering-sized plant is unlikely to have been seed-grown.

Many gardeners, and all true trillium enthusiasts, do grow plants from seed. An interesting aside to this process, and one that may be useful in keeping dinner-table conversations lively while plants are growing to blooming size, is that trillium seeds are myrmecochorous, which means they have a mutually beneficial relationship with ants. Each tiny seed has an edible lipid-rich appendage called an "elaiosome," there only for attracting ants. Ants respond by carrying seeds to the nests, where larvae consume the elaiosomes, leaving the embryos in the seeds undamaged. The seeds are left to germinate within the ant nest or after being discarded to waste piles.

Trilliums are exceptionally long-lived perennials and naturally increase slowly by underground rhizomes. The speed of their spread varies with different species and among seedlings within a species. Though it is also a slow method, division is a viable way of propagating trilliums.

After the hurdles of propagation have been cleared, the good news is that most trilliums are easy plants to grow. There are a few whose needs are very exacting, such as painted trillium, *Trillium undulatum*, which may be best appreciated in their native habitats. A beautiful plant with white flowers that are elegantly red-marked, painted trillium grows only in very cool, moist, acid soils at high elevations, conditions that are difficult to approximate outside of the mountains. Some others, including snow trillium, *Trillium nivale*, grow naturally only in association with limestone. Many of the showiest trilliums are among the easiest in cultivation and will persist for decades if provided moist, richly organic soil at near-neutral or only slightly acid pH, and dappled sunlight.

Of the approximately thirty-five species native to eastern North America, great white trillium, *Trillium grandiflorum*, is the largest and showiest, occurring naturally over a vast range from Quebec to Minnesota south to Pennsylvania, Ohio, and Indiana, and in the mountains to Alabama and Georgia. It is typical of the pedicillate trilliums: those whose flowers are elevated on a stalk (called "peduncle" or "pedicel") above the leaves. It does best on near-neutral soils but is very adaptable and cold hardy to zone 3.

Another common and widely adapted pedicillate trillium is red trillium or purple trillium, *Trillium erectum*. It is also wide-ranging in moist woods from Quebec and Ontario south into the mountains of North Carolina, Georgia, and Tennessee. Cold hardy to zone 3, it prefers acid soils. Its flowers are typically red and slightly malodorous at extremely close range but frequently vary to white and all combinations in between.

Other distinctive pedicillate trilliums include nodding trillium, *Trillium cer-*

TOP RIGHT Flowering in our Pennsylvania garden in late April, this clump of great white trillium, *Trillium grandiflorum*, has been slowly increasing in size for more than a decade. The clump began as a division from a friend who'd grown this adaptable plant for nearly thirty years. Extremely long lived, trilliums may be passed through generations of gardening friends.

CENTER RIGHT The clear white of great white trillium is gradually suffused with pink as the flowers age.

BOTTOM RIGHT Red trillium, *Trillium erectum*, blooms in late April in the Smoky Mountains of North Carolina along with fringed phacelia, *Phacelia fimbriata*.

TOP LEFT Red trillium, *Trillium erectum,* is a very variable species, with flower color ranging from red to white and all shades in between within a large natural population. The name *trillium* refers to the plant parts being arranged in threes. In this clear white form, it is easy to distinguish three petals and three sepals, which are held on a pedicel above three leaves.

CENTER LEFT This bicolored form of red trillium is among myriad beautiful variations that may occur in natural populations or in garden plants grown from seed.

TOP RIGHT A spreading group of yellow trilliums, *Trillium luteum,* blooms in the shade of a North Carolina woodlands in late April. This is the most common sessile trillium in the Great Smoky Mountains National Park, where it may be seen blooming in large drifts and masses each spring.

nuum, with white flowers mostly hidden under the leaves; Catesby's trillium, *Trillium catesbaei,* with slightly nodding flowers that are typically light pink; and Vasey's trillium, *Trillium vaseyi,* with broad red-maroon petals.

Many species have flowers which sit directly on top of the leaves, not elevated on stalks, and these make up the sessile group of trilliums. Though a few pedicillate *Trillium* species occur in eastern Asia, sessile trilliums are exclusively North American. Leaves of pedicillate types are typically solid green, but sessile trilliums are known for their exquisitely marked or mottled foliage. One of the most common and easy to grow in this group is the yellow trillium or yellow toadshade, *Trillium luteum,* native to moist woods from North Carolina and Georgia west to Tennessee and into Kentucky. Preferring near-neutral soils, it is cold hardy to zone 4. Purple toadshade or whippoorwill-flower, *Trillium cuneatum,* typically has dark red-purple flowers but is otherwise very similar in appearance. Yellow-flowered forms occur and have led to much confusion in garden literature between these two species. Cold hardy to zone 5, purple toadshade is native to rich woods from North Carolina to Kentucky and south to Georgia and Mississippi, widely adaptable to acid or near-neutral pH.

Other distinctive and adaptable sessile trilliums include *Trillium sessile*, called toad trillium or sessile trillium, which is low-growing with small red-purple flowers, and *Trillium recurvatum*, a stiffly erect species with strongly marked leaves, dark red flowers, and unique sepals which are strongly curved downward.

Tsuga
HEMLOCK
PINACEAE, PINE FAMILY

No other native coniferous tree can match the graceful form and dark green foliage of hemlock. Among the most shade-tolerant evergreen trees, hemlocks are also among the few that are often naturally integrated in otherwise deciduous eastern woodlands. Unfortunately, the fate of North American hemlocks is currently in the balance and tilting unfavorably. Both Canada hemlock, *Tsuga canadensis*, and Carolina hemlock, *Tsuga caroliniana*, have proved extremely vulnerable to an introduced pest, the wooly adelgid. This insect has been responsible for the decline and death of innumerable Canada hemlocks in gardens and native habitats in the northeastern United States, and its range is continuing to spread. At the time of this writing, the only controls available involve routine spraying with oil, and such treatment is expensive and impractical for the average residential gardener and impossible in larger landscapes. In affected and threatened regions, planting hemlocks is a risky proposition. Though it is significantly different in color and texture, American holly, *Ilex opaca*, is sometimes a reasonable alternative for a shade-tolerant evergreen tree in the woodland garden.

Uvularia
BELLWORT, MERRYBELLS
LILIACEAE, LILY FAMILY

As a group, bellworts are among the easiest flowering woodland perennials, attractive both in bloom and for their clean, graceful foliage, which lasts through summer. All are unusually shade tolerant.

Whenever I've come upon the large-flowered bellwort, *Uvularia grandiflora*, in its native habitat, it has been accompanied by one or more *Trillium* species and often by blue cohosh, *Caulophyllum thalictrioides*, and maidenhair fern, *Adiantum pedatum*. Largest and most dramatic of all the bellworts, it is native to rich

Purple toadshade, *Trillium cuneatum*, is very similar in appearance to *Trillium luteum*, except the flowers are usually dark purple-red and, if yellow, still have traces of purple pigment.

Large-flowered bellwort, *Uvularia grandiflora*, blooms in Virginia in early May. The flowers are the deepest yellow of all the bellworts.

woods from Quebec to Minnesota and South Dakota, south to Oklahoma, Alabama, and Georgia, growing up to eighteen inches tall. Though often occurring naturally on limestone soils, it is widely adaptable in the garden, and one of the easiest and longest-lived woodland wildflowers. Cold hardy to zone 3, it is tolerant of the deep shade of a dense deciduous canopy and will even grow readily below shrubs and trees. The foliage looks best when plants are grown in evenly moist soil, but large bellwort is also tolerant of dry summer shade. Individual leaves are perfoliate, meaning the stem appears to run through the leaf blade, and this characteristic is shared by *Uvularia perfoliata*. Simply called perfoliate bellwort, this latter species is similar in its cultural and appearance but much smaller in all parts. The flowers are also a lighter yellow.

The two remaining *Uvularia* species are also fine plants for the woodland garden, with very light yellow flowers and attractive foliage. Sessile bellwort, *Uvularia sessilifolia*, is native to rich woods from Nova Scotia to Minnesota and

TOP LEFT By late May, the foliage of large-flowered bellwort has expanded into a clean, beautifully textured mass, as here in our Pennsylvania garden where it is growing directly under shrubs and trees.

BOTTOM LEFT In May, after the flowers have passed, the neat foliage of sessile bell-wort makes a fine textural combination with royal fern, *Osmunda regalis*, in a north-facing bed along our shady front walk.

RIGHT Sessile bellwort, *Uvularia sessilifolia*, blooms heavily in shade at the base of a mountain laurel, *Kalmia latifolia*, at Mount Cuba Center in Delaware in early May.

South Dakota, south especially in the mountains through the Carolinas and into Louisiana and Florida. Growing up to twelve inches tall, it is cold hardy to zone 3. Its leaves are sessile, meaning they are attached directly to the stems without separate stalks, or petioles. Mountain bellwort, *Uvularia puberula*, is nearly identical but slightly smaller. More common to mountain woods, it prefers slightly cooler growing conditions. I've admired this in early May in the Virginia mountains, flowering along with dwarf blue iris, *Iris verna*, and below roseshell azalea, *Rhododendron prinophyllum*.

Vaccinium
BLUEBERRY
ERICACEAE, HEATH FAMILY

Though often relegated to the fruit or vegetable garden, highbush blueberry, *Vaccinium corymbosum*, is a surprisingly adaptable woodland shrub, with autumn color to rival the best. Native to swamps, bogs, and upland woods from Nova Scotia to Michigan, south to Texas and Florida, highbush blueberry is cold hardy to zone 3 and easily grown on moist, well-drained acid soil in sun or partial shade. Its white, urn-shaped May flowers develop into juicy blueberries by July, and these

ABOVE Highbush blueberry, *Vaccinium corymbosum*, blooms in May in New Jersey.

LEFT The mid-November foliage color of highbush blueberry stands out from a wet woodland edge in northern Delaware.

Pendent clusters of deerberry, *Vaccinium stamineum*, bloom in this late-May image from an upland woods in West Virginia.

ABOVE New foliage of false hellebore, *Veratrum viride*, erupts from a Pennsylvania floodplain in mid April looking very much like an Art-Deco motif from an architectural frieze.

RIGHT In early May, the foliage of false hellebore has expanded on a floodplain in northern Delaware. This huge sweep is growing in standing water.

are favorites of birds as well as humans. Provenance is important for best performance, and many cultivated varieties have been developed for various regions.

Deerberry, *Vaccinium stamineum*, is another attractive woodland species very different in appearance from highbush blueberry. Its pendent flowers are wider, like little flared bells, and the foliage varies from green to strikingly glaucous blue-green. It grows three to five feet tall, in well-drained soils in dry upland woods, ranging from Maine to Indiana, south to Florida and Texas. It is cold hardy to zone 5.

Veratrum
FALSE HELLEBORE
LILIACEAE, LILY FAMILY

Like skunk cabbage, with which it is often associated, false hellebore, *Veratrum viride*, is a large plant of wet woods and partly shaded swampy areas. Though its green flowers are unremarkable, its foliage, from the moment it bursts above the

soil until it begins to go dormant in mid summer, is fascinatingly beautiful. Occurring naturally from Quebec to Ontario south to North Carolina, false hellebore is often found in large sweeps occupying pockets of high moisture. It can be propagated by division and is an interesting choice for naturalizing where conditions are suitable. It is cold hardy to zone 3.

Veronicastrum

CULVER'S ROOT
SCROPHULARIACEAE, FIGWORT FAMILY

I've often encountered Culver's root, *Veronicastrum virginicum*, along forest roadcuts in the southern mountains, its slender white spires shooting out from the woodland edge in July. Culver's root ranges naturally from Vermont to Manitoba and south to Louisiana and Georgia, in moist or dry upland woods and into full sun in prairies. Though tolerant only of light or part-day shade, it is a superb perennial for adding summer flowering interest to edge and transition areas in the woodland garden. It is easy to grow in a variety of soil and moisture conditions, and cold hardy to zone 3. The flowers are typically white, though light lavender-pink forms are frequent in large populations. It is easy to propagate by division.

Culver's root, *Veronicastrum virginicum*, blooms in late July along a woodland edge in the North Carolina mountains.

Viburnum

CAPRIFOLIACEAE, HONEYSUCKLE FAMILY

The native viburnums are a beautiful and diverse group with some of the most unusual and nuanced autumn coloration in the eastern deciduous forest. Ranging in size and habit from multistemmed shrubs to small trees, most are extremely cold hardy and adaptable to a wide range of soil and moisture conditions in sun or shade. The majority of viburnums spread slowly by woody rhizomes, with some species capable of forming extensive groups and colonies over time, but none are aggressive in the woodland garden. Flowers are typically white or cream-white domed clusters appearing in early spring, though some species bloom in early summer. Ranging in color from translucent scarlet to bloomy blue or glossy black, the edible berrylike fruits add significantly to the plants' appeal. Some are used in making jellies or sauces, and all are important food for woodland wildlife. Native viburnums are sometimes called haws be-

TOP LEFT Mapleleaf viburnum, *Viburnum acerifolium*, blooms in late May in dense shade in northern Delaware.

TOP RIGHT Growing four to six feet tall on a shaded slope along a Pennsylvania creek, mapleleaf viburnum nears its autumn color peak in late October. The foliage hues nicely set off the glossy black fruits.

BELOW LEFT Leaves of mapleleaf viburnum glow when held up to the late-October sun against a natural background of shadows, their blue-purple tints clearly evident.

cause of their fruits and their sometimes-horizontal branching patterns, both of which are reminiscent of hawthorns, *Crataegus*.

I've long believed mapleleaf viburnum, *Viburnum acerifolium*, to be among the finer but underutilized native shrubs. Spreading and suckering to sometimes form large colonies as it often does in native woodlands, it can bring an amazing range of autumn colors into the shadiest situations, including light salmon, grayed pink, and deep purple. The leaves are quite maplelike and are held in flat tiers on spreading branches, topped by cream-white flower clusters in May and June. Native to both moist and dry woods, it occurs from Quebec to Minnesota and south to Louisiana and Florida, and is cold hardy to zone 4 and easy to grow on a wide range of soils. When sited in shade, it will be loose and open, but when exposed to direct sun it becomes full and bushy. It's also surprising how tolerant this woodland species is of urban conditions.

Another running species I've often admired is hobblebush, *Viburnum alnifolium*, which has a very spare, open branching pattern and large rounded leaves, up to eight inches across, resulting in an elegant but bold-textured overall appearance. Appearing in April and May, the white flower clusters are fertile at the center and are ringed by showy sterile florets. This viburnum adapts only to shade conditions but is a fine choice for growing under and among large trees. Native

to cool, moist woods from Nova Scotia to Michigan and south to North Carolina and Tennessee in the mountains, it is cold hardy to zone 3 but does not do well in regions with warm summers. When grown in cool northern climates or at higher altitudes in the mountains, the foliage often becomes strongly red-bronze-tinted by mid summer, and in autumn the color brightens to peach and rose-gold hues.

LEFT Hobblebush, *Viburnum alnifolium*, blooms in late April under a deciduous canopy at Longwood Gardens. This species is variable in height, growing from five to twelve feet tall depending upon conditions.

TOP RIGHT Fruits of hobblebush are glossy red in early August, on a plant growing at the edge of a New York woodland. They will eventually ripen to purple-black.

BOTTOM RIGHT Larger than peaches but similar in hue, the leaves of hobblebush brighten a woodland streambank in the Pocono Mountains of Pennsylvania in early October.

TOP Arrowwood, *Viburnum dentatum*, blooms white against deep green foliage in late May in northern Delaware.

BOTTOM The black berries of arrowwood are suspended in ornamental clusters against its vivid pink and purple foliage in early November in a southern Delaware forest.

Arrowwood, *Viburnum dentatum*, is an extremely variable and wide-ranging shrubby species that is often split taxonomically into a number of separate species and botanical varieties. In the broadest sense, arrowwood ranges from Maine to Illinois and south to Florida and Texas. It is cold hardy through zone 3 and easily cultivated in warm regions if proper attention is paid to plant provenance. Tolerant of shade or full sun, arrowwood is a good choice for grouping or massing at woodland edges. The leaves are distinctively toothed, as the botanical name *dentatum* suggests. Berries are blue-black, and fall color varies from deep burgundy to pink and blue-purple.

Viburnum nudum is often called witherod, for its flexible branches which were once used in cane and basketwork. Ranging from Newfoundland to Manitoba and south to Texas and Florida, it blooms later than many viburnums, usually in June and July. It is shrubby, growing six to twelve feet tall. Two botanical varieties are usually recognized. Swamphaw or smooth witherod, *Viburnum nudum* var. *nudum*, is more common in the southern part of the range, typically growing in swamps and wet woodlands, often on the coastal plain, and is cold hardy to zone 5. It has exceptionally glossy foliage which can turn deep burgundy red in fall. In its native habitat, swamphaw is often seen with sweet pepperbush, *Clethra alnifolia*, which turns a highly contrasting golden yellow in autumn. Though tolerant of wet or poorly drained soils, swamphaw needs steady moisture in summer if exposed to full sun. Possum haw or smooth witherod, *Viburnum nudum* var. *cassinoides* [synonym *Viburnum cassinoides*], is the more northern and upland variety often found in mountain habitats. It is cold hardy to zone 3 and more drought tolerant than the typical variety. Its leaf surfaces are dull, but autumn color is still handsome.

The leaves of black haw, *Viburnum prunifolium*, look quite like cherry leaves, as the botanical name implies. This viburnum may be multistemmed and shrubby or can grow as a single-stemmed tree up to twenty-five feet tall. Native to woods and streambanks from Connecticut to Wisconsin, south to Texas and Georgia, it is cold hardy to zone 3 and very tolerant of summer heat if plants are selected from the appropriate regional provenance. Southern black haw, *Viburnum rufidulum*, is very similar but more southern in distribution, ranging from Virginia to Ohio south to Texas and Florida, often in dry, rocky woods. It is cold hardy only to zone 5 but very heat and drought tolerant.

Sometimes considered the distinct species, *Viburnum trilobum*, American cranberry bush may alternately be grouped with the European cranberry bush and listed as *Viburnum opulus* var. *americanum*. It is among the minority of viburnums whose flower clusters are conspicuously ringed with sterile florets. It ranges widely across the northern portion of the continent, from Newfoundland to British Columbia south to Oregon and New York. Cold hardy to zone 3, it typically grows as a large multistemmed shrub up to twelve feet tall. The leaves are strongly three lobed and turn rich red in fall. The translucent red fruits are sometimes used as substitutes for cranberries in the making of jellies and sauces. They remain attractive in the winter landscape until taken by birds.

LEFT TOP AND BOTTOM Swamphaw, *Viburnum nudum* 'Winterthur', undergoes dramatic color shifts in late summer and autumn. In mid September, the leaves are green and berries are light pink. A little more than a month later, the berries are bright blue against deep burgundy-red foliage. Viburnums are not dioecious; however, they tend to be self-incompatible, requiring pollination by other genetically distinct individual plants for effective fertilization and fruit production. Compact growing with outstanding autumn color, 'Winterthur' was selected by Hal Bruce and represents the coastal variety of *Viburnum nudum*.

CENTER Black haw, *Viburnum prunifolium*, blooms in early May in the Virginia mountains.

RIGHT TOP AND BOTTOM In mid October, foliage on a large black haw at Ashland Hollow is a deep, lustrous merlot color and the berries have turned from bright red to purple-black. Bare branched in late January, the same tree casts long shadows on the snow.

TOP White sweet violet, *Viola blanda*, flowers nearly at ground level, spreading below bishop's cap, *Mitella diphylla*, and nodding trillium, *Trillium cernuum*, on a moist woodland slope in northern Delaware in early May.

BOTTOM Creamy violet, *Viola striata*, blooms in early May in Maryland.

Viola

VIOLET

VIOLACEAE, VIOLET FAMILY

In almost any woodland garden, violets come with or without invitation. Most are prolific seeders, and their spread is accelerated by the explosive dehiscence of their seed capsules: they literally throw seeds in all directions with wild abandon. The most aggressive types, such as the common blue violet, *Viola sororia*, and its lighter blue-gray variant the Confederate violet, *Viola sororia* var. *priceana*, can become utterly pervasive, sometimes overrunning plantings of more delicate herbs. At home, we spend more time than we'd wish weeding these from where they're unwanted, but it is worth it to have them create virtual sheets of blue in moist paths and shaded turf areas. Even woodland gardens can have lawns, and if they're maintained chemical-free, one of the best springtime rewards is a spontaneous admixture of blue violet blooms.

Many violets are better behaved and can be integrated in woodland plantings with minimal management required. Their ability to bring flowers and foliage interest to some of the shadiest interiors is a true asset.

There are too many violets to be covered here, but among the best whites is Canada violet, *Viola canadensis*, with white flowers sharply etched with purple. Blooming in spring, it's among the tallest species, usually twelve inches in height or more. Canada violet ranges widely in rich woods, from Newfoundland to Alaska south to Arizona and Alabama and is cold hardy to zone 3. Similarly hardy and slightly shorter with cream-white flowers, the creamy violet, *Viola striata*, is often found along stream banks or other wet shady places, from Massachusetts to Wisconsin south to Oklahoma and Georgia. My favorite of the white violets is the white sweet violet, *Viola blanda*, a diminutive species with basal leaves nearly flat to the ground and fragrant white flowers held two to three inches high on leafless stems. It spreads gently by creeping rhizomes and is often found in patches and drifts. Native to cool, moist woodland slopes and ravines, it is often found growing in a thin layer of humus on top of rocks. It ranges from Maine south to Indiana and New Jersey, and then further south in the mountains to Tennessee, South Carolina, and Georgia. It demands sharp drainage and constant moisture, and is cold hardy to zone 4.

One of the brightest colored and most common yellow violets is the yellow forest violet, *Viola pubescens*, which usually grows six to ten inches tall. Native to rich woods from Nova Scotia to North Dakota and south to Georgia and Texas, it is cold hardy to zone 3. Though sometimes called downy yellow violet, this is a misnomer, since plants may be either downy or completely smooth. The round-leaved violet, *Viola rotundifolia*, is one of the earliest to bloom, with small bright yellow flowers appearing almost naked above the unexpanded lower leaves. The leaves eventually grow to nearly four inches in diameter, lying nearly flat on the ground and making an interesting mosaic. Native from Quebec to Ontario and south in the mountains to South Carolina and Georgia, it is cold hardy to zone 3. Another yellow violet I've admired is halberd-leaved violet, *Viola hastata*, a species that prefers cool, moist woods. Its leaves are triangular in outline, and in some forms, the leaves are strongly patterned with silver gray.

Long-spurred violet, *Viola rostrata*, is among the showier blue-purple violets and is easily recognized by its heart-shaped leaves and long-spurred flowers. Native to moist woodlands from Quebec to Wisconsin and south to Alabama and Georgia, it is cold hardy to zone 3. The wood violet, *Viola palmata*, is also blue-purple-flowered and has distinctive leaves that are often deeply lobed or dissected, looking something like crow's feet. It is cold hardy to zone 3.

Wisteria

FABACEAE, PEA FAMILY

Much more manageable than its notoriously aggressive Asian relatives, American wisteria, *Wisteria frutescens*, is an intriguing option for bringing rich blue-purple color into the mid and upper levels of the woodland garden in spring. Though the flower clusters are not as large or as fragrant as those of Japanese or Chinese wisteria, they can be quite prolific and showy when vines are exposed to strong sunlight. The handsome foliage is not as large as that of the Asian species, and its smaller scale is often easier to fit into residential garden designs.

American wisteria grows naturally at the borders of lowland woods and along streams, and occurs over a wide range, from Illinois to Virginia and south to Texas and Florida. It is cold hardy to zone 5 and adaptable to a wide range of soil and moisture conditions in the garden. Though once separated into two species, *Wisteria frutescens* and *Wisteria macrostachya* (sometimes called Kentucky wisteria), current classification lumps all American wisterias together, which makes

TOP Long-spurred violet, *Viola rostrata*, blooms in late April in a moist North Carolina woodlands.

BOTTOM Halberd-leaved violet, *Viola hastata*, blooms in late April in a moist North Carolina woodlands. Though this plant has solid green leaves, some forms have foliage attractively patterned in silver gray.

American wisteria, *Wisteria frutescens*, blooms in late May at Longwood Gardens.

Yellowroot, *Xanthorhiza simplicissima*, blooms in early May at Longwood Gardens. The flowers appear before the leaves and last for a while as the new foliage expands. They are never showy, but subtly interesting.

sense to me since there is overlap in nearly all the supposedly distinguishing characteristics. Flowers appear in May and June, in grapelike clusters typically six to eight inches long. Blossoms are most often rich blue-purple; however, many cultivars have been selected with colors ranging from light lilac-blue to pure white. American wisteria blooms in direct proportion to the amount of sun it receives, so vines must be placed in full sun, on an arbor or trellis, or allowed to climb high into an open-growing tree to find sunlight if flowering is the goal. It can be pruned anytime after flowering or during the dormant season, since it blooms on new growth.

Xanthorhiza

YELLOWROOT

RANUNCULACEAE, BUTTERCUP FAMILY

Though rarely if ever spectacular, yellowroot, *Xanthorhiza simplicissima*, is an uncommonly useful shrub in the woodland garden. Running strongly but not aggressively by bright yellow woody roots which give the plant its name, yellowroot will attractively cover flat or sloped areas with a low mass of deciduous foliage that is clean green in summer and brightly hued in autumn. Native to moist woods, particularly in the mountains, it ranges from New York to Pennsylvania and Kentucky and south to South Carolina, Florida, and Alabama, growing one to three feet tall. Cold hardy to zone 3, it is virtually pest- and disease-free, and grows easily in a variety of soil and moisture conditions. Yellowroot will grow in dense deciduous shade or in nearly full sun if kept moist. If shaded, it is very heat and drought tolerant. Division is easy and successful in spring or fall, and yellowroot can be propagated by root cuttings.

LEFT Serving as a woody ground cover along a shady path at Mount Cuba Center in northern Delaware, yellowroot turns gold in mid November.

ABOVE Autumn foliage of yellowroot is richly colored when exposed to direct sun at a woodland edge or opening, as here in Pennsylvania in early November.

Plant Sources

Following is a partial list of nurseries or organizations that specialize in North American native plants and that produce a catalog or plant list. No endorsement is intended, nor is criticism implied of sources not mentioned. An asterisk before a name indicates the nursery sells wholesale only.

*Apalachee Nursery
1333 Kimsey Dairy Road
Turtletown, Tennessee 37391
423-496-7246

*Appalachian Nurseries
P.O. Box 87
Waynesboro, Pennsylvania 17268
717-762-4733

Appalachian Wildflower Nursery
Route 1, Box 275A
Reedsville, Pennsylvania 17084
717-667-6998

*Arrowood Nursery
870 West Malaga Road
Williamstown, New Jersey 08094
856-697-6044

Boothe Hill Wildflowers
921 Boothe Hill
Chapel Hill, North Carolina 27514
919-967-4091

Bowmans Hill Wildflower Preserve
P.O. Box 685
New Hope, Pennsylvania 18938
215-862-2924

Brandywine Conservancy
P.O. Box 141
Chadds Ford, Pennsylvania 19317
610-388-8327

Cold Stream Farm
2030 Free Soil Road
Free Soil, Michigan 49411
231-464-5809

*Doremus Wholesale Nursery
Route 2, Box 750
Warren, Texas 77664
409-547-3536

*Dry Shave Mountain Nursery
57 Dry Shave Road
McMinnville, Tennessee 37110
931-692-3117

Eastern Plant Specialties
P.O. Box 226W
Georgetown, Maine 04548
732-382-2508

Eco-Gardens
P.O. Box 1227
Decatur, Georgia 30031
404-294-6468

Enchanter's Garden
HC77, Box 108
Hinton, West Virginia 25951
304-466-3154

Forest Farm
990 Tetherow Road
Williams, Oregon 97544
541-846-7269

Georgia Wildlife Federation
11600 Hazelbrand Road
Covington, Georgia 30014
770-787-7887

LaFayette Home Nursery
1 Nursery Lane
LaFayette, Illinois 61449
309-995-3311

Lamtree Farm
2323 Copeland Road
Warrensville, North Carolina 28693
336-385-6144

*Maryland Natives Nursery
9120 Hines Road
Baltimore, Maryland 21234
410-529-0552

Missouri Wildflowers Nursery
9814 Pleasant Hill Road
Jefferson City, Missouri 65109
573-496-3492

Native Gardens
5737 Fisher Lane
Greenback, Tennessee 37742
865-856-0220

*Natural Landscapes Nursery
354 North Jennersville Road
West Grove, Pennsylvania 19390
610-869-3788

Niche Gardens
1111 Dawson Road
Chapel Hill, North Carolina 27516
919-967-0078

North Carolina Botanical Garden
University of North Carolina
    at Chapel Hill
CB 3375, Totten Center
Chapel Hill, North Carolina 27599
919-962-0522
(seed list provided with membership)

*North Creek Nurseries
388 North Creek Road
Landenberg, Pennsylvania 19350
610-255-0100

*Octoraro Nursery
6126 Street Road
Kirkwood, Pennsylvania 17536
717-529-3160

Plant Delights Nursery
9241 Sauls Road
Raleigh, North Carolina 27603
919-772-4794

Prairie Nursery
P.O. Box 306
Westfield, Wisconsin 53964
800-476-9453

Prairie Ridge Nursery
9738 Overland Road
Mount Horeb, Wisconsin 53572
608-437-5245

Shooting Star Nursery
444 Bates Road
Frankfort, Kentucky 40601
502-223-1679

Sunlight Gardens
174 Golden Lane
Andersonville, Tennessee 37705
800-272-7396

Sunshine Farm and Gardens
Route 5
Renick, West Virginia 24966
304-497-2208

We-Du Nurseries
2055 Polly Spout Road
Marion, North Carolina 28752
704-738-8300

Wild Earth Native Plant Nursery
P.O. Box 7258
Freehold, New Jersey 07728
732-308-9777

Virginia Natives
P.O. Box D
Hume, Virginia 22639
540-364-1665

Woodlanders
1128 Colleton Avenue
Aiken, South Carolina 29801
803-648-7522

Yucca Do Nursery
P.O. Box 907
Hempstead, Texas 77445
979-826-4580

One of the best ways to learn about sources of native plants for your region is to contact local native plant societies, nature centers, and botanical gardens. Many of these institutions maintain lists of reliable, ethical sources of native plants, and many post listings on their websites. The following two organizations maintain lists of native plant societies in the United States and Canada:

The Michigan Botanical Club
The University of Michigan Herbarium
North University Building
1205 North University
Ann Arbor, Michigan 48109

http://michbotclub.org/

New England Wild Flower Society
180 Hemenway Road
Framingham, Massachusetts 01701
508-877-7630

http://www.newfs.org/

The following organization maintains a members' list of botanical gardens and arboreta in the United States and Canada:

AABGA (American Association of Botanical Gardens and Arboreta)
351 Longwood Road
Kennett Square, Pennsylvania 19348
610-925-2500

http://www.aabga.org/

USDA *Plant Hardiness Zone Map*

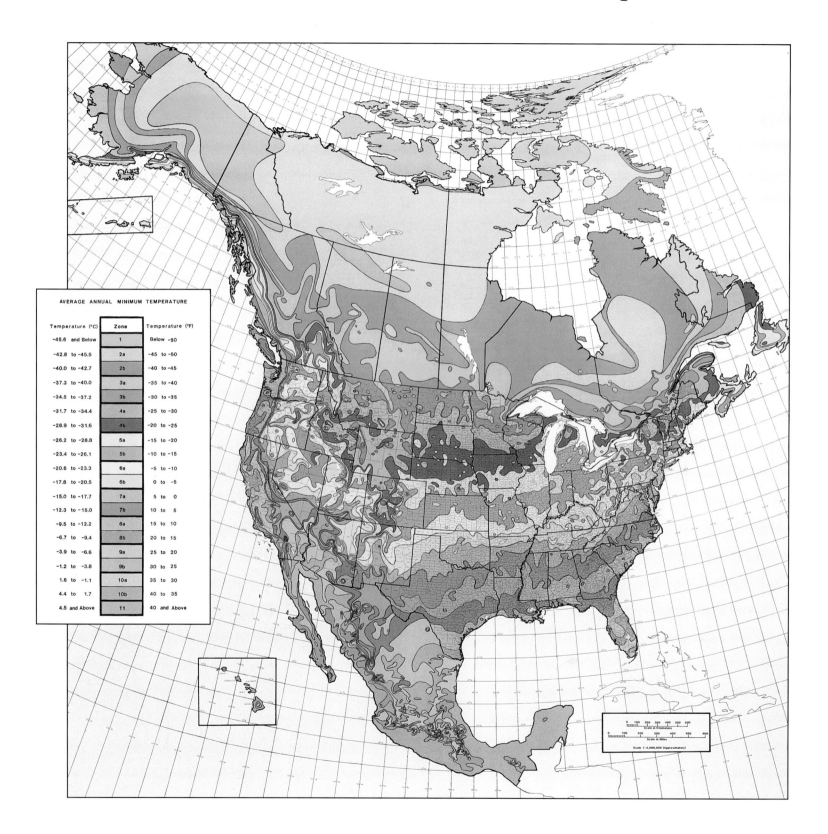

AVERAGE ANNUAL MINIMUM TEMPERATURE

Temperature (°C)	Zone	Temperature (°F)
-45.6 and Below	1	Below -50
-42.8 to -45.5	2a	-45 to -50
-40.0 to -42.7	2b	-40 to -45
-37.3 to -40.0	3a	-35 to -40
-34.5 to -37.2	3b	-30 to -35
-31.7 to -34.4	4a	-25 to -30
-28.9 to -31.6	4b	-20 to -25
-26.2 to -28.8	5a	-15 to -20
-23.4 to -26.1	5b	-10 to -15
-20.6 to -23.3	6a	-5 to -10
-17.8 to -20.5	6b	0 to -5
-15.0 to -17.7	7a	5 to 0
-12.3 to -15.0	7b	10 to 5
-9.5 to -12.2	8a	15 to 10
-6.7 to -9.4	8b	20 to 15
-3.9 to -6.6	9a	25 to 20
-1.2 to -3.8	9b	30 to 25
1.6 to -1.1	10a	35 to 30
4.4 to 1.7	10b	40 to 35
4.5 and Above	11	40 and Above

Scale in Kilometers

0 100 200 300 400 500 600

Scale in Miles

0 100 200 300 400 500 600

Scale 1:40,000,000 (Approximately)

Glossary

ACID (soil): having a pH measure lower than 7.0. Acid woodland soils typically have a pH of 5.6 to 6.5.

ALKALINE (soil): having a pH measure higher than 7.0.

ALLUVIAL (soil): deposited by the action of water currents or waves.

ANNUAL: a plant which completes its entire life cycle (from seed to seed) in one year.

ANTHER: the pollen-producing part of the stamen, located at the tip of the slender stalk called the "filament."

BERRY: a fleshy or pulpy fruit developed from a single ovary, and containing one or many seeds.

BLADE: the flat, expanded portion of the leaf above the sheath.

CALCAREOUS (soil): containing much higher than average amounts of calcium or lime.

CALYX: the collective term for the sepals of an individual flower.

CANOPY: in the forest, the high covering comprised of treetops (crowns).

CIRCUMBOREAL: around the world's northern regions.

CLONE: an asexually reproduced individual, genetically identical to the original organism from which it was produced.

CLONAL: genetically identical.

COLONIAL: forming colonies, often used to describe shrubs or trees which spread by underground roots or rhizomes.

CONIFER: a plant which bears seeds in a conelike reproductive structure, as opposed to an ovary.

CROWN: the top or head of a tree.

DECIDUOUS: shedding or otherwise losing all leaves annually, as opposed to evergreen

DIOECIOUS: having male and female flowers on separate plants.

DIPLOID: having two sets of chromosomes. Most plants are diploid.

DRUPE: a fleshy fruit with a single seed enclosed in a hard case.

DUFF: the decaying vegetable matter on the ground of a forest such as leaves or twigs.

ELAIOSOME: an oily, often fleshy appendage on a seed.

ENDEMIC: restricted to or occurring only in a particular place. Sometimes used in a broader sense to mean native; not introduced or naturalized.

EQUINOX: the precise time when the sun crosses the earth's equator, making the day and night everywhere of equal length. The vernal equinox occurs about March 21 and the autumnal equinox occurs about September 22.

EVERGREEN: remaining green or living throughout the year.

EXFOLIATING: the shedding of layers.

EXOTIC: foreign or extraneous; having the charm or fascination of the unfamiliar.

FILAMENT: in a flower, the threadlike stalk which bears the anther at its tip. The filament and anther comprise a stamen.

FLORET: an individual flower in an inflorescence.

FORB: a broad-leaved herbaceous flowering plant, as opposed to grasses, sedges, and rushes.

FRUIT: a ripened ovary containing seeds, along with any parts fused (adnate) to the ovary.

GLAUCOUS: covered with a waxy bloom, which often imparts a bluish appearance.

GRASS: a member of the grass family, Poaceae.

HARDWOOD: a tree that produces a hard, dense wood as opposed to a conifer which produces soft wood.

HERBACEOUS: lacking true woody tissue.

HUMUS: a brown or black substance resulting from the partial decay of leaves and other vegetable matter; the organic part of the soil.

INDIGENOUS: belonging by birth.

INFLORESCENCE: the flowering portion(s) of a plant, complete with any associated bracts.

LATERAL BUD: a bud located along the side of a branch or stem.

MONOCULTURE: a population or planting consisting of only one type of plant.

MYCORRHIZA: a fungus that grows in a symbiotic relationship with plant roots, aiding in the uptake of nutrients.

MYRMECOCHOROUS: having seeds evolved and adapted for dispersal by ants (from the Greek *myrmex* meaning "ant").

NAKED BUD: one without scales.

NODE: a point on a stem where a leaf or branch is attached.

OVARY: the enlarged lower portion of the female organ, containing the ovule(s).

PEDICEL: the stalk of an individual flower or fruit.

PERENNIAL: a plant which lives for more than two years.

PERFOLIATE: the leaf blade surrounding the stem, so that the stem continues through the leaf.

PETAL: a unit of the inner whorl of parts in a typical flower, often colored other than green.

PETIOLE: a leaf stalk.

pH (soil): a numerical measure of soil acidity. The neutral point is pH 7.0. All pH values below 7.0 are acid and all above are alkaline. Technically, pH is the negative logarithm of the hydrogen ion activity in a soil.

PHOTOTROPIC: growing toward the source of light.

PIEDMONT: the foot of the mountains. In the United States, it is the eastern region lying between the Appalachian Mountains and the coastal plain (literally translates *foot-mountain*)

POLYPLOID: having more than the standard two sets of chromosomes.

PROVENANCE: in plants, their ecological origin.

RHIZOMATOUS: spreading by rhizomes.

RHIZOME: an underground horizontal stem.

SEDGE: a member of the sedge family, Cyperaceae.

SEED: a fertilized ovule usually containing an embryo.

SELF-INCOMPATIBLE: requiring pollination by other genetically distinct individual plants for effective fertilization and fruit production.

SEPAL: a unit of the outer floral whorl of parts in a typical flower, often green and leafy.

SESSILE: attached directly to the stalk or stem, without a petiole or pedicel.

SOFTWOOD: a coniferous tree, typically producing wood that is soft, not dense.

SOLSTICE: the time at which the sun is at its greatest distance from the earth's equator. In the Northern Hemisphere, the winter solstice is on December 22 and the summer solstice is on June 21.

SPADIX: a thickened spike in an inflorescence, often covered by a spathe.

SPATHE: a leaflike appendage of an inflorescence, typically enclosing a spadix.

STAMEN: the male organ of a flower, consisting of a slender stalk called the "fila-ment," and the pollen-producing anther.

STERILE FLORET: an individual flower in an inflorescence that is not reproductively functional.

STIGMA: the pollen-receiving structure. The stigma may be located directly at the top of the ovary, or may be separated from the ovary by a short stalk called the "style."

STOLON: an aboveground horizontal stem, often rooting at the nodes where it contacts the soil.

STOLONIFEROUS: spreading by stolons.

STYLE: a short stalk projecting from the top of the ovary, usually terminating at the stigma which receives pollen.

SUCKER: a shoot arising from the roots or from beneath the ground surface.

SYMPODIAL: a type of branching pattern in which the new growth extends from lateral buds instead of from terminal buds as is typical with most woody plants.

TEPAL: a flower part that cannot be distinguished as either a sepal or a petal.

TERMINAL BUD: a bud located at the tip or top end.

THROAT: the opening into the tubelike section (of a flower) formed by fused petals.

TUBER: an enlarged portion of a stem or root, typically subterranean.

TUBEROUS: having tubers.

UNDERSTORY: plants growing below the canopy.

VARIETY: in botanical nomenclature, a taxonomic rank beneath species having minor but distinguishable characteristics that are generally consistent in offspring.

WOODY: having well-developed woody tissue. Technically, wood is made up mostly of xylem tissue, produced by the cambium.

Bibliography

Aiken, George D. 1935. *Pioneering with Wildflowers*. New York: Stephen Daye Press.

Armitage, Allan M. 1997. *Herbaceous Perennial Plants: A Treatise on Their Identification, Culture, and Garden Attributes*. 2nd ed. Champaign, Illinois: Stipes Publishing L.L.C.

Bailey, Liberty H., and Ethel Z. Bailey. 1976. *Hortus Third: A Concise Dictionary of Plants Cultivated in the United States and Canada*. Rev. and exp. by staff of Liberty Hyde Bailey Hortorium. New York: Macmillan Publishing.

Barnes, Burton V., Stephen H. Spurr, D. R. Zak, and S. R. Denton. 1988. *Forest Ecology*. 4th ed. New York: John Wiley and Sons.

Barry, John M. 1980. *Natural Vegetation of South Carolina*. Columbia: University of South Carolina Press.

Bell, C. Ritchie, and Anne H. Lindsey. 1990. *Fall Color and Woodland Harvests: A Guide to the More Colorful Fall Leaves and Fruits of the Eastern Forests*. Chapel Hill, North Carolina: Laurel Hill Press.

Blake, Harrison G. O., ed. 1887. *Winter: From the Journal of Henry David Thoreau*. Cambridge, Massachusetts: Riverside Press.

Blake, Harrison G. O., ed. 1892. *Autumn: From the Journal of Henry David Thoreau*. Cambridge, Massachusetts: Riverside Press.

Blakeslee, A. F., and C. D. Jarvis. 1911. *New England Trees in Winter*. Storrs: Connecticut Agricultural College.

Bolgiano, Chris. 1998. *The Appalachian Forest: A Search for Roots and Renewal*. Mechanicsburg, Pennsylvania: Stackpole Books.

Brown, Clair A. 1945. *Louisiana Trees and Shrubs*. Baton Rouge, Louisiana: Claitor's Publishing Division.

Brown, Lauren. 1977. *Weeds in Winter*. Boston, Massachusetts: Houghton Mifflin Company.

Brown, Melvin L., and Russell G. Brown. 1984. *Herbaceous Plants of Maryland*. Baltimore, Maryland: Port City Press.

Brown, Russell G., and Melvin L. Brown. 1972. *Woody Plants of Maryland*. Baltimore, Maryland: Port City Press.

Bruce, Hal. 1976. *How to Grow Wildflowers and Wild Shrubs and Trees in Your Own Garden*. New York: Alfred A. Knopf.

Case, Frederick W., and Roberta B. Case. 1997. *Trilliums*. Portland, Oregon: Timber Press.

Chapman, Alvan W. 1883. *Flora of the Southern United States: Flowering Plants and Ferns of Tennessee, North and South Carolina, Georgia, Alabama, Mississippi, and Florida*. New York: American Book Company.

Cocker, William C., and Henry R. Totten. 1937. *Trees of the Southeastern United States*. Chapel Hill: University of North Carolina Press.

Cole, Rex V. 1965. *The Artistic Anatomy of Trees: Their Structure and Treatment in Painting*. New York: Dover Publications.

Correll, Donovan S., and Marshall C. John-ston. 1970. *Manual of the Vascular Plants of Texas*. Renner: Texas Research Foundation.

Cullina, William. 2000. *The New England Wildflower Society Guide to Growing and Propagating Wildflowers of the United States and Canada*. Boston, Massachu-setts: Houghton Mifflin Company.

Darke, Rick. 1979. *Winter Botany*. Kennett Square, Pennsylvania: Longwood Gar-dens.

Deam, C. C. 1940. *Flora of Indiana*. Indi-anapolis, Indiana: Department of Con-servation, Division of Forestry.

Dirr, Michael A. 1998. *Manual of Woody Landscape Plants*. Champaign, Illinois: Stipes Publishing L.L.C.

Durand, Herbert. 1925. *Wild Flowers and Ferns: In Their Homes and in Our Gar-dens*. New York: G. P. Putnam's Sons.

Eastman, John. 1995. *The Book of Swamp and Bog: Trees, Shrubs, and Wildflowers of Eastern Freshwater Wetlands*. Mechan-icsburg, Pennsylvania: Stackpole Press.

Eaton, Leonard K. 1964. *Landscape Artist in America: The Life and Work of Jens Jensen*. Chicago, Illinois: University of Chicago Press.

Embertson, Jane. 1979. *Pods: Wildflowers and Weeds in Their Final Beauty*. New York: Charles Scribners Sons.

Emerson, Ralph W. 1876. *Nature Addresses and Lectures*. Cambridge, Massachu-setts: Riverside Press.

Farb, Peter. 1963. *Face of North America: The Natural History of a Continent*. New York: Harper and Row.

Fernald, Merritt L. 1987. *Gray's Manual of Botany*. 8th ed. Portland, Oregon: Tim-ber Press.

Ferreniea, Viki. 1993. *Wildflowers in Your Garden*. New York: Random House.

Foster, F. Gordon. 1964. *The Gardener's Fern Book*. Princeton, New Jersey: D. Van Nostrand Company.

Gleason, Henry A. 1952. *The New Britton and Brown Illustrated Flora of the North-eastern United States and Adjacent Canada*. Lancaster, Pennsylvania: Lan-caster Press.

Gleason, Henry A., and Arthur Cronquist. 1964. *The Natural Geography of Plants*. New York: Columbia University Press.

Gleason, Henry A., and Arthur Cronquist. 1991. *Manual of the Vascular Plants of Northeastern United States and Adjacent Canada*. 2nd ed. Bronx: New York Botanical Garden.

Godfrey, Michael A. 1980. *A Sierra Club Naturalist's Guide to the Piedmont*. San Francisco: Sierra Club Books.

Goldsworthy, Andy. 1990. *A Collaboration with Nature*. New York: Harry N. Abrams.

Great Plains Flora Association. 1986. *Flora of the Great Plains*. Lawrence: University Press of Kansas.

Grese, Robert E. 1992. *Jens Jensen: Maker of Natural Parks and Gardens*. Baltimore, Maryland: Johns Hopkins University Press.

Gupton, Oscar W., and Fred C. Swope. 1981. *Trees and Shrubs of Virginia*. Char-lottesville: University Press of Virginia.

Harlow, William M. 1959. *Fruit Key and Twig Key to Trees and Shrubs*. New York: Dover Publications.

Holmgren, Noel H. 1998. *Illustrated Com-panion to Gleason and Cronquist's Man-ual: Illustrations of the Vascular Plants of Northeastern United States and Adjacent Canada*. Bronx: New York Botanical Gar-den.

Houk, Rose. 1993. *A Natural History Guide: Great Smoky Mountains National Park*. Boston, Massachusetts: Houghton Mif-flin Company.

Jackson, John B. 1984. *Discovering the Ver-nacular Landscape*. New Haven, Con-necticut: Yale University Press.

Jackson, Kenneth. 1985. *Crabgrass Frontier: The Suburbanization of the United States*. New York: Oxford University Press.

Jacobs, Don L., and Rob L. Jacobs. 1997. *Trilliums in Woodland and Garden*. Decatur, Georgia: Eco-Gardens.

Jelitto, Leo, and Wilhelm Schacht. 1990. *Hardy Herbaceous Perennials*. 2 vols. Portland, Oregon: Timber Press.

Jensen, Jens. 1939. *Siftings*. Chicago, Illi-nois: Ralph Fletcher Seymour, Pub-lisher.

Jones Jr., Samuel B., and Leonard E. Foote. 1990. *Gardening with Native Wild Flow-ers*. Portland, Oregon: Timber Press.

Kaufmann, Edgar. 1986. *Fallingwater: A Frank Lloyd Wright Country House*. New York: Abbeville Press.

Lanner, Ronald M. 1990. *Autumn Leaves: A Guide to the Fall Colors of the North-woods*. Minnetonka, Minnesota: North-word Press.

Lawrence, George H. M. 1951. *Taxonomy of Vascular Plants*. New York: Macmillan Publishing.

Lay, Charles D. 1924. *A Garden Book for Autumn and Winter*. New York: Duffield and Company.

Lellinger, David B. 1985. *A Field Manual of the Ferns and Fern-Allies of the United States and Canada*. Washington, D.C.: Smithsonian Institution Press.

McClelland, Linda F. 1993. *Presenting Nature: The Historic Landscape Design of the National Park Service*. Washington, D.C.: National Park Service.

Midgley, Jan W. 1999. *Southeastern Wild-flowers: Your Complete Guide to Plant Communities, Identification, Cultivation, and Traditional Uses*. Birmingham, Alabama: Crane Hill Publishers.

Oelschlaeger, Max. 1991. *The Idea of Wilderness: From Prehistory to the Age of Ecology*. New Haven, Connecticut: Yale University Press.

O'Malley, Therese, and Marc Treib, eds. 1995. *Regional Garden Design in the United States*. Washington, D.C.: Dunbarton Oaks Research Library and Collection.

Parsons, Frances T. 1899. *How to Know the Ferns: A Guide to the Names, Haunts, and Habits of Our Common Ferns*. New York: Charles Scribners Sons.

Radford, Albert E., Harry E. Ahles, and C. Ritchie Bell. 1968. *Manual of the Vascular Flora of the Carolinas*. Chapel Hill: University of North Carolina Press.

Rhoads, Ann F., and Timothy A. Block. 2000. *The Plants of Pennsylvania*. Philadelphia: University of Pennsylvania Press.

Rickett, Harold W. 1965. *Wildflowers of the United States: The Northeastern States*. 2 vols. New York: McGraw-Hill Book Company.

Rickett, Harold W. 1967. *Wildflowers of the United States: The Southeastern States*. 2 vols. New York: McGraw-Hill Book Company.

Roberts, Edith A., and Julia R. Lawrence. 1935. *American Ferns: How to Know, Grow, and Use Them*. New York: Macmillan Company.

Roberts, Edith A., and Elsa Rehmann. 1929. *American Plants for American Gardens*. New York: Macmillan Company.

Robichaud, Beryl, and Murray F. Buell. 1973. *Vegetation of New Jersey: A Study of Landscape Diversity*. New Brunswick, New Jersey: Rutgers University Press.

Sauer, Leslie J., and Andropogon Associates. 1998. *The Once and Future Forest: A Guide to Forest Restoration Strategies*. Washington, D.C.: Island Press.

Sellars, Richard W. 1997. *Preserving Nature in the National Parks: A History*. New Haven, Connecticut: Yale University Press.

Shephard, Odell. 1927. *The Harvest of a Quiet Eye: A Book of Digressions*. Cambridge, Massachusetts: Riverside Press.

Smith, Richard M. 1998. *Wildflowers of the Southern Mountains*. Knoxville: University of Tennessee Press.

Snyder, Lloyd H., and James G. Bruce. 1986. *Field Guide to the Ferns and Other Pteridophytes of Georgia*. Athens: University of Georgia Press.

Sternberg, Guy, and Jim Wilson. 1995. *Landscaping with Native Trees: The Northeast, Midwest, Midsouth, and Southeast Edition*. Shelburne, Vermont: Chapters Publishing.

Steyermark, Julian A. 1963. *Flora of Missouri*. Ames: Iowa State University Press.

Stilgoe, John R. 1998. *Outside Lies Magic: Regaining History and Awareness in Everyday Places*. New York: Walker and Company.

Stokes, Donald W. 1976. *A Guide to Nature in Winter: Northeast and North Central North America*. Boston, Massachusetts: Little, Brown and Company.

Stone, Hugh E. 1945. *A Flora of Chester County, Pennsylvania*. Vol. 1. Philadelphia, Pennsylvania: Academy of Natural Sciences.

Strausbaugh, P. D., and Earle L. Core. 1997. *Flora of West Virginia*. 2nd ed. Grantsville, West Virginia: Seneca Books.

Stupka, Arthur. 1964. *Trees, Shrubs, and Woody Vines of the Great Smoky Mountains National Park*. Knoxville: University of Tennessee Press.

Sutton, Ann, and Myron Sutton. 1985. *Eastern Forests*. New York: Alfred A. Knopf.

Swink, F., and G. Wilhelm. 1994. *Plants of the Chicago Region*. 4th ed. Indianapolis: Indiana Academy of Science.

Taber, William S. 1937. *Delaware Trees*. Dover: Delaware State Forestry Department.

Tatnall, Robert R. 1946. *Flora of Delaware and the Eastern Shore*. N.p.: Society of Natural History of Delaware.

Trelease, William. 1949. *Winter Botany*. 3rd ed. Champaign, Illinois: S. B. Trelease.

U.S. Department of Agriculture, Natural Resources Conservation Service. 2001. The PLANTS Database, vers. 3.1 (*http://plants.usda.gov*). Baton Rouge, Louisiana: National Plant Data Center.

Vanderpoel, Emily N. 1903. *Color Problems: A Practical Manual for the Lay Student of Color*. New York: Longmans, Green, and Company.

Van Dersal, William R. 1942. *American Ornamental Shrubs*. New York: Oxford University Press.

Wells, B. W. 1967. *The Natural Gardens of North Carolina*. Chapel Hill: University of North Carolina Press.

Wessels, Tom. 1997. *Reading the Forested Landscape: A Natural History of New England*. Woodstock, Vermont: Countryman Press.

Wharton, Mary E., and Roger W. Barbour. 1973. *Trees and Shrubs of Kentucky*. Lexington: University Press of Kentucky.

Wherry, Edgar T. 1961. *The Fern Guide: Northeastern and Midland United States and Adjacent Canada*. Garden City, New York: Doubleday and Doubleday Company.

Whitney, David, and Jeffrey Kipnis, eds. 1993. *Philip Johnson: The Glass House*. New York: Pantheon Books.

Wofford, Eugene B. 1989. *Guide to the Vascular Plants of the Blue Ridge*. Athens: University of Georgia Press.

Wolschke-Bulmahn, Joachim, ed. 1997. *Nature and Ideology: Natural Garden Design in the Twentieth Century. Regional Garden Design in the United States.* Washington, D.C.: Dunbarton Oaks Research Library and Collection.

Wright, Frank L. 1954. *The Natural House.* New York: Horizon Press.

Wunderlin, Richard P. 1998. *Guide to the Vascular Plants of Florida.* Gainesville: University Press of Florida.

Wyman, Donald. 1969. *Shrubs and Vines for American Gardens.* New York: Macmillan Publishing Company.

Wyman, Donald. 1990. *Trees for American Gardens.* New York: Macmillan Publishing Company.

Index